The Edwardian Woman

THE EDWARDIAN WOMAN

by Duncan Crow

ST. MARTIN'S PRESS
NEW YORK

Library of Congress Cataloging in Publication Data
Crow, Duncan.
    The Edwardian woman.

    Includes index.
        1. Women—Great Britain—History.   2. Women—Great
Britain—Social conditions.   3. Women's rights—Great
Britain—History.   4. Great Britain—History—
Edward VII, 1901-1910. I. Title.
HQ1592.C76   301.41′2′0941   77–83847
ISBN 0–312–23912–2

FM

Contents

Illustrations

❦

The illustrations come from the author's own collection with the exception of No 14 from *Maternity*, No 15 from *Women's Work and Wages* and No 17 from *The Cause*.

9

Chapter 1

TO THE EDGE OF THE
VOLCANO

It has become a convention, acceptable to most, that the Edwardian age outlived the king who gave it his name and lasted until the outbreak of the 'Great War'. If an exact date has to be given, the Edwardian period ended on 4 August 1914. But this is too abrupt a demise. The Edwardian age, it seems to me, fizzled out in the slush and slaughter of the trenches, somewhere around Festubert and Neuve Chapelle, at Kinky Roo and Loos, and out along the Menin Road. Its *coup de grâce* was given by Kitchener.

And when did it begin? There is a straight-forward answer that it began on the day the old Queen died, on 22 January 1901 in the middle of another war, for until then Albert Edward, Prince of Wales, who the following day chose to be called Edward VII, had never pushed too hard at the doors of his heritage. As Prince of Wales he had lived the first sixty years of his life as a non-event in monarchical terms. The Queen was the Queen and shared nothing of the majesty with her eldest son. She treated him as a poor substitute for his father, Prince Albert with his exemplary characteristics, of whom his son never spoke without respect – though he spoke of him but rarely. As Sir Charles Petrie has written in *Scenes of Edwardian Life*, 'instead of rejoicing that he should take the place of his dead father she resented the fact, and tried to keep him in the background.'* Consequently when the unbelievable actually happened at Osborne that January day and Albert Edward, known

* Eyre & Spottiswoode, 1965, p. 3.

to his family as Bertie, did at last become King, his accession to the throne and to the vast influence of monarchy produced an immediate change – psychologically as much as in any visible way. He drew the curtains and opened the windows of the monarchy, letting air into the dusty old rooms where his mother had been sitting in seclusion for forty years. There is much validity therefore in arguing that a new age had begun with a new century.

Nonetheless, although Albert Edward had not been pushing too hard at the doors of his heritage, others had been doing so for him. Not in the sense that they had been agitating for the abdication of the Queen and her replacement by himself – though that had been mooted more than once when her popularity was at rock-bottom, before Jubilees and the mystique of extreme old age had restored the charisma of regality. What they had been doing, certainly in the 1890s and back into the 1880s, was to create the new infrastructure of the Edwardian age.

They had taken the internal combustion engine (and the compressed ignition engine, too, for that matter) and had built motor cars. They had examined the hydro-dynamics of submersibles and had built the submarine. They had studied the aerodynamic theories of Cayley and the other pioneers and were on the edge of heavier-than-air flight. They had invented the explosive shell and the machine gun. They had discovered X-rays and the properties of radium. They had adopted an empirical approach to sociology, developed new surgical techniques. They had begun to light their towns and their homes with electricity. They had invented the kinematograph and the phonograph or gramophone.

In the Introduction to *The Victorian Woman* I wrote that Victoria came to the throne at the dawn of the modern world when the contact techniques of steam and telegraphy which were to transform the scale of human, economic and social operations were just being evolved. Before the end of her reign industry had sifted through the discoveries of science and was creating the new technology.

In other ways, too, the characteristics of the Edwardian age were in existence before the old Queen died. The popular press had arrived in the 1880s with Stead's *Pall Mall Gazette*, T. P.

O'Connor's *Star,* with *Tit-Bits, Answers* and *Pearson's Weekly.* Alfred Harmsworth (later Lord Northcliffe) had started *Answers* in 1888, had bought the London *Evening News* in 1894 and transformed it into a popular paper, and had launched the *Daily Mail* in 1896. This was the new journalism, selling for a ha'penny, full of features to give an interest and an excitement to the dull day of the average man – and the average woman, too, for it was a cardinal point in Harmsworth's policy to attract women readers – furthermore, both Harmsworth and Pearson had laid the foundations of the twentieth century mass circulation women's weeklies.

Women had become a market; not simply in the traditional way as buyers of food, clothing, fuel, domestic raw materials and other essentials of the family life, but as a prime area for consumer exploitation in their own right. It was the entertainment and advertising industry that called women into being as a market at the turn of the century. It was not only as buyers and readers of newspapers and magazines that they became important. Musical comedy and matinées were invented for them. The Kinematograph, which quickly shed its walk-on party as an item in the music-hall and became an entertainment in its own right, transformed the lives of millions of women by offering them hours of enchantment and story-teller's magic in surroundings which, if they were not yet as palatial as they were to become twenty years later, nonetheless encouraged the feeling of opulence by their Arabian Nights' names and by the change they offered from drab rooms and drying clothes.

This exploitation of women as a market was not matched by a similarly significant change in their 'civil life'. Women, especially married women, were no longer, it is true, without civil rights as they had been when Victoria came to the throne, when a woman's legal existence was suspended on marriage and became incorporated into that of her husband so that she became, in fact, legally dead and could not carry on any business on ordinary commercial terms. 'Such has been the remarkable change in the position of women during the last fifty years,' wrote a legal expert in 1896, 'that it may be safely said, that no social legislation of any previous age has had such an effect upon society as the laws concerning women passed since the accession of Queen Victoria.'

13

These legislative changes were of two broad categories: the first concerning the protection of working women's welfare; the second giving women a limited amount of 'civil life'. The first category had begun with the Mines Act of 1842 which made it illegal for women and children to work underground in the pits. The second, despite a Divorce Act of 1857 which for the first time made divorce obtainable by a woman in Britain without recourse to a special Act of Parliament, did not begin significantly until after 1870 when legislation was passed giving some women certain political rights, as, for example, the right to fill a number of public posts including overseer, guardian, churchwarden, sexton, governor of a workhouse, medical officer of a workhouse, surveyor of highways, inspector of factories, member of a school board, member of a parish council, and, from the late 1880s, the entitlement to vote in the majority of municipal elections.

And in the matter of property, which the law still held to be almost more important than human life, there were important changes. Three Married Women's Property Acts of 1870, 1882, and 1893 successively granted married women, first, full rights over their own earnings made subsequent to their marriage and, finally, over all their own property so that a husband had no rights whatsoever over the property of his wife. The law also removed many of the disabilities under which married women had formerly existed as, for instance, in the matter of suing and making contracts.

These legislative remedies were the codified recognition of the change that was taking place in the ground-swell of social attitudes towards women and towards their occupation in life. During the Edwardian period there were no such fundamental changes in the law applying principally or exclusively to women – only the Trades Boards Act of 1909 in the first category, and nothing at all in the second. It may be argued that this was not surprising in view of the comparative periods involved – thirty years, at a minimum, from 1870 to the turn of the century; only half that time, at a maximum, during the years of the Edwardians. On the other hand, it is equally relevant that the surge of reform having started, it might well have been expected to continue at an increasing rate, especially since 1906 ushered in a Liberal government dedicated to reform. But whereas the legislative progress towards women's rights was virtually nil, the ground-swell of social attitudes towards change grew ever stronger. Paradoxically, the evidence of this vast desire for change is to be found in the refusal to grant it.

Take divorce. The laws of marriage and divorce, which had remained unchanged since 1857 and which were not the sort of thing discussed in polite circles, all at once became a matter of public concern, largely because of the bills Lord Russell introduced into the House of Lords and his previous tribulations which had ended in imprisonment. Lord Russell's initiative was followed in 1903 by the foundation of the Society for Promoting Reforms in the Marriage and Divorce Laws of England and the foundation shortly afterwards of the Divorce Law Reform Association, both of which merged into the Divorce Law Reform Union in 1906, with Sir Arthur Conan Doyle as its president. Divorce, too, became an important theme with novelists and playwrights – Arnold Bennett and Bernard Shaw among them. In 1909 the concern about marriage and divorce had reached such proportions that the Government appointed a Royal Commission on Divorce and Matrimonial Causes, and, incidentally, in making its appointments gravely offended Edward VII who, although a well-known latitudinarian in anything to do with sex so long as it was kept private and, best of all, gave him personal satisfaction, was a rigorous puritan when it came to 'the thing' being talked about publicly. Majesty took offence because two of the Royal Commissioners were ladies – Lady Frances Balfour, the ex-Prime Minister's sister-in-law and daughter of the Duke of Argyll, and Mrs H. J. Tennant, sister-in-law of the current Prime Minister's wife. Divorce, he told the Home Secretary, Herbert Gladstone, was a subject 'which cannot be discussed openly and in all its aspects with any delicacy or even decency before ladies'.

The appointment of a Royal Commission on Divorce so comparatively soon after the matter had come to the forefront of public discussion is not to suggest that the Government was anxious to do anything in the way of reforming the existing laws. It has long been government's method of damping down controversy to appoint a Royal Commission, to let it work sedulously for as many years as possible, and then to add its resultant Blue Book to the dusty stack upon the shelf, pleading as it does so that the whole matter had been shown to be so contentious that time for further consideration is essential to a proper handling of this vital aspect of public business. This is exactly what happened with the Report of the Divorce Commissioners. After holding seventy-one hearings and examining 246 witnesses the Commission presented its report in November 1912, three years almost to the day after it was appointed. Despite a private bill and questions to the Prime Minister from time to time over a period of fifteen months the answer, though couched in different phrases, was always the same: there would be no bill to reform the divorce law.

This refusal was important for its own sake because it left the issue 'still hopelessly unresolved, still unjust'. But the importance of the Royal Commission in the present context is that divorce and marriage had become such a dominant issue that government had to take notice of it and deploy its Fabian defence.

Even more publicised than the divorce question was the suffragette campaign. It is not often that a mass of women have become so polemic that they erupt into physical warfare against the strait-jacket of life in which they are, or feel themselves, to be held. But in 1908 the flavour of revolt was so much in the nostrils of one band of women that suddenly the quiet anger that had rippled through decades of head-patting sympathy and decorous speech-making erupted into a civil war.

The actual legal advancement achieved by this rioting, burning and destruction before the explosion of Europe snuffed it out overnight, was, like the Divorce Commissioners' work, absolutely nil. But, as in that other case, the mere fact that the arguments were abroad and the stones flying was proof of the volcanic rumblings of the time. The Edwardian period, particularly its latter part, saw the rejection of old leaders and old habits.

To later generations the Edwardians were people who lived in a Golden Age of long hot summers, summers of crackling hay and crisping leaves that fell drought-stricken from the trees, summers that seemed to be epitomised by L. P. Hartley's *The Go-Between*, summers of the country-house and diabolo, of cucumber sandwiches and tea on the lawn.

The glorious summer weather, it is a phrase that occurs

again and again in descriptions and reminiscences of that long
Edwardian decade that lasted into the first years of the Great
War. Mind you, the attitude to a glorious summer depends
rather on whether one is sweating in an office, humping coal,
or playing cricket every day. It may seem to later generations
that everybody lay under a tree and had a picnic, but the
sybaritic life was only for the few.

So what of those famous Edwardian summers? 1901? The
legend is perfectly correct. There was, the *Annual Register*
reported, 'an excess of bright sunshine'; it was a glorious
summer just as it had been in 1900 when L. P. Hartley's young
hero was sweating about in Norfolk in school clothes that were
most unsuitable for the heat of that troubled war-time summer.
1902? Nothing worth noting. 1903? Abnormal rain. 1904? Very
sunny. 1905? Nothing. 1906? Ah, 1906! Well, in 1906 the beginning of August saw a week of remarkably high tempera-
tures. Great heat was recorded over most of England, the shade
temperature reaching 91°F in London, and 92° in Canterbury
and Norfolk. 1907 and 1908? Nothing to report. 1909? If you
had asked anyone in the street at the end of that year what the
weather had been like you would have been told that not only
had the summer been appalling but that the whole year had
been wet and sunless. That was the impression people had, but
the meteorologists would have denied it. 'The popular belief,'
said the *Annual Register*, 'is not borne out by the records.' And
1910? Nothing. In 1911 there was another glorious summer. In
1912 the summer was wet and cold; in 1913 July and August
were below the average temperature; in 1914 the summer sunshine was normal – it was all that was!

The glorious Edwardian summers were not a complete myth;
neither were they a total reality. Popular belief was the key.
After the black chasm of the Great War and the holocaust of its
successor the Edwardian years seemed to radiate a serenity that
was symbolised in the warmth and sunshine of a few summers;
the intervening bad or nondescript ones were elided, so that
there were people in their old age in the insecure later years of
the century who looked back to a long-lost Arcadia in their
youth.

For many Edwardians at the time, however, the matter was
somewhat different. Their mood was one of anxiety. For them

the heat of the long hot summers carried with it the apprehension of thunder below the horizon.

There were many reasons for this deep-set unease. At home there was the threat of rebellion in Ireland, the growing belligerence of the industrial trade unions, the rise of the Labour Party, the challenge of the suffragettes and the strange destructive policies of the Liberal Party which seemed to please no-one. The Liberals were originating the Welfare State with Act after Act: school meals, school medical inspection, town planning, old-age pensions, national insurance and the 'People's Budget'. For those who wanted to keep to the old ways it was far too much, but for those who wanted a new form of society it was not enough. The refusal of a so-called reforming government to accede to moderate demands resulted in resentment and the rise to power of militants. 'The petitioners for change,' as Cole and Postgate said in *The Common People*, 'were sent away empty-handed.'* In consequence, the petitions in many cases then gave way to violent protest.

There was also a feeling that the country was becoming progressively decadent. This took such hold of official thinking that in 1904 an Inter-Departmental Committee was appointed to enquire into the reasons why two-thirds of the recruits enlisting for the Boer War had had to be rejected because they were medically unfit. This figure was tossed into the public arena by F. B. Maurice, who later, as General Sir Frederick Maurice and Director of Military Operations, was to fall foul of Lloyd George in 1918 over manpower figures. In the event the proportion of two-thirds was shown to be somewhat of an exaggeration – a result that could not have surprised Lloyd George, whose vehement denunciation of Maurice was that his statistics were habitually suspect!

But the worry behind the figure was genuine enough. The report of the Inter-Departmental Committee showed that as far as the rejection of recruits was concerned about one half of the 35 per cent who were rejected on medical grounds had been turned down because they were under the required height or weight or had defective vision or bad teeth. Clearly the working class, basic fodder for the army, were physically deficient.

Poor in physique as all these rejected recruits demonstrably

* Methuen, Fourth Edition, 1949.

were, 'and poor in mental capacity and power of application as many of them must be, what becomes of them?' asked one eminent Scottish doctor who gave his views to the Committee. 'Many of them,' he said, answering his own question, 'probably marry girls as weak as themselves and have children, some of whom go to swell the lists of infant mortality, some to join the criminal classes, while others grow up more weak and incompetent than their parents.'

That there was a progressive deterioration of the working class was also the view of Francis Galton and the Eugenics Society. But the Royal College of Physicians disagreed. The general improvement in food, clothing and housing (partially evidenced by the greatly lowered death-rate), 'together with the diminution of general pauperism', meant in effect that it was only the very poor and hence those most likely to be unfit who would be driven by necessity to volunteer for the army. However, what the Royal College forgot to mention in pursuance of its argument, sensible as that might be, was the call of patriotism and adventure that stimulated many volunteer recruits for the Boer War – and a large number of these were certainly not the very poor.

The progressive deterioration of the race was not accepted by the Committee. Nonetheless it agreed that the condition of poorer urban schoolchildren was 'serious'. They were shorter in stature than children from higher-class homes and those living in the country, and many of them were suffering from the diseases of poverty – for example, lice, bad teeth, suppurating ears, ringworm and tuberculosis. The causes were the conditions that poverty imposed; above all malnutrition.

To this mélange of anxieties and frustrations from the crowding pressures of the political and economic situation at home where the rich seemed to be getting richer and the poor poorer, there were added other frighteners from the world outside. The Boer War had shown the suspect quality of British military might and had severely impaired national complacency about the army, their generals, and the country's capacity to wage a successful war against even a small nation; the silhouette of the German High Seas Fleet looming over the horizon could make one wonder whether the Royal Navy was as powerful as it should be; there were the warnings of future economic problems in the huge pressure, subtle but indisputable, that Germany and the United States were exerting on the structure of world trade; and allied to this immanent competition which, the pessimists said, would eventually topple England from its paramount throne, were the undoubted deficiencies of English technical education especially compared with that in Germany.

Indeed, in a word, a major worry was Germany.

Chapter 2

THE YELLOW RICH

When at last Edward VII came to the throne half-way through the Boer War he found himself the monarch of a country that, in its basic economic characteristic, had changed fundamentally from the nation his mother had been summoned to rule. Of England at Victoria's accession in 1837 George Eliot had written that its industrial towns were 'but crowded nests in the midst of the large-spaced, slow-moving life of homestead and far-away cottages and oak-sheltered parks'. England was an agricultural country stretching north from the southern downlands with its two arms spreading round the Pennines, rolling up on the east past the sky-swept fields of Norfolk, through Doncaster, across the Humber and the flat miles of the North Riding until it crawled left-handed over Berwick bridge into the Lothians, and, on the west, moving up that broad fertile plain which even today is a pasture land of sheep and cows and endless miles of arable criss-crossed with rivers and canals, a path that is slowly hemmed in from the further west by the encroachment of Wales and blunted in the north by the barrier of Shap.

The national procession from country to town started sooner and moved much faster than is generally realised. By 1851, when the Crystal Palace in Hyde Park was housing that heterogeneous clutter of 'the Works of Industry of all Nations', which was to capture the nation's imagination as the Great Exhibition, Britain was already bursting the bonds of its rural and small town past and was emerging into the first industrial urban economy in the world, its shires and farming acres threaded by railways, its 'crowded nests' swelling out around the textile mills and iron foundries, its foreign trade (already substantial) doubling in a decade. In the late 1850s agriculture accounted for 20 per cent of the gross national product; forty years later that percentage was down to six, and whereas in 1851 more than one fifth of the population had been employed in agriculture, by Edward's accession less than one tenth gained their living from the land. By that time only 23 per cent of the population was rural. More than three-quarters were living in towns and urban districts. Thus the vision of the Edwardians lolling their long decade away under the ilex trees while Raffles made a century and then bowled the others all out for 43 before rifling his host's family jewels is more nostalgia than a true picture of the balance between town and country in England after the turn of the century.*

Edward VII inherited the leading industrial nation of the world, and one which had gathered into its grasp a mighty empire over which, so the poet proclaimed, the sun never set. It was certainly the largest empire there had ever been, covering a fifth of the earth's land surface and containing a quarter of its population. The country's overseas trade was immense, and the fact that it had an adverse balance of imports over exports created no problem because the world was its debtor. 'Invisible' earnings more than made up for the visible deficit, leaving a large annual surplus for further investment overseas. Edwardian Britain was a prosperous country, the richest in the world, and the key to its prosperity lay in trade. The toffee-nosed ranks of Society might sneer at those in 'Trade' and ban them from their clubs and golf-courses and gatherings. But it was trade that paid for their luxuries and extravagances. In 1894, exports reached the nadir of their fortunes after the slump of the Great Depression which spanned the last quarter of the nineteenth century. Including re-exports they amounted to £284 million – and it should be remembered that in those days money was money and not an inflationary imprecision, so that the comparison between 1894 and 1913 is a valid one in monetary terms, unlike a comparison between 1957 and 1977 – or even a comparison between 1976 and 1977! In 1900 exports amounted to £354 million and in 1913 they reached £635

* As that superb litterateur Oliver Edwards wrote in *The Times* of 22 March 1956: 'Chronologically, of course, Raffles was Victorian, but in spirit he was Edwardian.'

million, of which all but £110 million were home-produced goods.

The composition of this export total is worth examining, because in it lay the seeds of Britain's later decline. Textiles accounted for one third, heavy industry for a quarter, but the trend was increasingly towards coal and machinery with which overseas customers could manufacture essential commodities for themselves. The new exports – those which took Britain through the next half-century – were only just on the move.

As to the visible deficit, the great increase in imports – essential to a nation with few natural resources and a new inability to feed itself – produced one of £160 million in 1900. But thereafter exports grew so much more rapidly than imports – a sign of more sophisticated techniques – that by 1913 there was a modest export surplus in goods and services. What won the race and made the nation so prosperous was the return on overseas investment: £2,000 million a year by 1913.

Britain was rich. As the *Illustrated London News* wrote in March 1901, on the question of a public subscription for some really grand and worthy memorial for the late Queen, 'circumstances are hardly altogether fortunate: the rise in taxation, especially in income tax, and the large funds raised for war charity, have made the pinch of diminished spare income felt', not to mention death duties and higher food prices. However, the article concluded complacently, there was no doubt that the subscription would be forthcoming because 'there is always plenty of money in this country'.

And so there was – for some. The 'rich', defined by economists of the time as those with over £700 a year, were less than one in every thirty of the population – and yet they received more than one third of the national income. The 'comfortable', with between £160 and £700 a year, who were about one-ninth of the population, received one seventh. So that these two economic groups taken together – some 14 per cent of the total population of 43 million people – received nearly half the national income. Over the whole population the average income per head was about £40 a year. Some people were very rich indeed; millions were very, very poor.

Between the poor and the 'rich and comfortable' there was fixed the Biblical gulf, and this gulf was the source of much unease. As a radical politician of the time recorded it: 'A scared and wealthy middle class confronts a cosmopolitan uprising of the "proletariat" whose discontent it can neither appease nor forget.'* But what he did not mention was that between the rich themselves, let alone between the rich and the middle class, there were gulfs across even more turbulent Tibers with bridges guarded by ladies whose courage on behalf of their Romes would have put Horatius to shame. The middle classes were at war with themselves, and the rich were trying to pauperise each other – though without avail, for this was the age of the new millionaires.

A critical observer of London Society and its attendant country-house life was Beatrice Webb who, as one of the famous nine Potter sisters, had been brought up in it, doing the *tourneé*, the visiting, the balls, the parties, the riding, dancing, flirting and dressing up – in short, the whole rigorous choreography of entertaining and being entertained, 'all occupations', she wrote primly in later life when she had eschewed her conservative background and had become a prime mover, with her husband Sidney Webb, towards the new world of Fabian Socialism – 'all occupations which imply the consumption and not the production of commodities and services'.

In her autobiography *My Apprenticeship* she defined, as a good sociologist should, the social entity of which she was so critical. Though the period of which she wrote was her youth of the 1880s, her analysis was still valid in Edwardian times.

'London Society appeared as a shifting mass of miscellaneous and uncertain membership; it was essentially a body that could be defined, not by its circumference, which could not be traced, but by its centre or centres; centres of social circles representing or epitomising certain dominant forces within the British governing class . . . persons who habitually entertained and who were entertained by the members of any one of these key groups could claim to belong to London Society.'†

There were four of these circles, all interlinked through an element of common membership. 'There was the Court rep-

* C. F. G. Masterman, *The Condition of England* (Methuen, 1909), p. 208.
† Longmans, Green, 1926, p. 46.

resenting national tradition and custom; there was the Cabinet, and ex-Cabinet, representing political power; there was a mysterious group of millionaire financiers representing money'; and there was the racing set with its headquarters in Newmarket. The centripetal force that kept these four intersecting social circles from floating apart like bubbles in the air was 'a curiously tough substance – the British aristocracy' – an aristocracy which, as a foreign diplomat once remarked to Mrs Webb, was

'the most talented, the most energetic and the most vulgar in the world; characteristics which he attributed to a perpetual process of casting out and renewal, younger sons and daughters falling out of social rank to sink or swim among their fellow-commoners, whilst the new rich of the British Empire and the United States were assimilated by marriage, or by the sale of honours to persons of great riches but with mean minds and mediocre manners, in order to replenish the electoral funds of the "ins" and "outs".'*

The main difference between Society from the 1880s onwards as compared with the earlier years of Victoria's reign was the inclusion of that circle which Beatrice Webb defined as 'the mysterious group of millionaire financiers representing money'. In the early part of Victoria's reign money could give no entrée to society; later in the nineteenth century it became, whatever its origin, an open sesame. In 1836 the wife of the American Minister found on her arrival in England that wealth, with which she and her husband were reasonably well endowed, was 'nothing, as to the rank it gives, tho' all important as to the comforts'. The Lucullian banquets given by rich merchants and money-men seldom moved them out of their own commercial circle into that unattainable Society that ran before them like a will-o'-the-wisp. As Lady Dorothy Nevill, that prolific recorder of her long age defined it, Society in the earlier part of Victoria's reign was an exclusive assemblage of people who

'either by birth, intellect, or aptitude, were ladies and gentlemen in the true sense of the word. For the most part fairly,

* *Ibid.*

though not extravagantly, dowered with the good things of the world, it had no ulterior object beyond intelligent, cultured and dignified enjoyment, money-making being left to another class which, from time to time, supplied a selected recruit to this *corps d' élite*'*

To say that, even under the moralistic umbrella of the Prince Consort, Victorian Society up to 1860 had no ulterior object beyond intelligent, cultured and dignified enjoyment sounds more like a selection of epistles from the *Morning Post* than a true bill of the times. Nonetheless the antipathy between the Upper Ten Thousand, as Gladstone called them, and the new rich was well-inferred. It was still violently alive in Edwardian times – and this despite the inclusion of self-defined *nouveaux riches* among the King's friends and accepted leaders of Society.

This antipathy is reflected in many novels of those years, among them at least two by Anthony Hope, better known to-day as the author of *The Prisoner of Zenda*. But Hope was an accomplished novelist, recording creatively the *esprit* of his times. While Galsworthy saw with cold charity the chills of middle-class men of property as they rose into power in Edwardian England, and Wells threw his huge creative mantle across the Kipps's, Mr Pollys and Dick Remingtons of his time, bringing the whole class snakes-and-ladders into the brilliant picaresqueness of the Ponderevos in *Tono-Bungay*, and Somerset Maugham wrote with the understanding sympathy of a doctor about young girls in Lambeth 'breaking their ankles' and the problems of human bondage – while these three and other novelists were noting the life around them in the *milieux* they had chosen, Anthony Hope was among those writing about that disputed area between the ten thousand and their challengers. Two of his books in particular illustrate the point: *The Intrusions of Peggy* and *Quisante*.

In the former, the eponymous Peggy is far less the actual heroine of the book than the lady who is introduced in the first chapter. While Peggy is a charming but vague catalyst to the story, the real feminine lead is Trix Trevalla. Trix has been widowed early after a short unhappy marriage to an alcoholic.

* Ralph Nevill, ed., *The Reminiscences of Lady Dorothy Nevill* (Ed. Arnold, 1906), p. 100.

Without the essential qualifications for immediate acceptance
she slides her way towards her ambition – a secure place in
Society:

'Here at Mrs Bonfill's she seemed to be in the world up to her
eyes. People had come on from big parties as the evening
waned, and the last hour dotted the ball-room with celebrities.
Politicians in crowds, leaders of fashion, an actress or two, an
Indian Prince, a great explorer – they made groups which
seemed to express the many-sidedness of London, to be the
thousand tributaries that swell the great stream of society.'*

People, it seems, were always 'calling in somewhere else first'
and then coming on 'at the tail of the evening'; those were the
phrases of the day. And there always seemed to be an explorer
about, based no doubt on the heroes of the day, Nansen, Scott,
Shackleton and Amundsen. Interestingly enough, when Vita
Sackville-West came to write her classic *The Edwardians* she too
had an explorer, Anquetil, who plays a vital part in the novel.
No doubt she was reflecting the spirit of the Edwardian age,
for the explorer-cum-clean-limbed adventurer seems to epitomise a dominant aspect of that spirit. The quietly handsome,
almost middle-aged, unobtrusively athletic hero, moving with
the ultimate of *sangfroid* through the hazards of wide open
spaces, be they snow-covered or thinly forested grass country –
or even into the diamond-stocked safes of plutocratic bedrooms – he, whether his name was Richard Hannay, or Raffles
or a member of The Burglars' Club, was the Edwardian hero.
And with him, except of course in polar regions or in places
where uncontrolled savages might put her in a predicament
that no story-teller could get her out of except at the cost of his
literary integrity – went the Edwardian girl-friend.

The Edwardian girl-friend was usually an upper-class tom-
boy – unless, of course, she was 'a good sort', in which case her
background was unimportant so long as she knew how to behave herself during a working-dinner at the Savoy. She
was slim, dressed always perfectly for the occasion, never
had inconvenient calls of nature, and although expressing a

* Anthony Hope, *The Intrusions of Peggy* (Smith Elder, 1906), p. 20.

challenging submission in her clear-set eyes or a defiance of the villain's demands, seldom had occasion to rue the day. Peggy of *The Intrusions* was one of those girl-friends.

Apart from the minor story that revolves around the essential attraction of Peggy, the theme of the book is people fighting their way into Society. There is Trix Trevalla herself – Trix who manages to get herself engaged to the Duke of Barmouth's heir, and then throws him over because she cannot stand the cant of the ducal establishment, a renegation that earns the fury of Lady Blixworth, Mrs Bonfill's ally and another adjudicator of Society's rules. Trix's obvious duty, Lady Blixworth tells Peggy, 'was to marry him, and please herself afterwards. We must have our rules kept, Peggy, else where should we be? And because we were all furious with him for becoming engaged to her, we're all the more furious with her for throwing him over. Nothing is more offensive than to see other people despise what you'd give your eyes to have'.* Then there are the Frickers. Sydney Fricker is a speculator, a financial buccaneer. His wife and daughter want desperately to become part of Society.† Sydney Fricker helps Trix financially in order that she will use her contacts to give the entree. But she welshes on her agreement, and he in turn sets out to ruin her. The attitude of the pillars of Society is expressed by the Duke of Barmouth, a pernickety, boring fellow, with a tall and majestic wife ('They had a very big house in Kent, within easy reach of London, and gave Saturday-to-Monday parties, where you might meet the people you had met in London during the week')‡ His Grace, and many like him, was disgusted at the whole motive of the Stock Exchange. Money was land and the rents from land; money was not gambling on pieces of paper – whether they even existed was a moot point – which might or might not be worth

---

* *Op. cit.*, p. 191.

† The difficulty for the female Frickers and for those like them was described in *The Lady's Companion* magazine of 10 March 1900. 'Society men will fraternise with the millionaire and ignore his misplaced "h's" and the absence of good breeding while they drink his wine, but the wives and daughters of those men will not visit his wives and daughters, nor receive them in their own homes if they lack refinement and culture.' (quoted in Cynthia L. White, *Women's Magazines 1693–1968* (Michael Joseph, 1970), p. 79.

‡ *Op. cit.*, p. 116.

a fortune if someone or other in some out-of-the-way place reported (and did they ever actually report?) that gold or diamonds or some obscure mineral had been proved to exist on the particular company's option. 'Resist the beginnings', he said firmly, ' – the beginnings' (for he had a habit of repeating what he considered to be the key word in his judgements). 'The habit of speculation is invading all classes. . . . Persons like these Frickers are pests – pests.' But Lady Blixworth took a more practical view – at least privately. 'If we cut everybody who's disreputable, we can all live in small homes and save up for Death Duties.'

The old rich, in fact, were worried. Compared with the latter half of the twentieth century their worries seem futile. But they were worried nonetheless. Death duties had been the first real worry. Introduced in 1894, under Lord Rosebery's premiership, with the assurance of the then Chancellor that they would 'only occur once in a generation' and were therefore of no devastating significance, they had since proved to threaten a mortal blow to the aristocracy. Boer bullets were no respecters of landowners and a generation proved to be of short duration in a major war. So great was the threat that the Dowager Duchess of Chevron in *The Edwardians* was moved to send for her man of affairs and dictate a letter to the Chancellor of the Exchequer registering a protest – with some justice, it may be argued, because the duties were incurred when her son, the present Duke's father, had been killed in the Boer War which was not something that had been included in Sir William Harcourt's argument about 'once in a generation'.*

It seemed more than unjust that one's family should be ruined just because one was honourable enough to die for one's country. It was a point of view that took on a more sinister aspect some years later when Europe set about committing suicide in the Great European War; especially so when the whizz-bangs and Jack Johnsons confined themselves to killing young men at the Front and avoided the fat profiteers slothing it out in comfort at home. Death duties, when they were first

---

* 'The only event that had ever been known to arouse her indignation was the death duty imposed by Sir William Harcourt in the Radical Budget of 1894.' V. Sackville-West, *The Edwardians* (Hogarth Press, 1930), p. 210.

introduced, could only be aimed at the landed gentry. Through-out history, wealth in England had meant land; it meant land that you got rents from – if it was land in the shires where things had been going badly since your father's time because of the agricultural depression you were in real trouble and death duties would finish you. As the Duke of Barmouth might have said, wealth was not a question of cash – after all it was vulgar to talk about money. No. Death duties meant breaking up the estates – the estates. And who was going to buy them? I'll tell you who's going to buy them, old boy. These bloody plutocrats, bloody men who work with money as if it were something worth having for its own sake. They find a gold mine, or a diamond mine, or lend some little pipsqueak the money to fight a Balkan war. Enough said. Our revered Sovereign has a few friends of that ilk: 'gone boating with his grocer', as I hear the Kaiser said. Death duties won't hurt them, old boy. We have to sell our estates to pay; these . . . these financiers, financiers – buccan-eers without guts would be a better name for them – all they have to do is hand over the right amount of shares in one of their cooked-up companies, then fiddle the exchanges around until they come out with a profit – a profit. And with the profit they buy our land.

Thus spake the aristocracy, the landed gentry, the men and women whose families had been in Burke's Peerage since its first edition – and many who were qualified for inclusion for centuries before that. Some of them, except when it came to the unavoidable necessity of 'doing the season' in order to bring out their daughters for the marriage market, did their best to keep their eye concentrated on the fox's brush and the keeper's habits and forget about the changing pattern of Society that was going on in London. Others accepted the challenge of the plutocrats, and partially out of an innate determination not to be worsted, and partially in an often subconscious urge to educate these interlopers as they married their money into the old cadres of Society, they looked them in the eye and outspent them at every turn. On the one hand were the Ponderevos, the Frickers, the 'boating grocers', the tea merchants and the news-paper magnates – for by 1905 the newspapers were at the height of their power, not merely a Fourth Estate but a foreclosing mortgagor on the other three.

Those were on one side, and on the other were the great dukes (some already married into the money of the American millionaires) and the men whose lesser titles disguised from the uninitiated the feudal powers they held over tens of thousands of acres.

The outcome of this monetary duel was a rapid acceleration in spending for show. As the fight went on between the gold lace hats and those who tried to buy hats which would outvie them in lace and gold and every expensive nonsense that could be crammed around their brims, the people outside the struggle who read their newspapers and crowded round the big London houses to see the famous arrive were rewarded with a panoply of ostentation. It is true that the consequences of this spending included a benefit to trade – or at least to those trades, and there were many, which catered for the ostentation of the rich. Among them were the new hand-maidens of fast travel – motor-cars, and at the end of Edward's reign, aeroplanes. It was 'last across the road' played with money.

C. F. G. Masterman, a junior minister in Asquith's first government, looked with distaste at the vulgarity of these new irresponsible rich. He abhorred the urban, industrial society which had been created by the aggressive capitalism of the later Victorians, and he bemoaned the lack of religious faith that accompanied it. He wrote in 1909 in *The Condition of England*

'We have called into existence a whole new industry in motor cars and quick travelling, and established populous cities to minister to our increasing demands for speed. We have converted half the Highlands into deer forests for our sport; and the amount annually spent on shooting, racing, golf . . . exceeds the total revenue of many a European principality. We fling away in ugly white hotels, in uninspired dramatic entertainments, and in elaborate banquets of which one is weary, the price of many poor men's yearly income. Yet we cannot build a new cathedral.'

Masterman equated fulness of bread with leanness of soul. Conspicuous expenditure was the order of the day.

Both the making and spending of millions was an Edwardian trait – a trait learnt by the American yellow rich some decades previously. This is not to suggest, of course, that no one spent millions before the Edwardians. There was many a gambling-mad marquess who put the family estates up the creek before the turn of the century. But making the millions was something different. It was the sole object of that financial buccaneering that thrived increasingly throughout the later Victorian decades and is still not entirely unknown. Nonetheless, even though financial buccaneering began before Edward VII actually reached the throne and continued long after he died, there is something typically Edwardian about it. No doubt it may be maligning the actual persons who created the legend, some of the King's friends among them. But they take their place in history in that guise.

There is no better book about financial buccaneering at this period than Wells's *Tono-Bungay* (1908). Edward Ponderevo begins with a little chemist's shop in Wimblehurst, a fictitious outer suburb of London. He chances his arm and loses the shop. He hides himself in the maw of London, invents a patent medicine called Tono-Bungay and from there, with his nephew George's help, rapidly emerges as a soaring rocket that bursts upon the firmament of City shares and mergers like a second advent. But money, he finds, brought its social obligations. One had to live up to one's money and behave as one's money demanded. The Ponderevos moved first to Beckenham, another London suburb, where everyone was pretending they were better than they were. From there it was Chislehurst, a little further out, with week-ending at plush hotels on the South Coast. One went there in one's motor and one's fellow-guests were learning the social conventions just as one was oneself. It was part of a swift and systematic conversion to gentility that was going on throughout the whole commercial upper middle class – the 'upper' being a definition of income, not of breeding or intellect. And from Chislehurst to a mansion folly called Crest Hill in the peerage belt of Sussex, with a vast apartment in a London hotel for the week-day deals and interviews. These were the sort of bases from which one sallied forth into the shops and markets of the world to plunder objects that one might not necessarily want but which were essential to the consolidation of one's new social position. Thus the Ponderevos. They learnt to spend money, part of a heterogeneous collection whose only common factor was that they were all moving, and particularly their womenkind were moving, 'from conditions in which means were insistently finite, things were few and customs simple towards a limitless expenditure and the sphere of attraction of Bond Street, Fifth Avenue, and Paris'. They bought everything they could lay their hands on, encouraged by the illustrated weeklies which guided them in everything they did. Acquisition became the substance of their lives and the world was organised to gratify that passion.

It happened to Uncle Teddy Ponderevo. At Beckenham and Chislehurst he was chiefly interested in amassing money. Then he began to shop – and 'to shop violently'. And then in the end the rocket's stars went fizzling out and the stick fell sadly to the ground. George helped his uncle to escape to France in a dirigible balloon which was part of his own aeronautical experiments; but they dropped to earth on the west coast of France and Uncle Teddy died in a small auberge along Les Landes somewhere north of Biarritz. It was a fitting area for an Edwardian financier to die in.

Plutocrats were not a unique feature of Edwardian Britain. They flourished in South Africa, they flourished in Australia, they flourished in France, and most of all they flourished in the United States where a firm but gentle critic christened them 'the yellow rich'. The critic was Owen Wister, remembered today, when remembered at all, as the author of *The Virginian*. In a way the Wild West might seem the last subject Wister would have chosen. He was by nature and upbringing a European. His grandmother – his mother's mother – was the great Fanny Kemble. His mother, a formidable lady, married one of Philadelphia's leading citizens. Owen was brought up in a house with family portraits by Reynolds and Lawrence and with framed letters from George Washington on the walls. He played the piano to professional standards, he composed music, he spoke perfect idiomatic French, and he began to write. When he was a young man he went to Europe, met Liszt and Liszt's son-in-law Wagner, hob-nobbed with the composer in Bayreuth, and, through his impeccable introductions moved, like an as yet unwritten Henry Jamesian character, through the couloirs and salons of European culture. Back in the United States he went to a ranch in Wyoming to recuperate from an illness, and it was here that in the saloons and on the ranches his warm humanity and imagination was seized by the sights and sounds and beauties of the West. Wondering why the West had not had its Kipling, he announced to a friend one fall evening in 1891, 'I'm going to try it myself'. From that determination came *The Virginian, Lin McLean, Red Men and White, When West was West,* and such immortal phrases as 'When you call me that, *smile*' – without which no Western movie seems to have been able to authenticate its dialogue since the phrase came into common parlance.

All this may seem a long way from the plutocrats. But the West was not the whole of Wister. There was still that sympathy for Europe, that cultural background of Mozart and salons. He was the friend and biographer of Teddy Roosevelt, and in the First World War he was an ardent pro-Britisher from the very outset – indeed he was the author of *The Pentecost of Calamity,* which looks with passionate sadness at the self-destruction of Europe. Thus, for those who knew him, the polite but scathing irony with which he put down the plutocrats in another of his books was no surprise.

Lady Baltimore, published in 1906, was Wister's silky-pawed attack on the current state of American Society. The title of the book, incidentally, derives not from some noble relict of the family that gave its name to Maryland's state capital but from an especially delicious sort of cake called Lady Baltimore that forms a fine thread of romantic narrative throughout the novel. In *Lady Baltimore* the plutocrats are compared unfavourably with the remnants of the old Colonial Society that still holds – to the death – to different values. Not that the follies of the old Colonial Society go uncriticised – although where the ladies are concerned their foibles are treated with the same tender admonishments that were accorded to Miss Matty in *Cranford.* Nor was Wister uncritical of some of the things that were going on in England, much as he loved that Jamesian paradise. In particular he did not take at all kindly to the steady trickle of dukes who crossed the Atlantic looking for duchesses whose fathers were millionaires, wherever those millions came from. Nor was the title-dollar market simply between English dukes and Chicago heiresses. Many a long-titled, spendthrift European Count, especially in Republican France, saw the advantages of one night in a marriage bed with a daughter of America's 'yellow rich'.*

Lady Baltimore is set in King's Port, South Carolina. The narrator is Augustus from Boston; the hero is John Mayrant, the heroine (in the romantic sense) turns out to be Eliza La Heu (the lady who bakes the Lady Baltimores), but the central character (who doesn't appear until half-way through the book, although she is continually referred to throughout its first half and who dominates it from start to finish) is a young-ish, short-knickered, cigarette-smoking, 'fast' lady called Hortense Rieppe. Hortense came originally from South Carolina, but she had thrown her hat at Newport, Rhode Island, society and her hat had been caught – and held more than once.

This was the 'new' Newport society, those, says Mayrant, 'who get into the papers, who dine the drunken dukes, and make poor chambermaids envious a thousand miles inland!' 'There should be a high tariff on drunken dukes,' Augustus counters.

'You'll never get it!' Mayrant declares. 'It's the Republican party whose daughters marry them,' and with the exception of Grover Cleveland's eight years of in-and-out Democratic presidency there had been Republican Presidents in the White House since 1869; so Mayrant had a point.

There were three sorts of Newport society, Mayrant explained to his friend: 'Those who have to sell their old family pictures, those who have to buy their old family pictures, and the lucky few who need neither buy nor sell, who are neither going down nor bobbing up, but who have kept their heads above the American tidal wave from the beginning and continue to do so.'

Those who had to buy their old family pictures were 'the re-placers', the 'yellow rich'. 'If you don't want to see yourself

---

* And lest one might feel sorry for the poor innocent daughters of rich America sacrificing their maidenheads to titled European roués, a glance at a du Maurier cartoon in *Punch* in 1881 will be sufficient to allay fears of Minotauran rape. A number of eligible young American damosels are about to set off for Europe. They are examining Debrett. 'What a pity', says Clara Van Deppenbeck, 'that they don't publish their photographs as well as their ages and titles.'

jolly well replaced,' says one of Augustus's more cynical friends, Beverley Rodgers, another Ivy League man, 'you must fall in with the replacers.' Newport society was the symbol for all that was going wrong. It was a world of boating grocers and beef barons, of sugar sharks and railroad robbers. And it was all the fault of the women. In an exchange of views that Augustus has with a Southern gentleman, Wister makes the point – at the same time flicking with his claw at the mores of Southern society.

'South Carolina, sir,' says the haughty Southern gentleman, 'South Carolina has never lacked sporting blood, sir. But in Newport – well, sir, we gentlemen down here when we wish a certain atmosphere and all that have always been accustomed to seek the *demi-monde*.'

'So it was with us until the women changed it,' said the sophisticated Augustus from Boston.

'The women, sir?'

He *was* innocent! thought Augustus.

'The "ladies",' he corrected himself. 'The "ladies" as you Southerners so chivalrously continue to style them. The rich new fashionable ladies became so desperate in their competition for men's allegiance that they – well, some of them would, in the point of conversation, greatly scandalize the smart *demi-monde*.'

Hortense Rieppe was one of those 'ladies'; and despite her South Carolinian background she had joined 'the replacers'. Another who had done so was Beverley Rodgers. 'Our blooming old republic is merely the quickest process of endless replacing yet discovered, and you take my tip', he tells Augustus, 'and back the replacers! That's where Miss Rieppe, for all her King's Port tradition, shows sense.' She showed it to the extent of marrying Charley the banker, and the bridal party (so the papers reported) sat on a dais and was composed exclusively of Oil, Sugar, Beef, Steel and Union Pacific – the 'yellow rich' in fact.

Whether John Mayrant was justified in dubbing them 'drunken' or not, his friend Augustus was certainly right in saying that British dukes were making a habit of going to the United

States to find heiresses as wives. Not only dukes but their brothers too. It was a habit that began in the 1870s. The first ducal house to risk a marital connection with the 'yellow rich' was the Marlborough's. In 1874 Lord Randolph Churchill, third son of the seventh Duke, married Jennie Jerome, one of the three daughters of Leonard Jerome of New York. Some years later Lord Randolph's eldest brother was divorced by his wife, the daughter of the Duke of Abercorn, and soon afterwards succeeded his father as the eighth Duke of Marlborough. Financially his heritage was strained. It was apparently Leonard Jerome, for whom he had a great regard, who suggested that he restore the family fortune by marrying a rich American. One of those available was the exceedingly rich and amiable widow, Mrs Lilian Hammersley. In 1888 the Duke went to the States and married his Lilian within a month. For four years he enjoyed the cornucopia of dollars she brought back to Blenheim – installing central heating, electric light and telephones, among other amenities, in the palace that Vanbrugh had built. Then he died. His widow had no intention of losing her rank and even when she married Lord William Beresford she continued to call herself Lilian, Duchess of Marlborough.

The ninth Duke of Marlborough continued the American bride tradition – and improved on it by marrying successively two rich heiresses. His first wife, who married him much against her will because she had fallen in love with a fellow-American during the marriage negotiations that were conducted by her mother, was Consuelo Vanderbilt. Consuelo was a great-granddaughter of the formidable 'Commodore' who had founded the family fortune. Her mother was Mrs William Kissam Vanderbilt, no less formidable as a social dragon. She came from the South, where she was born Alva Erskine Smith. After the Civil War her father, who was ruined by the liberation of his slaves, moved to Paris where she became enraptured by France and the glamour of nobility. As her own daughter began to grow up she decided that Consuelo would be a duchess – and that was that. She ordered her to marry the Duke, and poor Consuelo wept throughout the morning of her wedding-day. In 1906, after eleven years of marriage during which their life together had only accentuated their differences the couple separated; in 1921 they were divorced. The Duke

thereupon married a second wealthy American, Gladys Deacon
of Boston, who had fluttered the heart of the German Crown
Prince 'Little Willie' on a visit to Blenheim at the turn of the
century.

After her separation Consuelo became involved in philanthropic activities, chairing charity committees and joining social
reform groups. She helped to implement the scheme for re-
moving Bedford College for women, part of London University, from Baker Street to its present location in the green acres
of Regent's Park where it is now a mixed college. She ran a
home for assisting the wives of first offenders in prison, and the
Mary Curzon Lodging House for Poor Women (named after
Lord Curzon's first wife, who was an American) was another
permanent interest. She recorded proudly in her autobiography
what a compliment it had been to be invited to join Beatrice
Webb's circle: 'she had the beauty of an eagle with finely chisel-
led features, while in her look one saw the soaring, searching
quality of her mind'. Sadly, Beatrice Webb did not reciprocate
this complimentary opinion. In October 1905 she wrote of the
Marlboroughs in her diary as 'somewhat futile young persons
floating aimlessly on the surface of society, both alike quite
unfit for their great position. . . . The little Duke is, I should
imagine, mildly vicious – the Duchess has charm and, I think,
goodness. . . . They reminded us of H. G. Wells's "little white
people" in *The Time Machine*'.

The Duchess also took an active part in politics and was a
member of the London County Council from 1917 to 1919. In
November 1913 she helped Gertrude Tuckwell and Margaret
Lawrence, two Trade Union officials, to organise a meeting at
her London home, Sunderland House in Curzon Street, to call
attention to the plight of women in sweated industries. 'Sweating' was the dominant social evil in public consciousness during the Edwardian period, just as prostitution was 'the social
evil' during the preceding Victorian years. The leaders of
opinion and ornaments of society who came at the Duchess's
call found that instead of taking part in the usual amiable and
platitudinous discussions which involved the enjoyment of a
superb collation they were there to listen to twelve old women
who each in turn related the details of their sweated working
lives.

The press was well represented at the meeting and one paper reported that

'the sweated women's conference which was organised recently by the Duchess of Marlborough has probably done more to advance the cause of female suffrage in Britain than the violent combined efforts of the militant suffragettes. It is evident that the Duchess of Marlborough understands the British public. She is in closer touch with the thrifty spirit of the nation, which abhors the house-burning and window-breaking methods of illuminating grievances, than any of her radical co-workers.'

As the result of this conference, the Duchess claimed, 'trade boards were opened to about eight more sweated industries'. Trade boards were created under a 1909 Act to secure a minimum wage for certain sweated industries. To start with the Act applied only to the tailoring, dress-making, and shirt-making industries, but provision was made for trade boards to be set up for other industries if the demand for them were made.* After her divorce Consuelo married Colonel Jacques Balsan of the French Air Force and together they went to the United States after the fall of France in 1940. Subsequently she wrote *The Glitter and the Gold*† in which she told the story of her ducal marriage and of her life at Blenheim Palace as well as of the happiness of her twenty married years in France.

Her mother, the redoubtable Mrs William Kissam Vanderbilt, who had a passion for building huge elaborate mansions in addition to dominating the commanding heights of Society, divorced her husband in the same year that she ordered her daughter to marry the Duke of Marlborough. She then married Oliver H. P. Belmont, a noted whip and man of taste in New York society, who died in 1908. Thereafter she became totally engrossed in the suffrage movement. 'To this end,' wrote her daughter, 'she sacrificed her time, her wealth, even her personal feelings.' She started by supporting the National American Woman Suffrage Association which for ten years until 1915 was led by Dr Anna Shaw, a qualified doctor and an ordained minister of a small Methodist sect, and in 1913 she and Consuelo

* See p. 102, below.
† Heinemann, 1953.

went to the Biennial Convention of the International Woman Suffrage Alliance in Hungary, where Dr Shaw preached a sermon on the virtues of woman's suffrage. By the time Dr Shaw was ousted from her leadership and had been replaced by Carrie Chapman Catt, whom she herself had supplanted at the end of 1904, Mrs Belmont had become disenchanted with the NAWSA as had the NAWSA with her. Arguments about strategy – whether suffrage should be sought by individual State legislation (nine States already gave women full suffrage), or by an amendment to the Constitution; the States route or the Federal route.

Arguments based on the perennial geographical rivalry between Easterners and Westerners with the South having its own racialist viewpoint. Arguments about whether Anna Shaw's approach was too moderate and too middle class. Arguments between Republicans and Democrats. And, perhaps above all, arguments that stemmed from private feuds and the desire for power. Mrs Belmont left the NAWSA and took her considerable personality and enormous fortune over to the militant Woman's Party. This had just been formed by the amalgamation of the Women's Political Union, founded in 1907 by Harriot Blatch who was the daughter of the pioneer women's suffragist Elizabeth Stanton, and the Congressional Union, formed in 1913 by Alice Paul. Both Blatch and Paul had been in England (Blatch for twenty years) and had seen the workings of the Pankhursts' Women's Social and Political Union – Paul indeed had served a fighting apprenticeship in it. The object of the WPU was to involve all working women in the struggle for the vote; its original title was the Equality League of Self-Supporting Women. The object of the Congressional Union was to campaign for the Federal route – the route that was ultimately successful when the Nineteenth Amendment was ratified in August 1920. Mrs Belmont's most spectacular exploit was during the presidential election when Woodrow Wilson was seeking re-election. The Woman's Party supported the Republican candidate Charles Evans Hughes, who had been persuaded to support the Federal route, known as the 'Anthony amendment' after Susan Anthony, whereas Wilson's support for woman's suffrage was through the action of individual states – the States route.

Mrs Belmont hired a train which she filled with upper class Eastern socialites and sent it through the West to campaign for Hughes. The resentment of the Westerners was roused and one Western suffragist picketed the train with the legend 'Which Goose Laid The Golden Egg?'. The train was thereafter dubbed the 'Golden Special'.

Through her mother Consuelo met some of the suffragette leaders including Mrs Emmeline Pankhurst. Christabel Pankhurst, who ran the British suffragette campaign in its later stages from Paris, often stayed with Mrs Belmont who had a home there. Christabel's later conversion to the Book of Revelations and her prophecy as a result of studying that vast landscape of the future that Armageddon would soon be upon us made Consuelo reflect that 'if so, women should don armour rather than exercise a futile vote'. Both Christabel Pankhurst and Mrs Belmont shared a common hatred for the male although both, as one might expect from that overall loathing, delighted in men's company. A letter written to a friend by Mrs Belmont explained why she was a male-hater. 'My first experiences in life gave birth to my belief in militant woman suffrage. I found even at the age of seven that boys looked down upon girls. I can almost feel my childish hot blood rise as it did then in rebellion at some such taunting remarks as: "you can't run." "You can't climb trees." "You're only a girl." But no young would-be masculine bravado ever expressed twice such slurring belittlements of me.' Mrs Belmont's solution for the problem of young prostitutes was blunt: 'Arrest the men,' she said.

The other dukes to marry rich American ladies were the eighth and ninth Dukes of Manchester and the eighth Duke of Roxburghe – eight and nine were clearly portentous numbers in ducal astrology or perhaps in ducal finances! The eighth Duke of Manchester, who succeeded his father in 1890, was married in 1876 to another Consuelo, Consuelo Vanderbilt's godmother, who died in 1909. This senior Consuelo was the daughter of Don Antonio Yznaga de Valle who hailed from Cuba, Louisiana and New York. In 1900 their son, who became the ninth Duke, married Helena Zimmerman, the daughter of a millionaire Cincinnati rail contractor. The Manchesters by this time were a fairly cosmopolitan lot:

the seventh Duke had married a German, Countess Louise von Alten of Hanover, the lady who later became known as the Double Duchess after she had married the eighth Duke of Devonshire in 1892 when they were both sexagenarians.

Helena Zimmerman, whom he divorced in 1931, was Manchester's second choice. His first choice was one he shared with many others. Her name was 'Baby May' Goelet. She eventually brought her millions to the eighth Duke of Roxburghe and went to live in another Vanbrugh creation, the Castle of Floors near Kelso. 'Baby May' had been courted by an eager flock of Counts and Grafs and Earls and others, as well as by the two Dukes, for it was not only dukes whose finances benefited from marrying dollars.

Not all American heiresses went to England to find a duke or lesser lord. Some went to Italy, some to Paris. Among the latter were Miss Adela Simpson, who married the Duc Charles Maurice de Talleyrand-Perigord bringing him a dowry of $7 million; Miss Forbes who brought the Duc of Choiseul $1 million; Miss Isabel Singer of sewing-machine money whose dowry was $2 million when she married the Duc Jean-Elie Octave Decazes; Miss Winarella Singer, another of the sewing-machine heiresses, who became the Princess de Polignac; the Duchesse de Chaulne *née* Miss Schautz; the Baronesse de la Sellière (Mrs Livermore); the Marquise de Choiseul (Miss Clara Coudert); the Comtesse Guy de Rohan Chabot (Miss Hayward); the Princesse Charaman-Chimay, *née* Clara Ward of Detroit, who eventually made off with a violinist called Rigo and then appeared at the Folies Bergères – that most sophisticated of Arcadias – in the traditional occupation of 'Poses Plastiques', clad in pink tights; and Anna Gould, the homely daughter of multi-millionaire Jay Gould who had fought 'Commodore' Vanderbilt for control of the Erie Railroad in 1867–8 and, with his partners James Fisk and Daniel Drew, had looted the Erie treasury when they were successful and who the following year had caused the Black Friday Wall Street panic by his attempt to corner the gold market. Anna married Comte Boniface de Castellane in 1894 and found the $15 million dowry she brought with her paying for some of the most resplendently lavish parties Paris had ever seen. Boni de Castellane was one of the pioneers of the trade in which an Old

World title was sold for a New World inheritance. So important did the trade become that when an unmarried American millionairess appeared in the Faubourg St Germain the unmarried noblemen praised Lafayette and murmured '*Merci, Christophe Colombe!*' Some years later Anna, who has been described as hopelessly plain and sallow, with heavy eyebrows that almost met over her nose and with scrawny arms that were covered with hairs in a dark fuzz that went clear up to her shoulders, divorced the Comte Boni, last of the dandies and refugee from eighteenth-century Versailles, and married his cousin, Helie de Sagan, Duc de Talleyrand.

There were other rich American ladies who had settled in Paris. One of the best known in the early 1900s was Madame Kate Moore. Parisian Society was as much entertained by her eccentricities and social climbing as by her fantastic parties. Among other flights of financial folly she used to take a villa at Biarritz year after year and eventually succeeded in giving a luncheon party there for Edward VII – the real object of her long drawn-out exercise. There had once been a Monsieur Moore and the story is told of how one morning he went for a walk. His wife, too, having checked that all was ready for her socially vital luncheon party for twelve, also went for a walk. When she returned home she was met by a footman who told her with horror, '*Monsieur est mort; tué par un autobus.*' '*Bon*', said Madame Moore with the greatest *sangfroid*. '*Enlevez un couvert.*' When she herself came to die it was found that she had left a large number of legacies to those who had helped her up her social path. Count Robert de Montesquiou, part model for Proust's Baron Charlus, commented: 'Mrs Moore left life as she left the Ritz – handing out tips.' She was silly, but she was kind, and she was an Edwardian to the ends of her fat little toes.

It has been estimated that by the end of the Edwardian era New World heiresses had enriched Old World husbands by some £40 million. But it was not only to America that dukes and the lesser nobility went to find wives who were not members of the usual aristocratic circle. Actresses, and especially Gaiety Girls, were also an important source, although in their case the attraction was not a mountain of money. As the diplomat remarked to Beatrice Webb, 'a perpetual process of casting out and renewal'.

The process was not acceptable to all the aristocracy. Lady Casterley, the matriarch in Galsworthy's *The Patrician* (1911), told her grand-daughter: 'All this marrying with Gaiety girls, and American money, and people with pasts, and writers and so forth, is most damaging. There's far too much of it and it ought to be stopped.'

Chapter 3

'PRETTY FACES AND LARGE FORTUNES'

Edward VII's Court was a continuation of the Marlborough House set that had gathered round him since his marriage to Princess Alexandra of Denmark in 1863. The marriage ceremony itself had been played in a low key because the Queen was in the deepest mourning for her husband's death and refused to listen to the call of public duty that demanded that Britain's future king should be married in Westminster Abbey with all the trappings, trimmings, and advantages to trade that such a royal occasion would produce. London wanted a show, one that would bring the colour back into the cheeks of the capital after all the dull flat months of mourning for that over-perfect Prince. And London meant both the day-to-day people shoving their way along the stinking streets and the 'establishment' (to use its latter-day connotation) who were anxious to dress themselves up in their knee-breeches and tiaras (as the case might be) and, whatever their ritual grumbling to the contrary, to demonstrate their vital places in the hierarchy of the nation.

But the Queen would have none of it. To hold the ceremony in Westminster Abbey would mean that she would have to appear in public. Unthinkable, with the Mausoleum at Frogmore hardly built. She insisted that the Prince of Wales be married in the semi-privacy of St George's Chapel, Windsor, where there could be only a few guests and even such stars in the aristocratic firmament as dukes and their duchesses would have to wait outside. The wheel was to come full circle with Edward's Coronation when the 'establishment' was determined

45

not only to have its money's-worth but nearly forty years of compound interest as well.

The Marlborough House set – so named from the Prince's London home on a corner at the end of Pall Mall, across the road from St James's Palace – was not the usual sort of clan that an heir to a throne gathers round him. Politically, apart from discreet furthering of specific issues at home and the Prince's own genuine concern for social reform together with an occasional exciting run into the intrigues of foreign policy, it was unimportant. Socially, in matters of dress, manners, attitudes, it was all-important – as all-important as Beau Brummell's cravat had been in the early years of the century. It did not flout convention in public, but it had little use for morality in private. Sport and fashion were the currency of its daily life, and by sport it meant hunting, shooting, a mild amount of fishing, and a great deal of racing. With racing went betting, and with betting went gambling on a grand scale.

Edward's circle, whether as a set around him as Prince of Wales or as a Court around him as King, was more eclectic than his mother's. Instead of Palmerston and Beaconsfield were Lord Randolph Churchill (off and on) and Lord Charles Beresford (more off than on). There were cronies like the Marquis de Soveral, the Portuguese Minister, and Christopher Sykes. There were financiers, some of whom were also cronies: the Rothschilds, the Sassoons, the Beits, Sir Julius Charles Wernher, Eckstein, Albu, Oppenheim, Baron Hirsch and the monetary genius Sir Ernest Cassel, who became one of the administrators of Edward's finances when he became king.

As well as these gentlemen and those of the King's household there were in the Marlborough House set a large number of attractive young men and women. For a time these included the ninth Duke of Marlborough and his young American wife, for Edward was as fond of Americans as he was of 'pretty faces and large fortunes'* and this predilection increased after 1898 when Mrs Keppel became his chosen lady, for Mrs Keppel, that supreme comforter of high office and kindest and most discreet of power-dispensers, who appears as Mrs Romola Cheyne in *The Edwardians*, had many Americans among her close friends.

* Philippe Jullian's phrase in *Edward and The Edwardians* (Sidgwick & Jackson, 1967).

Lady Paget, born Minnie Stevens, Jennie Jerome, now Lady Randolph Churchill, Mrs Cavendish-Bentinck, and the Duchess of Manchester as well as the other Consuelo Duchess, were the core of the American element in the small smart coterie of the Marlborough House set. In July 1901 this American contingent chartered and equipped the *Maine* as a hospital ship for the Boer War.

Philippe Jullian has listed the qualities that the King expected of his courtiers as 'an impeccable sense of dress, the ability to play a good hand at bridge, some knowledge of the Turf, fluency in both French and German, powers of conversation capable of preventing a lapse into silence'. They were a close-knit clan. They had their own slang, reproduced by V. Sackville-West in *The Edwardians*, with English words being given Italianate endings: 'partnerino, dinnare, dansare, lovelare' and so on. Everyone had a nickname. The Marquis de Soveral was the Blue Monkey, the King was Tum-Tum (though it was unwise to call him so to his face and Mrs Keppel's daughters were on safer ground calling him Kingy). Extramarital activities within the accepted range of people were carried on in such an organised fashion that a hostess's chief responsibility at a week-end house party – and the week-end party was very much an Edwardian innovation – was to ensure that there was not too much padding down midnight corridors but that those with a common interest should be comfortably contiguous in the matter of bedrooms. In Mrs Keppel's immortal words: *'à chacun sa chacune.'*

Alice Keppel, daughter of an admiral, bridge fiend, ally of Sir Ernest Cassel who managed her money for her, and wife of a brother of the Earl of Albemarle, was the third of the ladies with whom Edward VII's name is traditionally linked. That there were a considerable number of others over the years is undoubted, but their identities have long since been lost in the conflagration of Edward's private papers and in the discretion which was obligatory if one was to remain in Society. The first of the ladies was Lillie Langtry, the 'Jersey Lily', so-called because she was born and brought up in that Channel Island, the Dean's daughter, from the boredom of which life she escaped at an early age by marrying a passing yachtsman. Within a short time she was in London Society, and before long she was Edward's mistress, having met him with her husband on 24 May 1877 at the house of an Arctic explorer, Sir Allen Young. The meeting was pre-arranged. Mrs Langtry was then aged twenty-six. The passing yachtsman drifted away and Lillie, after a bad patch both socially and financially, had a highly successful career on the stage and, later, in Hollywood. In due course she became Lady de Bathe.

The second of Edward's great ladies was Lady Brooke. Christened Frances Evelyn but known as Daisy from her childhood, she was the heiress of her grandfather, the last Lord Maynard, and from him inherited a huge fortune including Easton Lodge and its estates in Essex. She married Lord Brooke, the Earl of Warwick's heir, in 1881. One of her first meetings with the Prince of Wales was at a ball in 1883, but it was not until 1886, when she was twenty-six years old, that she and her husband became part of the Marlborough House set. Years later, when she had long been a member of the Labour Party, she wrote scathingly of 'that glamorous circle which was so much discussed, so much envied, and so sadly overrated. Outwardly it was a life of idle pleasure, and was condemned in consequence. This was only true in part, for duty was a big word in those days. We took a personal interest in our tenants, their families, and their affairs'. But despite this respect for duty she later resented 'the waste of time, the waste of energy, and most of all, the waste of brain-power that such an existence entailed'. Shopkeepers were not so critical. 'Our patronage was sought by tradesmen, eager to gratify our every caprice for the honour of serving us, while waiting indefinitely for our money. In those days, bills were presented yearly, sometimes triennially.'

During the London season

'. . . the special achievement of the Marlborough House set was to turn night into day. We would dine late and long, trifle with the Opera for an hour or so, or watch the ballet at the Empire, then "go on" to as many houses as we could crowd in. The extravagance involved in country-house entertainment was so considerable that some of Royalty's friends could not afford it. In certain houses of unlimited wealth, it had become customary to have a Royal suite specially refurnished on the occasion of each visit, in order that the note of novelty might be maintained. The chef who served for ordinary occasions would be replaced by a specialist, whose skill was equalled only by his wastefulness. . . . Added to the cost of entertaining the guests was the expense of caring for the cohorts of servants that their visit entailed.'

One thing that was not kindly taken to was brains. 'As a class, we did not like brains.' And while acknowledging that there were people whose job it might be to paint pictures or write books, or administer the law 'we did not see why their achievements entitled them to our recognition; they might disturb, over-stimulate, or even bore'. Nonetheless, she did concede that the Marlborough House set had glamour, 'indeed glamour was its particular asset. It created the atmosphere which intrigued the public. I can feel something of the same sense of enchantment, in recalling it, that children experienced when they watched the transformation scene at the panto-mime'.*

Edward, as Prince of Wales, was not the only one to fall for the bubbling charms of the extravagant Daisy. Another of her admirers was Lord Charles Beresford, a pugnacious naval officer who had been the Prince's boon companion for many years. Daisy was the cause of a personal quarrel between the two men. She wrote an indiscreet letter to her ex-lover, Lord Charles, which fell into the hands of Lady Charles, who used it to threaten Daisy if she caused the Beresfords any further annoyance. Edward, appealed to by Daisy, called on Lady Charles to ask her to destroy the letter. But she refused. The Prince ceased to invite Lady Charles to parties at Marlborough House, and her husband took violent umbrage at this social boycotting of his wife and on one occasion almost struck the Prince. In the end the Prime Minister, Lord Salisbury, achieved a settlement and the letter was returned to Daisy for burning in March 1892. It had been an unhappy affair, lasting for more than two years, and it was not the only occasion on which letters to or from 'my darling Daisy' were to cause trouble.†

* Frances, Countess of Warwick, *Afterthoughts* (Cassell, 1931), Chapter 4 *passim*.

† See Margaret Blunden, *The Countess of Warwick* (Cassell, 1967) and Theo Lang.

In 1893 Lord Brooke succeeded his father as fifth Earl of Warwick and Daisy became known by the name by which she is most familiar, the Countess of Warwick. Although she probably ceased to be Edward's mistress about this period it was not until just before the birth of her son Maynard in March 1898 that Alice Keppel appeared on the scene. By this time her philanthropic work was well under way. It began in 1890 with the foundation of a needlework school at Easton for local girls. The following year, to provide a show-room for their marvellous embroidery which included the lingerie for the future Queen Mary's trousseau, she opened 'Lady Brooke's Depot for the Easton School of Needlework' in Bond Street, the heart of London's fashionable quarter; thus becoming one of the first of the lady shopkeepers who were to proliferate around the West End. That Lady Brooke had 'taken up shop' caused much sneering gossip in Society, despite the justifications which she wrote in an article for the *Queen* magazine. The Bond Street shop was sold in 1902, more the victim, as were other schemes in her life, of her lagging interest and lack of business ability than of idle gossip. In 1897 she started a co-educational school on the Easton estate which provided the only secondary education in the locality with a bias towards science and agriculture. The following year she opened a hostel in connection with the University Extension College at Reading for the training of women in the lighter branches of agriculture such as horticulture and apiculture. Five years later the Lady Warwick Hostel at Reading was moved under her direction to Studley Castle in Warwickshire, where it was re-named the Studley Agricultural College for Women.

Lady Warwick had a succession of lovers among whom were reputed to be Haig, Rosebery, and Captain J. F. Laycock. Another of her close male friends, though their relationship was what is usually, and curiously, called platonic, was the crusading editor W. T. Stead, whom she met at a dinner in 1892. She often turned to Stead for advice and help and it was his influence which made her take an interest in radicalism. But the person who really changed her attitudes and turned her away from the conspicuous waste of the Marlborough House set was the ex-sergeant of the Dublin Fusiliers, Robert Blatchford, who started the famous Socialist *Clarion* in 1891. She met him in

February 1895, marching in to his office at the drab end of Fleet Street to complain about an article he had written castigating an extravagant ball she had given at Warwick Castle. This was the beginning of a ten-year political journey that culminated in her joining the Labour Party in 1905.

The true quality of the circle that surrounded Edward, both as Prince of Wales and as eventual King, wrote Philip Magnus, was

'. . . obscured in a hothouse world of game preservation, gold plate, jewels and other luxuries, and their sense of complete security was buttressed by the gaping servility of a host of inferiors. Some, in those circumstances, had recourse to gambling and other absorbing hazards, and most convinced themselves that they personally embodied English history; that the Empire belonged peculiarly to them; and that the future of both, as well as their own survival, depended upon the maintenance of privileges which they accepted as rights.'*

Nor was its sybaritic existence confined to those who were in the King's immediate circle. It spread through all the interlinking circles of Society, although in the case of the political sets it was tempered with the discussion and practice of government.

Chief among these political sets in the 1890s and the early years of Edward's reign was a group of friends known as The Souls, with Margot Asquith at the helm. In her *Autobiography* she wrote that no one ever knew how she and her particular friends were called 'The Souls', but the reason is obvious within the pages of her own book. In 1889 George Nathaniel Curzon, who was to become Viceroy of India ten years later, had to leave for a stay in Switzerland on account of his health. On the eve of his departure he gave a dinner party at the Bachelors' Club to his friends, who were referred to by themselves by the somewhat uninspired name of 'The Gang'. Curzon wrote a set of verses, a copy of which was laid at each guest's place. In this 'doggerel appalling', as he called it, he mentioned them all, and included those who were unable to be present. Part of two stanzas of the poem are:

* Sir Philip Magnus, *Edward VII* (Penguin, 1975), p. 230.

'Around that night –
Was there ere such a sight?
Souls sparkled and spirits expanded;
For of them critics sang,
That tho' christened the Gang,
By a spiritual link they were banded.

Souls and spirits, no doubt
But neither without
Fair visible temples to dwell in!'

And the last stanza is:

'And blest by the gang
Be the rhymester who sang
Their praises in doggerel appalling;
More now were a sin –
Ho, waiters begin!
Each soul for consommé is calling!'

'The Souls' immediately presents itself as a much more original collective noun. There were at least fifty of them.*

* Those who belonged to 'The Souls' – who were listed in Curzon's poem – were: himself, Margot Asquith ('the wit and the wielding of it, That makes her the joy of a party'), Arthur Balfour ('Prince Arthur' to his friends), Mr and Mrs Harry White, the fourth Duke and Duchess of Sunderland (who was Daisy Warwick's half-sister), Colonel and Mrs Lawrence Drummond, the Duke and Duchess of Rutland, the Earl and Countess of Pembroke, the Hons Evan and Alan Charteris, the Earl and Countess of Brownlow, Sir John and Lady Horner, Lord and Lady Elcho, Lord and Lady Wenlock, Godfrey Webb, the Hon. Mrs Edward Bourke, the Hon. Spencer Lyttelton, Sir Edgar Vincent (later Lord D'Abernon), Mrs Graham Smith (one of Margot's surviving sisters), Lord and Lady Ribblesdale (her other surviving sister), the Hon. Alfred Lyttelton (whose first wife, Margot's sister Laura, died in childbirth), the Hon. St. John Brodrick (later Earl of Midleton) and his wife Lady Hilda, Mr and Mrs Willy Grenfell (later Lord and Lady Desborough), A. G. C. ('Doll') Liddell, Harry Cust, the Earl and Countess de Grey (later the Marquess and Marchioness of Ripon), the Earl and Countess Cowper, Miss Ponsonby (later Mrs Montgomery, daughter of Queen Victoria's private secretary Sir Henry Ponsonby), Countess Grosvenor, George Wyndham MP, Lord Ferdinand de Rothschild, Viscount Chaplin (the most accomplished gourmet since Lucullus), the Marchioness of Plymouth, the

They belonged to both political parties. Arthur Balfour once told Margot Asquith that prominent politicians of opposite parties seldom if ever met one another. It was The Souls, he suggested, that had made a dialogue possible. Unlike the Marlborough House set – at least as it was described by Lady Warwick – The Souls did not object to 'brains'; 'everyone met,' Lady Asquith wrote in her *Autobiography* waving her pen with a broad sweep, 'Randolph Churchill, Gladstone, Asquith, Morley, Chamberlain, Balfour, Rosebery, Salisbury, Hartington, Harcourt and, I might add, jockeys, actors, the Prince of Wales and every ambassador in London. We never cut anybody – not even our friends – or thought it amusing or distinguished to make people feel uncomfortable; and our decision not to sacrifice private friendship to public politics was envied in every capital in Europe.'* Whether that was an exaggeration or not there is no doubt that for more than a decade in the 1890s and beyond they were the butt of those beyond the pale. Lady Warwick underestimated their number, but expressed the antagonism when she wrote that 'there were only about a dozen members, but all of them wrote poetry and explained their emotions to each other. A shamelessly inquisitive world eavesdropped when it could – especially during the explanations. It was inclined to let the poetry alone'.†

As a matter of fact, trivial as it may seem, the characteristic of The Souls that really got the Lady Warwick down was the way they passed the after-dinner hours. Instead of bridge and baccarat they went in for rather intellectual and literary games which could not help but display a certain bottom of education. Pretentious indeed they were to be intelligent and witty; to be educated as well was social anathema. 'As a class we did not like brains.'

Apart from The Souls the political set revolved round the reigning hostesses: the three great Marchionesses – Londonderry, Lansdowne, and Salisbury – and the Duchesses of Devonshire and Buccleugh among the Conservatives; Lady Spencer

* Eyre & Spottiswoode, 1962 edition, p.92.
† *op. cit.*, p. 126.

Hon. Mrs. Alfred Lyttelton (*née* Edith Balfour, nicknamed D.D.), Mrs Chanler (American novelist, later Princess Troubetzkoy). Lionel Tennyson was another Soul.

(of The Souls) and Lady Tweedmouth among the Liberals. Even Lady Warwick admitted that the Liberal Party was never able to give such splendid entertainments as its Conservative rivals. But she allowed the importance of them all:

'From the time I married (1881) down to the era of the Great War, these hostesses were a dominant factor in English politics. They had vast resources, had been trained almost from birth in the art of entertaining, and were excellent judges of character.... They exercised their power largely through their pull over their own sex. A man might start his political career with every intention of being independent. . . . But if he proved too difficult, there were many ways of bringing him to heel, and the most effective was by cutting him off from the social centre! This might not matter to him, but it mattered terribly to his wife and daughters, who could be counted upon to bring domestic pressure to bear. Hence the political hostess owed much of her influence to her hold on the wives of politicians, and the rest of it to her natural talents and capacity for diplomacy.'*

Among those who had recourse to gambling and the absorbing hazard of racing was Lady Sykes, wife of Sir Tatton Sykes. She, like Edward VII, was bitter about the flibbertigibbet Society women who went out to South Africa to follow the drum. Nominally they were nurses, in practice they helped themselves to as good a time as they could get. For myself, in another war, I bless them for the tedium they relieved. But King Edward was not so thankful. 'I am told,' he said, 'that they walk about the streets of Cape Town dressed as though they were at Ascot or Monte Carlo. One would suppose that if they were not prevented by a sense of the fitness of things, they would at least be deterred by a sense of humour.'

Jessica Sykes, Christina Anne Jessica to give her all her Christian names, was the elder daughter of the Rt. Hon. George Augustus Cavendish-Bentinck, MP, fourth son of the third Duke of Portland. Her mother was Penelope Leslie, sister of John Leslie, MP, to whom Disraeli gave a baronetcy for services to the Conservative cause in Ulster, and aunt of the famous Beresfords whose mother, Christina, was Penelope's

* *Op. cit.*, p. 45.

sister and whose father was a wild and violent Irish rector, who in 1849 became the fourth Marquess of Waterford. It is recorded that when his son Lord William Beresford was given a banquet after winning the VC he said he would rather face an army of Zulus than his Christian father in a bad temper. The Beresford brothers, who were extravagant in all things, did not take kindly to the parsimonious streak in their Aunt Penelope's nature. They felt that when they went to her house for lunch on Sundays there was not enough to eat for the guests. Lord Charles Beresford made the point clear to his aunt by taking his bulldog with him and throwing it the joint before anyone had been served: 'He's had his,' he declared, 'Now where's ours?' There were many tales told of Aunt Penelope – most, no doubt, apocryphal: of how she furnished her dinner table with flowers she had garnered at a funeral she had attended earlier in the day; and of how at a family ball she had dawdled so long on the steps with her daughter Jessica that the Beresfords, whose duty it was to see the guests off, became so exasperated that they bundled the two ladies into the carriage along with the link-boy with lighted torch. Aunt Penelope's dress went up in smoke and she sent in a bill for damages. But Lord Charles Beresford sent more up in smoke than his aunt's dress before he was finished – which is little to be wondered at in a naval officer who had the Waterford Hounds in full cry tattooed down his back with the brush of the fox disappearing where one might well expect as it went to earth.

In 1874 Jessica Cavendish-Bentinck married Sir Tatton Sykes, fifth baronet, who was then aged forty-eight. He had succeeded his father eleven years earlier. Jessica was scarcely out of her teens. Sir Tatton was an eccentric in the established tradition of that genre which was once considered to be such an essential part of British society – provided the eccentricity was a trait of a gentleman or scholar. He was at school at Harrow where his fag-master was Penelope Leslie's brother, later to become the first Sir John Leslie, Bart. Sir Shane Leslie, the first Sir John's grandson, recorded in his memoirs that it was John Leslie who gave Tatton Sykes his first toothbrush. In later life Tatton evolved an excellent method of dressing to meet the vagaries of English weather. He would wear several pairs of trousers and several overcoats at the same time and, assuming

55

that he had started at the minimum temperature, he could always adjust his dress towards the maximum by taking off the odd pair of trousers or overcoat as the thermometer demanded.

Jessica's wooing was somewhat unusual. The story is that Sir Tatton was invited to accompany Jessica on the train from York to London. They were met at King's Cross by Penelope who, it seems, must have been unaware of Jessica's travelling companion, because Sir Shane records – and clearly the family would undoubtedly know the truth – that the baronet was 'guileless' and that there was 'no predilection on the daughter's part and no subterfuge by the mother.' Be that as it may, and whether Jessica had a word to remark to her mother about the journey, whether her mother knew of Tatton's eccentricities when the temperature rose, or whether the mere fact of spending some hours together in a corridorless carriage was sufficient – as it may well have been according to the conventions of the time – when Penelope saw Jessica getting off the train with the over-trousered Tatton she instantly announced the match.

Jessica, it appears, was bewildered by the whole thing and was never consulted about what was to happen to her. She was not asked for her opinion nor did she show any particular enthusiasm for it. Tatton, on the other hand, wriggled a bit and appealed to his brother Christopher to get him off the hook.* But to no avail. Travelling with innocent and unchaperoned young girls in corridorless railway carriages in that day and age was tantamount to an announcement of marriage, as the guileless Tatton was to find out.† As the engagement wore on Tatton became increasingly restive, but in the end he accepted

---

* Christopher Sykes was one of Edward VII's close companions when he was Prince of Wales. The price Sykes paid for this royal favour was high. He was the sad butt for many of the King's practical jokes and oafish pranks and the cost of entertaining him when he descended on him – as he frequently did – became so high that eventually it brought him to the edge of bankruptcy.

† The following year, 1875, Colonel Valentine Baker of the 10th Hussars was arraigned at Croydon for attempting to ravish a young lady on a train travelling between Liphook and London. He was aquitted on this charge but was found guilty of indecent assault and common assault and was sentenced to one year's imprisonment and a fine of £500. He was also cashiered from the Army. As a direct result of the Baker case the corridor train was introduced.

the inevitable. On his wedding day his mother-in-law called for him in a brougham and transported him – in one pair of trousers only, one presumes – to Westminster Abbey where, in Sir Shane Leslie's words 'the amazing marriage was solemnized amid ambitious Cavendish-Bentincks, amused Beresfords, unprotesting Sykes, and wondering Leslies'* and 'to the surprise of Yorkshire'. On 16 March 1879 their only child was born. This child, Mark, was to achieve international fame during the first World War as an adviser to the British Government on Middle Eastern affairs and as co-author of the secret Sykes-Picot Agreement of 1916 which delimited the spheres of influence of the British and French Governments in the territories at that time under Ottoman control.

The Sykes were Woldsmen and owned 34,000 acres at Sledmere, between Malton and Great Driffield in the East Riding of Yorkshire. The great house was built in 1784 and in it Tatton's grandfather, Sir Mark, collected a magnificent library of Elizabethan plays and poems which was sold in 1832 by Tatton's father, 'old' Sir Tatton, for over £10,000. The sale was made in order to save the famous pack of Sykes hounds, each branded with Sir Tatton's S. Books versus hounds. Hounds were more in old Sir Tatton's line. So was bloodstock. His stud became one of the finest in England and he bred the Derby winner St Giles, while his son Tatton bred two more, Doncaster and Spearmint. Despite the sale of the Elizabethan treasures the great house, severe and repellent outside, still had a magnificent library and was full of priceless furniture. Between one o'clock and five on the afternoon of 23 May 1911, however, it was gutted by fire, though many of the treasures were saved.

Neither Tatton nor his son Mark spent much time in their ancestral home, for both were perennial travellers around the world. Indeed Tatton was probably the most dedicated globetrotter of his day, and on most of his travels he would take his wife and son with him. Each year Jessica paid for a children's tea-party in Hull and the extent of her wanderings with her husband and son can be gauged from the fact that her cheque for the tea-party would arrive from Jerusalem or South Africa, from Brazil or Cairo or Mexico. She had been to Assouan (at

---

* *The Film of Memory* (Michael Joseph, 1938), p. 126.

that time almost the Dervish frontier), to India, to the Arabian desert, to the Mexico of Porfirio Diaz.

Jessica was a woman of whirlwind moods whose kindness, like everything else about her, was almost riotous. She was a daunting enthusiast and an inveterate rusher-about. There was no question of her being dragged unwilling about the world on Tatton's journeys. She loved travelling as much as her husband and her son and often initiated expeditions herself. When Mark was at Beaumont she would descend on the school like a thunderbolt, generally half-way through a term, and announce that she proposed to take her son away on some journey or other of indefinite length and for an indefinite period. Despite opposition from the equally pugnacious Rector, Father Heathcote, on this and on other subjects, she habitually achieved her end.

Because of these forays Mark Sykes, as his kinsman Winston Churchill wrote, was 'a unique product. His parents gave him the advantage of a public school education in sparing and sporadic instalments, with the result that his originality was never cramped, and he afterwards enjoyed a University career without becoming a slave to the conventions which it not infrequently implants in susceptible youth. He failed to acquire the standing of a Master of Arts perhaps because he was really proficient in so many of them'.

One of those arts was the art of conversation which he had inherited from his brilliant mother. The epithet is not idly used. Churchill used it, Shane Leslie used it (she was, he wrote, 'the most startling and brilliant relative . . ., a linguist and a conversationalist attractive to such great monologuers as Gladstone and Lord Randolph Churchill'). She was able to read in four languages and her enthusiasm for the literature of those languages extended over the whole period of their existence. She could have passed an examination in Balzac and had a huge admiration for Dickens and Swift. She was indeed something of a Dickensian character herself – broad strokes, clear characteristics, memorable in her vitality though it might alarm and even repel. One of her many friends was the Princess of Monaco and one of her admirers, so it appears, was John Ruskin.

How long the manner of his engagement rankled with Sir Tatton is unknown; but one aspect of his marriage left a long train of bitterness. On 25 November 1882 Jessica was received into the Roman Catholic Church and with her from the Church of England she took her three-year-old son. Mark's conversion had no less a seal of approval than that of Cardinal Manning who had experienced a similar conversion himself. Mark's godparents that November day were Henry Duke of Norfolk and Mary Caroline Talbot. According to Shane Leslie, while baby Mark was unwittingly received into the Church which he defended in the years to come against all heretics and scoffers, Jessica

'. . . had thoroughly appreciated the intellectual reasons for her act, which was not a piece of feminine sentiment, for her brain was always masculine in its processes and decisions. She used, however, to attribute her conversion on the mystic side to the fact that her great-grandfather, Charles Powell Leslie, had voted in the Dublin Parliament against the Act of Union, and thereby secured a larger share of Divine favour to his posterity than if he had acted otherwise'.*

Apart from travelling and his famous stud, Tatton's other main interest in life was the designing and building of neo-Gothic churches in which there was a great deal of interest in the 1870s and 1880s. To mark his permanent protest of disapproval of the religious beliefs that his wife had adopted and that his successors would be brought up in, he built Sledmere Church as a bastion of the Anglican faith. Nevertheless he is reported to have proposed that a reproduction of Milan Cathedral be built on the site in London where Westminster Cathedral now stands. Possibly Sir Tatton's interest in church architecture overcame his repugnance for the Roman Catholic Church – or possibly it was Jessica who made the proposal on his behalf.

Between Tatton and Jessica acrid quarrels developed. As well as religion, though no doubt linked with it, another cause of argument was Mark. Each endeavoured to suborn their son away from the other. Tatton wanted him to go to Harrow; his mother insisted on Beaumont. Instead of taking him to the pantomime his father would take him to hear criminal trials,

* *Mark Sykes: His Life and Letters* (Cassell, 1923), p. 6.

and instead of holidays in south coast resorts he would whisk him off to Lebanon and the Jordan. His mother, on the other hand, who was a passionate gambler, took him racing to Doncaster and Newmarket and sat him beside her during her long spells in her favourite casinos. The effect of his father's regime was to nurture his interest in human nature and plant the seeds of wanderlust. His mother too, made him eager to be always on the move, but her gambling habits soon created a strong aversion. Newmarket and Monte Carlo were not for him. He left Beaumont at sixteen and went to the Jesuit School at Monaco; then to the Institut St Louis in Brussels. When the time came for him to go up to the university Tatton wanted him to go to Oxford, for this was the home of the Gothic revival. But Jessica in her usual flurry of action swept Tatton's proposal away and Mark was sent to Cambridge accompanied by his closest friend, George Bowles, who was actually going to Oxford but whose destination was hurriedly changed at Jessica's command.

Resisting Jessica was something altogether unknown. Lord Howard de Walden, a kinsman and near contemporary of Mark who, for a short time, was a close friend, admitted that despite her brilliance Jessica 'partially caged and embittered, was terrifying'. De Walden's mother became afraid of her and that fear, added to the difference of religion between them, brought the friendship of the two boys to an end.

In due course the acrimony between Tatton and Jessica resulted in a law suit. Tatton refused to honour a bill for £60,000, averring that the signature on it was not his. Nor was it, in all probability. One of Tatton's eccentricities – or perhaps native wisdoms – was that he refused to sign cheques and it was Jessica who always wrote his name, just as it was she who officiated at Sledmere when guests had been invited. Especially was this so during Doncaster week when Yorkshire's Derby, the St Leger, is run. Doncaster week was a time for open house at Sledmere and Jessica entertained the cream of Society's gamblers while Sir Tatton retired to distant parts of the house to reflect on his stud and his church designs and avoid the mishmash of baccarat and poker.

During the trial Jessica's cheque stubs were sent for and when they arrived counsel realised with acute embarrassment that one of the first cheques for a large amount in settlement of a baccarat debt had been paid to the presiding judge himself, who was one of the gamblers who always stayed at Sledmere during Doncaster week. In the event Jessica's cheque stubs did not have to reveal their secrets in open court because Mark organised a peace between his parents. Throughout the long tug-of-war of his childhood and adolescence he had managed to avoid succumbing to the zeal of either. As far as possible he kept them both in ignorance of what really interested him. At the time of the trial he was still an undergraduate at Cambridge but had managed so to persuade the authorities that he was given permission to spend his Lent terms travelling in the eastern Turkish provinces. Arriving back from Kurdistan, he brought the trial to an end by shouldering the debt himself on his own prospects.

When the Boer War broke out in October 1899 Lady Sykes having, as she wrote, a few months to spare (she had to be back in England for Mark's 21st birthday in March) decided to go to South Africa as a voluntary worker in a hospital. Such help was not popular with the army medical authorities but being who she was Jessica ended up at the forward hospital at Estcourt, between Pietermaritzburg and Colenso where she saw the aftermath of the Colenso battle, the third disaster for the British army in that 'Black Week' of December.

The inefficiency of the Army's logistics may have been appalling enough in the Crimea, but the state of affairs in South Africa during the first part of the Boer War was no better. Jessica Sykes' description of the attitudes of the medical officers in Estcourt hospital could well have been written by Florence Nightingale half a century earlier. And for the rest: crates of comforts piled up at the docks, cavalry regiments with their bridles on other transports still at sea; at the forward hospitals no blankets, no cutlery, no plates, no washing facilities, no food even (except for that which was bought with their own money by voluntary helpers like Jessica Sykes), Christmas parcels stagnating at the station, no clean shirts to give to the wounded, and – as always in the conduct of human affairs – a host of insufferable little men standing on their dignity and pushing paper forms about.

In this particular case it appears that the insufferable little men were all army medical and transport officers. The civilians in the hospital and on the railways were efficient and helpful (provided they weren't black!); and as for the naval officers and Bluejackets who were manning the guns at Estcourt every one was a paragon.

Jessica Sykes was at Estcourt when the wounded were brought down from Colenso. Train after train came through. In the afternoon, at the hottest time of a scorching day, she and her colleagues went to the station for the arrival of yet another train. They distributed the bread, butter and tea provided by the Government, and some soup, jelly, cigarettes and cocoa provided by themselves, together with pails full of condensed milk for those who were too weak to take soup.

'This train', she noted in her diary, 'was in charge of one of the most offensive little Jacks-in-office it has ever been my lot to encounter, in the shape of a doctor attached to some volunteer regiment. Mr Green, the contractor at the refreshment rooms, was a most capable and kind man. I am sure he gave away that day alone, out of his own pocket, £10 or £12 worth of tobacco and provisions to the wounded, and had assisted us to prepare pails of Bovril, condensed milk, and many other things which we were proceeding to distribute to the occupants of the train, together with tobacco, chocolate and jelly. After we had been so employed for about ten minutes, the little doctor walked up to us and said very fussily in an extremely insolent manner:

"Now you good people doubtless mean well, but I object entirely to this kind of thing. It is quite unnecessary, besides against discipline, that the men should receive anything not actually provided by the Government."'

'He further added that there was a waggon at the back of the train containing whisky, soda-water, ice, champagne, and every possible luxury which he could give his men – if he considered they really required it.'

Lady Sykes' comment on this latent cornucopia was that it brought very forcibly to her mind the old story of Mr Squeers when he described, with deep regret, the unfortunate demise from fever of one of his pupils: 'I don't know why he died. The boy had every comfort; warm tea provided for him when he could not swallow it, and the best dictionary in the house for a pillow.'

On her return to England she wrote *Sidelights of the War** (which, incidentally, is listed in *Who Was Who* as by Sir Tatton Sykes). Later she wrote *The New Reign of Terror in France* (1903) (also listed as by Sir Tatton) and at least two Society novels, *The Macdonnells*, which was believed to be a *roman à clef* about the Leslies, and *Mark Alston* about the Bentincks and their relations the Lowthers; Mark Alston himself was John Ruskin. 'The families concerned,' wrote Shane Leslie, 'preferred to ignore or destroy all available copies.'†

Two female relations of Jessica's went to the Boer War as well as herself. These were Dosia and Olive, sisters of the second Sir John Leslie and sisters-in-law of Leonie, one of the three Jerome sisters, the others being Jennie who married Lord Randolph Churchill, and Clara who married Moreton Frewen and was the mother of Clare Sheridan the sculptress. Both Dosia and Olive were nurses in South Africa and Dosia recorded her experiences in *Shadows of the War*. One of those whom Olive nursed was a young officer called Jackson. The Hon. F. S. Jackson was W. G. Grace's successor as the idol of English cricket and he survived the Boer War to captain England and win the toss all five times against Australia in the 1905 Test Matches. England won the series without losing a match and Jackson headed both the batting and bowling averages.

* Fisher Unwin, 1900.
† *Film of Memory*, p. 127.

Chapter 4
'A GODDESS TO MANY'

With the experience of the Marlborough House years as a guide there were some who expected Edward's move along the road to Buckingham Palace to be accompanied by a certain laxness in Court life. They were mistaken. The man who could rebuke a minister in the Foreign Service by telling him that 'knee-breeches are never worn on board a man-of-war', or reprove his assistant private secretary for wearing a tail-coat to a private view before luncheon when 'everyone must know that a short jacket is always worn with a silk hat at a morning view', who could make a cutting remark about some tiny error in an esoteric order of military dress, was not going to relax any single item of the regiment's tradition now that he had become the colonel after so many years of cherishing minutiae in that most neutered of all appointments, the second-in-command. Nonetheless, although *lèse-majesté* became a greater crime than ever in a social sense there was an atmosphere of informality about the Court. It became more cosmopolitan, and although Edward still paid his dietary homage to the German spas, the stiffness and formality that had arrived at court with his over-conscientious father and the puritan mentor Baron Stockmar suddenly disappeared. So too did that Calvinistic feeling of perpetual mourning, not only for life in general but specifically for the death of Albert, that had made the Crown into an ancient monument.

That things were going to be a little different was obvious from the first day when the new King announced to the Privy Council on 23 January 1901, 'We have decided to be known by the name of Edward, a name carried by six of our ancestors.' No mention of Albert! And smoking enormous cigars with the

Kaiser and the King of the Belgians in Victoria's drawing-room at Windsor! A little different indeed.

The first state occasion of the new reign after the Proclamation was the Opening of Parliament on Thursday, 14 February 1901. There were five open carriages (four of which were each drawn by six bay horses, and in the fifth black horses were harnessed); then came the King's Marshalmen walking two by two and His Majesty's footmen in State liveries; then came the State Coach drawn by eight cream-coloured Hanoverian horses with postilions and walking men in attendance and two equerries riding in attendance instead of the usual one (this was a refinement dredged up from some arcane protocol by the King himself). Finally came escorts and guards of honour found by the three regiments of the Household Cavalry (the 1st and 2nd Life Guards, and the Royal Horse Guards.) It was a parade in honour of the horse almost as much as it was one in honour of the sovereign and his Parliament.

The number of horses in Britain reached its peak, not as one might suppose in those coaching days and coaching ways so charmingly and nostalgically celebrated by Outram Tristram and Hugh Thomson, but at the beginning of the Edwardian era. Bearing in mind the fact that the railway age was at the height of its prosperity this might seem to be a paradox. The explanation lies in the huge amount of new traffic created by the railways themselves. The railways brought people to the towns, brought food to the people in the towns, carried raw materials to the factories and took goods from the factories to the seaports. Branch line after branch line was opened. Railways and urban growth and industrialisation were an ever-widening circle like the sparks of a catherine wheel revolving at a faster and faster rate. And the concomitant of all this was an ever-increasing dependence on the horse. In 1901 there was one horse in Britain to every ten of the population.

The machine that killed the horse was the petrol engine in the motor-car. The motor, as the Edwardians called it and many a latter-day Edwardian still called it for the next half-century, came to Britain from the Continent of Europe. No one person 'invented' the motor-car, although Edmund Benz has the greatest claim to this distinction as he was the first to design and produce light self-propelled carriages for sale in 1885.

At all events the foundations of the motor industry were laid in Germany and France; any development of a British industry was paralysed by the Red Flag Act of 1865.* In 1896, however, the Act was repealed and the speed limit was increased from walking pace to fourteen miles an hour. With this repeal the motor age began in Britain and into the leisured world of the horse and carriage with its appalling crashes and seven tons of dung per horse per year there came the strange noise of the early petrol engine: 'ta-pocketa, ta-pocketa, ta-pocketa', it went, on account of the action of its valves.

Early motoring demanded two basic things. One was money; the other was time. You needed money because motoring was an expensive occupation. You needed time – and plenty of it – for running repairs, not only for a succession of punctures, but for continual mechanical faults of varying severity as well. Needless to say therefore, the places where most of the early motor-cars were to be seen, when they were not broken down by the roadside or juddering along in a cloud of dust, were on the drives and in the parklands of the well-to-do. You might motor over to tea with a friend and then find that you had an hour to spare walking round the garden yet again while your husband in braces and with his shirt-sleeves rolled up was wrestling with the motor's engine in front of the carriage house. Or it might be that you could leave such things to your chauffeur – a new breed of men who caught the imagination both of Shaw and Proust, men whom 'nobody disparages, toiling on horseless carriages'.† Sometimes the help of the local blacksmith had to be summoned. King Edward was an enthusiastic motorist, so too was Queen Alexandra, although neither, one need hardly add, ever attempted the 'toiling' themselves. When Edward went on a motoring picnic in France he had the embarrassing habit of choosing a spot for it beside a busy thoroughfare so that what might have been a pleasant relaxa-

* Its cardinal clause was that any vehicle on the public highway, other than a horse-drawn vehicle, must be preceded by a man carrying a red flag to warn oncoming traffic of the snorting monster behind him; this Act was the railways' final and most effective blow against the road 'steamers' whose threat of competition had been worrying them for years.

† Lawrence Durrell, whose poem 'The happy filth of garages', appears as one of his character's writings in *Monsieur or The Prince of Darkness* (Faber and Faber, 1974), p. 206.

tion for his companions, who usually included Mrs Keppel on
these occasions, turned out to be a public exhibition. The King
was a speed fiend and encouraged his chauffeur to pass everything on the road. He was proud of having exceeded sixty miles
an hour on the Brighton road in 1906. He also had a four-key
cornet horn which the superintendant of the royal cars, who sat
in front, had to play as the King's car zoomed along.

Queen Alexandra, too, loved speed, especially during this
first regnal summer of 1901 when, having at last reached the
throne, she told her friends that she was going to do exactly as
she liked. She was, however, the original back-seat driver.
Writing to her son the Duke of York and Cornwall she said, 'I
did enjoy being driven about in the cool of the evening at fifty
miles!! an hour! I have the greatest confidence in our driver. I
poke him violently in the back at every corner to go gently and
whenever a dog, child or anything else crosses our way.'*
Edward had several cars, all of which were painted in his own
royal claret colour. But he refused to let her have one. 'There
was a kind of chivalry in this', one of her biographers suggests,
'an anxiety for her safety and perhaps also he felt that the sight
of the Queen smothered in white road dust would be undigni-
fied.' Whatever the reason, the Queen was irritated by her de-
prival when she 'saw many of her female friends travelling
about in smart cars while she ambled after them in a carriage'.†
After borrowing cars from friends to the anxiety of the Court
she eventually persuaded the King to let her have one of her
own.

Apart from mechanical problems there were others to con-
tend with. A major one was the dust, and the dust had its
effect upon fashion. 'Motoring,' said the *Illustrated London News*
in March 1901, 'is a distinct feature in the arranging of fashion
nowadays.' As often as not the driver was a lady, for lady drivers
were early on the scene. But even as passengers, before em-
barking on any expedition ladies had to dress themselves up in
veils and linen dust-coats – of course they were kept 'spotlessly
clean' said the *Illustrated London News* hopefully. The men had
to muffle themselves up to their eyes and don their goggles.

* Quoted in Georgina Battiscombe, *Queen Alexandra* (Constable, 1969),
p. 241.
† E. E. P. Tisdall, *Unpredictable Queen* (Stanley Paul & Co., 1953), p. 200.

Once they had done all that it was well worth it. As H. G. Wells' Mr Hoopdriver said in 1895, when setting out on his cycling tour of the south coast of England, 'Oo knows what the wheels of chance will bring?'

You could climb into the Baby Peugeot or the De Dion Bouton and then motor off with your family or your friends for a picnic at some nearby beauty spot or a visit to a sporting event where you would leave your vehicle in the motor enclosure. Or you might go farther afield – as far as the open road beckoned, as far even as the great roads if you were a real enthusiast taking part in an international race from Paris to Madrid, or Berlin or even to Peking. No longer were you restricted to the fifteen miles there and fifteen miles back which was the horse's limit for a day. On and on you could go – as long as the petrol held out! This was another problem. There were few filling stations (though the bicycle trade was increasingly turning its attention to this new method of transport); so it was a wise precaution to carry spare cans of petrol with you, especially as there were few other motorists on the road to help you when you were in difficulties, and the reaction of other road-users who passed you in your plight was likely to be facetious or disparaging at the best. In case of accident the motorist was always wrong. Yet another major problem were the police traps that stemmed from the letter of the law, and which took nourishment from the pro-horse anti-motor benches of JPs in many districts.

In 1903 came a sign that the motor-car in Britain was no longer a passing craze of the idle rich. Authority took notice of it. Until then there had been no numbers, no licences, nothing of that sort. But from now, and hence-forward, every car must carry a registration number. The owners were indignant. They objected to being labelled like so many hackney carriages. But the objections were ignored. The number stayed and initiated yet another 'collecting game' – motor-car numbers, to add to engine numbers. In passing it may be remarked that until 1920 the owner not the car was licensed. So in Edwardian days the number stayed the same from car to car – from the Peugeot to the Swift, from the Swift to the Palladian. By the end of that first year (1903) 8,500 motors were licensed in Britain.*

---

* The registration number A1 was allocated to Earl Russell.

The Opening of Parliament in February 1901 was followed by other state processions. On such occasions the horse was still supreme and the motor-car or electric brougham was hidden away in the mews for the day. These ponderous, fancy-dress caravans wound their way between the packed pavements of London, each one an excuse for the 'roughs' to rifle pockets and the patriotic to cheer their genial, phallic, gambling, sports-loving monarch who, as George Dangerfield has written, was 'the living excuse for their own little sins'.* At the end of October the Duke and Duchess of Cornwall and York (King George V and Queen Mary to be) were welcomed back from their seven month visit to the Colonies – to Ceylon, Singapore, Australia, New Zealand, Mauritius, South Africa, Canada and Newfoundland. It was another royal occasion, wriggling along like a grotesque worm from Victoria Station up past the Wellington Arch and along Piccadilly to St James's Street and then down to Marlborough House, for the son had taken his father's old house – though in no way had he taken over the cachet that had gone with it.

The Empire of Edwardian Britain contributed towards that illusion of stability that existed ambivalently with feelings of anxiety in those who had been brought up in the classics to know that Nemesis was lurking somewhere. But the Empire was reassuring and it was more than ever real. Edward was the first monarch ever to be formally proclaimed as 'King of the British Dominions beyond the Seas'. For those who could appreciate such things it was clear that enormous wealth was being drawn from the Empire; it was the pot of gold at the foot of the rainbow. What the Empire proved, and proved by the fact that so many British families, high, low and indifferent had sons and brothers, daughters and sisters, nieces, nephews, cousins and second cousins twice removed now living in the Empire, was that one was not alone. Grouped around old England were India and the Dominions, tied by links of blood and service; and peripheral to that great majesty of power were the Colonies. But whether Dominions or Colonies they were a loyal *cordon sanitaire* against the inroads of the barbarians.

* *The Strange Death of Liberal England* (MacGibbon & Kee, 1968).

The Edwardian decade was the high point of British emigration to the Empire. In the decade from 1891 to 1900 only 28
per cent of the emigrants from the British Isles (including Ireland) went to countries within the Empire; two-thirds of them
went to the United States. But from 1901 to 1912 the percentage of total emigrants remaining within the Empire increased
to 63, and in 1913 it went up to 78. There were a number of
reasons for this. On the negative side the United States no
longer offered the opportunities it once had to the emigrant
from the British Isles. Less Irish were emigrating both because
Ireland's population was no longer too large for its resources
and because the work previously done in the United States by
the Irish, and by unskilled labourers in general, was now being
done by the flood of emigrants from Southern Europe. On the
positive side much had been done by the Dominions, especially
Canada, to tell people about the opportunities which they
offered, and the success stories were beginning to filter back
home through letters and visits.

Openings of Parliament (there was another on 16 January
1902) and other royal processions were mere pipe-openers for
the great occasion that was to take place on 26 June 1902 when
the King was to be crowned. London filled up with emperors
and kings and princes, programmes were printed, places allotted, rehearsals held. Then the rumour went round that the
King was seriously ill. Despite his determination not to disap-
point his subjects and to get to Westminster Abbey on time
even, so it is said, if he had to leave Queen Alexandra at home –
for she was pathologically unpunctual – and even if it killed
him, the King was at last over-ruled by his doctors and on the
24th he had to undergo an operation for peritonitis.

The Coronation eventually took place, in a shortened form,
on 9 August. By that time most of the foreign potentates had
departed and the stars of the state procession were Lord Roberts
and Lord Kitchener, the heroes of South Africa, whose names
appeared in the official programme in the same large size capital letters as Their Majesties. On the whole everything passed
off satisfactorily although there were a few contretemps. The
Marchioness of Londonderry, doyenne of Society's political
hostesses, was sworn at rudely by a taxi driver on the way to the
Abbey and on arrival suffered a lengthy embarrassment when

her diadem fell into the pan of the only convenience provided for peeresses and could be retrieved without damage to the stones only by the use of a pair of gynaecological forceps which took some time to find. This rescue operation caused an impatient queue of peeresses to form outside the haven where they were seeking to take precautions for the long vigil ahead. When they heard the Marchioness, who was turned sixty, calling for forceps they feared that the heat must have affected her.

During the ceremony itself the Duchess of Marlborough, who was one of the four duchesses bearing Queen Alexandra's canopy, noted that when the peers had to put on their coronets some of these weighty baubles which had been made for their ancestors with bigger heads than the present holders of their titles slid ignominiously down to their chins. No such ludicrous disaster afflicted the Duchess herself for she had had her coronet especially made so that it balanced becomingly on the top of her tiny head at the end of her long swan's neck. The Duchess also noted that the sacred oil with which the Queen was being anointed ran down on to her forehead causing her, so the Duchess thought, some anxiety lest it spoil her discreet maquillage; but, wrote the Duchess, she was able to reassure her Queen with a look that all was well. The Duchess, however, according to Georgina Battiscombe, had misinterpreted the incident:

'To Queen Alexandra the chief meaning of the Coronation was a religious one. . . . The true version of this incident is still current in the family of Archbishop Maclagan of York, who, contrary to custom, crowned the Queen, the Archbishop of Canterbury being so frail that it was thought unwise to impose on him the double strain of crowning both the King and the Queen. Before the Coronation Queen Alexandra sent for Archbishop Maclagan to explain to him her predicament. Like most women of her age [she was fifty-seven] and generation, she augmented her own hair with a *toupet*. If she were to be properly anointed she felt that the holy oil must actually touch her own body, not merely this erection of false hair; she therefore begged the Archbishop to be sure that some of the oil ran down on to her forehead. This he did; and on returning to

Buckingham Palace she refused to wipe the oil off, wishing to bear the mark of her anointing as long as possible.'*

Queen Alexandra was noted for her obstinacy – among other characteristics. This obstinacy was well in evidence over the arrangements for the Coronation. It had been sixty-four years since the last one and the field was open for the historians and traditionalists to decree what everyone should do and everyone should wear. As to what she would wear the Queen, who absolutely refused to be called the Queen Consort, had made up her own mind. 'I know better than all the milliners and antiquaries. I shall wear exactly what I like and so will all my ladies,' she announced to the Comptroller of the Lord Chamberlain's Department. Of the ladies she was going to choose four of them herself, whatever the claims of precedent. These were the four who were to carry her canopy. They were to be four Duchesses and they must all be tall like herself; they must all be beautiful – again like herself, for Alexandra's beauty was such that it made people gasp when they looked at her; and they must all have a certain similarity of appearance. Indeed she had the instincts of a George Edwardes or Flo Ziegfield in the blending of beauty. It was to be her Coronation as much as the King's and she was implacable about many points, including the height of her footstool in the Abbey. But they were practical points. Four ladies of unequal size would have made the canopy lop-sided. Four ladies shorter than herself would have made her look as ridiculous as the peers with their coronets over their noses. Too high or too low a footstool would have had a similarly ludicrous effect.

The Queen's beauty caused a sensation at the Abbey just as she had done at the State Opening of Parliament the previous year when 'the packed assembly saw a tall girlish figure with the crown gleaming above a black Mary Stuart coif and the deep black of her gown standing out from the brilliant State robe, a great rope of pearls falling to below her knees and the Koh-i-noor flashing in the golden light'.† The King's coronation robe was made of the finest velvet ever woven. Beneath the thrones was a great blue coronation carpet. Four years later, on a visit

* *Op. cit.*, pp. 249–50.
† E. E. P. Tisdall, *op. cit.*, p. 195.

to home-workers in the sweated industries of London's East End, Clementina Black met the man who had woven the coronation robe. He was a descendant of the Huguenots, a silk-weaver, but also one of the very few hand-weavers of velvet still left in Britain. The carpet, too, has its historical interest. Whereas the weaver was the link with the past, the carpet pointed towards the future – not in its making, but in its cleaning.

Although the invention of labour-saving devices to lighten the drudgery of household tasks began early in the nineteenth century, it was not until the fractional-horsepower electric motor* had been developed towards the end of the century that mechanisation in the home became practicable. The impetus for its spread came from the worsening of what their employers called 'the servant problem' – the difficulty of getting servants.

The first of the great labour-saving devices to be generally accepted and mass-produced was the vacuum cleaner. It was invented in 1901 by an English engineer, H. C. Booth. Booth saw a demonstration of an American machine in the Empire Music Hall, London, where it was being used to clean the carpets. This machine worked by blowing air into the carpet. Booth immediately felt that the suction principle would be a more efficient method of cleaning, but he was told that suction had been tried in the United States and had failed to work. Unconvinced, he made his own experiment by 'sucking with my mouth against the back of a plush seat in a [London] Victoria Street restaurant, with the result that I almost choked'. The discomfort proved his point. He designed a pump which would provide the necessary suction and then fitted it into a mobile machine which was parked in the street outside the building where the vacuum cleaning was to be done. Long flexible hoses with the now familiar vacuum cleaner nozzle on the end were connected to the machine and passed through the doors and windows. With two of these machines half a ton of dust was removed from a large West End store in a single night.

Needless to say the new machine met opposition; not, as might be supposed, from human cleaners who thought their

* That is, an electric motor with horsepower of about one or less.

jobs might be at risk, but from the police who prosecuted the company using Booth's machine on the grounds that they had no right to operate on the public highway, and from the owners of cab horses who claimed damages because their animals were being frightened – an unforgivable solecism in Edwardian times when, as Mrs Patrick Campbell said in another connection, one could do what one liked provided one didn't frighten the horses in the street.

Booth's pump, known as 'Puffing Billy' and now an exhibit in the Science Museum, South Kensington, was in constant use from 25 February 1902 to 13 October 1903. Despite the police and the frightened cab horses the idea caught on, especially after the machine was successfully demonstrated to King Edward at Buckingham Palace and to the Emperor of Austria at Hofburg Palace, Vienna. So successful was it that one of its first and most spectacular operations was to clean the great blue coronation carpet beneath the monarch's throne in Westminster Abbey on the eve of the coronation. Booth's machine was the precursor of the modern portable vacuum cleaner.

A week after the ceremony in Westminster Abbey a further instalment of the Coronation celebrations took place with a Review of the Fleet at Spithead on 16 August. Unfortunately for the good name of British seamanship, the day ended somewhat badly. The *Carthage*, a P and O liner carrying some 500 guests of the Admiralty, including ambassadors and diplomatists, had an accident on its return to Southampton in the evening. A tug which was taking the liner into harbour failed to clear the dock wall and the *Carthage* crashed into it. Her bows were smashed and torn at the water-line and the passengers, so the *Naval Review* reported, 'were alarmed. Many of them, principally the ladies, were thrown down on the deck and suffered bruises and contusions, the wife of the Chinese Minister being among the number'.

Queen Alexandra was noted for her strange ideas as well as for her obstinacy. One of the strangest – in the opinion of those involved – had been her idea to give the biggest banquet in history. As her own contribution to Queen Victoria's Diamond Jubilee in 1897, she had proposed to invite 400,000 of the London poor to a meal. Far from being by invitation only, any hungry person who cared to come would be fed. She opened a subscription list, but there was no rush to be connected with something that was clearly destined to be a folly of stupendous proportions. It was the 'boating grocer' who saved the day. Thomas Lipton sent her a cheque for £25,000 and a menu, with prices, which he promised he could provide at one and the same time for 400,000. It would take 700 tons of food and 10,000 waiters; he was still working out how many gallons of beverages would be required. Lipton's professional blessing and his cheque made the idea practical. The monster feast took place the day after the Diamond Jubilee procession at the same hour in halls all over London. Alexandra visited three main centres: the People's Palace in the Mile End Road, and the Central Halls in Clerkenwell and Holborn. Shattered by the misery and starvation she saw, she started, once again with Lipton's help, the Alexandra Trust which, for one penny, provided a helping of hot food to the destitute and for two or three pennies a large meal.

Nursing was always a keen interest with her. She was the first royal personage to be actively interested in hospitals and it is said that this concern stemmed from the time when, at the age of twenty-two, she had rheumatic fever. Although she visited a number of hospitals she early adopted the London Hospital in the East End of London as her own, and it was from the London that she sent twelve nurses to South Africa at the end of 1899 at her own expense, insisting that they should wear the same uniform as the military nurses. Later she sent another twenty, although she complained because in their case she was not allowed to select them as she had selected the first twelve. These nurses were the forerunners of Queen Alexandra's Imperial Nursing Service (now called the Queen Alexandra's Royal Army Nursing Corps) which she created under the War Office in 1902. They were 'my nurses' to the degree that she personally devised the badge they wore.

The monster feast of the Diamond Jubilee had clearly put into her mind the way to make a public gesture for the underprivileged. Soon after she had become Queen she linked her name with another great area of women's work. She decided to hold a remarkable series of Queen's Teas for 10,000 London servants. Having asked who were the most ill-used women in the country she was told, 'The slaveys, Ma'am; the Maids-of-all-work.' 'Then I'll give them a tea,' she replied.

Once again Lipton, who had been knighted soon after the monster feast, was the practical tower of strength. This time, however, the donations were quickly forthcoming. The problem was to ensure that no undeserving girls received the royal invitation – for this time there were to be invitations. The Bishop of London, to whom the Queen gave the unrewarding task of selecting the Lower Ten Thousand (for perhaps that figure was chosen as a direct antithesis to Gladstone's Upper Ten Thousand) embarked on the project by handing the whole thing over to the various voluntary societies which befriended and helped young servant girls, among them the Metropolitan Association for Befriending Servant Girls, the Girls' Friendly Society and the Ladies' Society for Aiding Friendless Girls. But this method of selection gave rise to much ill-feeling. Those who did not belong to any of the Societies, nor indeed had ever had anything to do with them, also wanted to be eligible. In the end Teas were held in some thirty districts of London. The servants wore their best uniforms and the Teas were served by ladies dressed in the height of fashion – it was rather like Christmas Day dinner in the army when the men are waited on by the officers and sergeants. Her Majesty put in an appearance where she could and the Bishop of London addressed them all (they were not all held on the same day) and the guests sent loyal greetings and thanks for the feast of tea and buns. Beside each plate was a brooch inscribed 'From the Queen'.

What exactly these Teas achieved, apart from the pleasure given by the food, the brooch and the mild entertainment, it is difficult to see. Certainly they did not bring mistress and servant any closer together in the long run than did Lord Loam's monthly tea parties in J. M. Barrie's *The Admirable Crichton* which appeared the following year. But it was a gesture in the right direction.

Deaf, beautiful, unpunctual, and a goddess to many, Queen Alexandra could be extremely tiresome to others and as pedantic as her husband about the minutiae of uniforms. Elizabeth Haldane, sister of the War Minister who created the Territorial Army in 1907, played a leading part in setting up a nursing service within the TA. To achieve this, however, was a difficult struggle against the Queen's dug-in reluctance, and without the Queen's approval the scheme could not go ahead. Indeed the objections to the creation of a Territorial Nursing Service were paralleled in the larger objections to the Territorial Army itself. There were other nursing schemes in existence which feared that if the TNS was set up they would either lose their separate identity or be completely disbanded. These other schemes had influential supporters (especially the Queen herself) and they rallied them in an endeavour to maintain their position, just as the Militia, Yeomanry and Volunteers enlisted the aid of their supporters to resist the Territorial and Reserve Forces Bill.

Even when a modification was made so that the old Nursing Reserve was retained, the Queen was not satisfied. A committee was set up to consider the problem. Naturally enough, for that was its purpose as it is generally the purpose of all committees, it produced a compromise scheme. This was eventually adopted, but eventually is the operative word. On the road to adoption one difficulty after another was encountered, because Her Majesty fought a strong rearguard action, raising a series of objections like a system of fortified trenches. And even when the scheme was adopted other problems still remained. Her Majesty now weighed in about the uniforms. She decided that the nurses would wear khaki. The nurses refused, 'for the very practical reason', commented Miss Haldane, 'that they, rightly, thought it unbecoming'. It took a long time and a great deal of tact before Her Majesty consented to the grey Territorial uniform with its touches of red. 'The red cape of the First Line nurses was considered to be sacred to them, and as was always in those days the case in the Army, there was constant fear that the Territorials . . . would usurp the rights of what many considered to be the real army.*

Nor was it only on the question of uniforms. Queen Alexandra's *amour propre* was invincible. In 1908, when the great Parisian couturier Poiret sent a copy of his book *Les Robes de Paul Poiret Racontée par Paul Iribe* to all the queens and princesses of Europe with a personal inscription, every one of them acknowledged the gift of this beautiful book except Queen

* *From One Century to Another* (Maclehose, 1937), p. 224.

Alexandra, who sent him a message through a lady-in-waiting
that in future he must refrain from sending Her Majesty things
of this nature.

There were, however, many homely touches about Queen
Alexandra. Daphne Fielding, the daughter of the fourth Lord
Vivian, had two aunts who were twins. One married Colonel
(later Field-Marshal Earl) Haig, the other remained single and
became lady-in-waiting first to Queen Alexandra and later to
Princess Victoria. As a child Daphne was often in royal circles
where, she recalled in her reminiscences, her behaviour

'seems to have been extremely uninhibited. I remember being
graciously put on the pot by Queen Alexandra, who took me
up to her bedroom followed by several Japanese spaniels. I
was unable to button the flap at the back of my drawers, so she
did it for me. It was repeated, to my embarrassment, for years
afterwards, that I had asked Her Majesty if she had the same
difficulty in buttoning up her own.'*

The style of life King Edward led was not acceptable to a
large number of his subjects. The Merrie England image may
have lifted the hearts of those who backed his winning horses,
and his gambling and mistresses may have brought an agreeable
freshness to replace the dowdiness of monarchy, but there were
many, especially in the north of England, who did not feel that
he was king enough in the standards of behaviour he set. The
less Puritan standards adopted by Society had not spread to the
middle classes, nor indeed to some of the 'backwoods' aristocracy. It was here that Queen Alexandra's importance lay as
far as the monarchy was concerned. It was left to her, wrote
Georgina Battiscombe, 'to preserve for the throne its aura of
Victorian respectability without in any way detracting from
its new, more decorative Edwardian air; she proved in her own
person that royalty could be both glamorous and good. . . . She
was the smartest of all Edwardian beauties and yet as virtuous
as Queen Victoria'. Apart from the virtue and 'a certain touching innocence' she was the standard Edwardian lady, writing
the same sort of letters, reading the same sort of books, enjoying
the same plays. 'Had she been more serious and intellectual,

* *Mercury Presides* (Eyre & Spottiswoode, 1954), p. 22.

preferring George Moore to Marie Corelli, Bernard Shaw to Pinero, she would not have personified as well as she did the Edwardian ideal of womanhood. The very mediocrity of her mind, flitting, impermanent, butterfly-like, made her the more typical of her generation.'* There were many other women, however, mostly from the middle classes, whose minds were far from mediocre and whose single-mindedness of purpose made them, if not typical of their generation, at least one of its vital phenomena.

* *Op. cit..* pp. 216 and 217.

Chapter 5

MILITANTS FROM MANCHESTER

As the nineteenth century approached its end the Women's Suffrage movement was in the doldrums in Britain, as indeed it was also in the United States. Bills continued to be introduced in Parliament, petitions were drawn up and signed by thousands, there were spasms of hope when women's suffrage was granted in New Zealand in 1893 and in South Australia the following year – but on the whole, except among the passionately committed like Mrs Fawcett and Miss Lydia Becker, the cause languished.

A depressing sign of its ineffectiveness was that the hostility of earlier years, the years of Mill's amendment to the Reform Bill of 1867 (which brought about the first parliamentary debate on women's suffrage) and Gladstone's determined opposition to Jacob Bright's Suffrage Bill of 1870, changed to ridicule and mirth. The enfranchisement of women was always guaranteed to raise a laugh in political debates. Furthermore the earnest homeliness, not to say uncouthness, of one or two of the early pioneers of the cause had given rise to the legend that the movement consisted solely of strident viragos with large feet and incipient moustaches. They were a gift to the comic press, and even *Punch*, which was not ill-disposed towards the cause, remarked that 'those who want women's rights want also women's charms'.

This feeling persisted throughout the long campaign and found its way into the novels of the day. 'I have been hunting all over London for a woman, beautiful, charming, exquisitely dressed, accustomed all her life to command the attentions and

the opinions of her fellow-men, and – a Suffragette,' Sir Christopher Bridburn told his cousin, the elegant Mrs Ilford in
Sybil Spottiswoode's novel *Hedwig in England* (1909).* 'I was
hoping that you,' he added gallantly, 'who fulfil all the other
requirements so admirably, would have also fulfilled the last. If
I might see you parading Hyde Park under a militant banner
and a French hat, screaming for an acknowledgment of the
power which you, as a charming woman, have possessed all
your life, I should begin to consider the matter seriously.' It was
a point of view that had a wide acceptance among men, but
there were suffragettes enough with French hats and the other
attributes that Sir Christopher demanded had he only cared to
look.

The men had their allies among the women too. Mrs Ilford's
theory was that 'if you could give the whole army of Suffragettes
lessons in dress, deportment, and how to make the most of the
few graces Heaven has given them, and then import enough
husbands to go round, nothing more would be heard of women's
suffrage. Of course,' she acknowledged loftily, 'there would be
some over whom you couldn't settle in this way, but they are
the specimens who are mentally unhinged, and without any
backing they would soon stop, and start shrieking about
Christian Science or anti-vivisection instead'.† The Shrieking
Sisterhood, Mrs Lynn Linton, one of the foremost literary
opponents of the Women's Movement, had called them in the
1880s. There were many jokes at their expense. 'Votes for
Women? What they need is Blokes for Women.' 'The only
right a woman should have is a bloke's left.' Among Wilkie
Bard's songs was one evoked by the suffragette movement,

> 'Put me on an island where the girls are few,
> Put me amongst the most ferocious lions in the zoo,
> You can put me upon a treadmill and I'll never fret,
> But for pity's sake don't put me with a suffering-gette.'

Apart from mockery, which could be borne, there was other
opposition against which even less headway could be made. It

---

* p. 53.

† Sybil Spottiswoode was a better prophet than she knew. Christabel
Pankhurst, one of those with all the attributes that Sir Christopher desired, eventually became a religious preacher for the Second Advent.

came from the Paulines. God, as interpreted by St Paul, had ordained that woman was subject to man – and that was the end of it. Even the British Houses of Parliament, all-powerful as they were over one-fifth of the world's population, did not have the power, even had they so wished, to alter this eternal decree. Against this faith and that of the Sentimentalists, who were convinced that giving women the vote would destroy 'the old landmarks of society' and 'unsex' the women, there was nothing to be done by debate, committees, or petitions.

Nor indeed was there much to be done against the blunt calculations of party politics. If women were to be given the vote, said the Tories, they'd be bound to vote Liberal. If women were to be given the vote, said the Liberals, they'd undoubtedly vote Tory. Not worth the risk, both parties agreed.

Nonetheless, women had become an important asset in politics. In 1883 the Corrupt Practices Act had been passed. This put an end to the previous system of conducting elections whereby the canvassing and clerical work had been done by men who were paid for the job. No longer was payment allowed. But the work still had to be done. Previously the only women involved in an election were the candidates' relatives – those of them, that is, with the temperament to survive in the bear-garden. Now the need became greater than the susceptibility. 'What was more natural,' asked Ray Strachey, 'than to discover that, after all, it was women's work? A whole new technique of election machinery came into being, and with the appearance of the volunteer women workers the modern type of electioneering began.'* Within a few years both parties had created women's organisations, their sole purpose being to clutch the women to the parties as unpaid helpers. There was no question of their being invited to give their views on political questions or to help in initiating policy. They were not wanted for any intellectual abilities they might have, but solely for the help they could give in the practical matters of fund-raising, canvassing, converting, disseminating propaganda, and keeping up registers.

In 1885 the Conservatives set up a Women's Council as part of the Primrose League which had been founded two years earlier and was named after Disraeli's favourite flower:

* *The Cause* (G. Bell, 1929), p. 279.

'With its knights and dames, its gamut of "office holders" of varying rank, dependent on the size of their contribution, its subtle admixture of the great and the noble, of garden fetes and soirées, it appealed to middle-class and lower middle-class snobbishness. At the same time it brought in the "lower orders", paying only nominal contributions. By this "union" of social classes and by the adroit mixture of refreshment, entertainment and a little politics the League gave the conservative working man, his wife, his sons and daughters, the experience of civility and apparent care by members of the middle class. And the local leaders, in turn, received their portion of civility and condescension on the part of a "real" Lady or perhaps a Cabinet Minister or ex-Cabinet Minister who might receive them in London or in their country houses.'*

Or, as Ray Strachey put it: 'Its paraphernalia of dames and garden parties was more effective in enlisting the great force of social snobbishness than in adding to the intellectual strength or representative nature of the Conservative Party.'†

The Liberal Party, too, had its women's organisations, 'to help our husbands', as Mrs Gladstone put it. But unlike their political opponents in the Primrose League the Liberal ladies proved to be not at all docile. To start with, the Home Rule split in the party in 1886 meant that there was almost immediately two organisations: The Women's Liberal Federation and the Women's Liberal Unionist Association. The President of the WLF was Mrs Gladstone then an old lady of seventy-seven. It was an office she accepted against her better judgement, because throughout all the years she had been connected with politics she had never personally taken any part in public life. However, to accept the office would mean that she would be helping her husband and she would never shrink from that however distasteful the task might be. Before long her forebodings proved justified. The members of the Federation were not content with the auxiliary role allotted to them. They began to discuss ideas, and especially the idea of Women's Suffrage. The arguments were bitter and throughout 1890 and 1891 the

* W. L. Guttsman, *The British Political Elite* (MacGibbon & Kee, 1963), p. 285.
† *Op. cit.*, p. 279.

struggle for control of the Federation went on. At the head of
the suffragist faction was a formidable lady, Rosalind, Countess
of Carlisle. She was as fanatical about Women's Suffrage as she
was about teetotalism, and the extent of her fanaticism in that
latter cause is amply illustrated by the fact that she had all the
priceless contents of the family cellar at Castle Howard poured
away into the fountain there. But although she tore the Federation in two and gained partial control of it the suffragists could
only achieve their full purpose by creating a new organisation,
the Women's Liberal Association, which was formed in 1893.
Only then was Mrs Gladstone able to resign her office, something she would gladly have done long before had she not been
persuaded that it was her duty to remain. Both organisations
flourished, the Federation supporting all Liberals, the Association supporting only those who pledged themselves to the
suffrage cause.

The important thing about these political organisations as
far as women were concerned was not so much that here and
there for those who wanted to do so the suffrage cause could be
pushed along a little further; more important was that these
organisations gave them experience of political methods and
furthermore exploded the old idea that politics was a male
preserve.

While the suffragists caused havoc in the ranks of women
Liberals they had also had their own divisive struggles over the
years. Mrs Josephine Butler's great crusade against the Con-
tagious Diseases Acts in the 1870s appalled some women's
rightists as much as it appalled all those who did not think that
prostitution was a fit subject for open discussion, let alone a
subject for the pamphlets and petitions which were being distributed throughout the country, so that gentlemen were
alarmed at what their wives might find waiting on the break-
fast-table.* Other suffragists felt equally strongly that the cause
for women's rights was a unity, it was one single campaign –
greater opportunities for employment, facilities for secondary
and higher education, the repeal of the CD Acts, the demand
for the vote: these were all part of the same struggle, the
Women's Movement was indivisible.

But, in fact, it had proved not to be. In 1871 the suffragists

* See *The Victorian Woman*, Chapters 14 and 15.

broke ranks. There were, in effect, 'Officials' and 'Provisionals', as there so often are in reformist or revolutionary
bodies. In this case the 'Provisionals' were the new Central
Committee of the National Society for Women's Suffrage who
supported Mrs Butler, and the 'Officials' were the old London
National Society which had been formed in 1867. The split
lasted for seven years. By this time the CD Acts were moving
towards their demise, though there were still some years to go
before they finally disappeared. Despite the vested interests of
honorary secretaries and honorary treasurers and an insuffi-
ciency of committee places to satisfy everyone, the London
suffragists were re-united. In due course they joined with the
provincial societies to form the National Union of Women's
Suffrage Societies with Mrs Millicent (later Dame Millicent)
Fawcett as President. In the end it was the NUWSS – with the
help of the Great War – that succeeded at long last in getting
the vote for women in Britain.

The record of parliamentary approval for women's suffrage
up to 1901 was not impressive. Gladstone had 'thrown the
women overboard' at the Committee Stage in 1870 after
Bright's Suffrage Bill had passed its Second Reading; in 1885
a Second Reading was carried with the knowledge that the
Bill could go no further; in 1897 Mr Faithfull Begg had introduced a Women's Suffrage Bill which, despite the watchfulness
and procedural ingenuity of its opponents, managed to reach a
Second Reading and actually to be passed at that stage with
a majority of seventy-one. Henry Labouchere, the boisterous
editor of *The World* and one of the two members for Northampton, was an assiduous opponent of votes for women. His ebul-
lient loquacity had killed more than one Private Member's
Bill for Women's Suffrage in the past and when Begg's Bill got
through its Second Reading it was the only occasion on which
Labby's verbal manoeuvrings broke down. But he made sure
that the failure was not repeated at the subsequent stage of the
Bill. He spoke at such length about verminous persons on the
appropriate parliamentary day that he managed to kill it on
the threshold of its Committee Stage.

The Boer War gave an opportunity with one hand and took
it away with the other. The war in the Transvaal was being
fought because the British Uitlanders in practical terms had no

representation in the Transvaal Parliament. If England could fight the Boers to give Englishmen the vote, surely English women had an innate right to the vote at home. That was the giving hand. But the taking-away hand touched something equally innate – the loyalty of women. The middle of a war, with 'our lads out there' and disaster threatening on every side – as indeed it did in the Black Week of Stormberg, Magersfontein, and Colenso – was no time to rock the boat by distracting government from its primary duty. Nevertheless, Mrs Fawcett, in her effective manner, took every opportunity of pointing the moral.

Meanwhile another strand was strengthening in the north. Manchester, that unholy hovel of Engels' manufacturing experience, had developed a powerful political consciousness that reflected its economic importance. Cotton was king. In 1901 one-third of Britain's exports came from cotton – and Manchester, or at least Lancashire, was cotton. Trade unionism was strong in the north, so too was the growth of the Independent Labour Party. Involved with both were feminists and women's suffragists. As the ILP moved towards effective parliamentary politics and the unions discussed a political levy which would be used for the furtherance of Labour policies and to which women who were trade unionists would contribute, the activists for women's suffrage began to emerge from the shadows of parliamentary frustration. The Tories would clearly stick to their 'chuck under the chin and smack on the bum' technique for turning aside suffragist importunities. The Liberals, though ostensibly a radical party, seemed resolutely determined to follow their dead leader in his traditional approach towards women. The new Labour Party must surely be the route forward.

To this end, the Manchester Suffrage Society turned its guns on the Labour Party. The thinking behind this policy was quite straightforward: we, the Suffrage Society, will do all we can to encourage factory workers to support you, the Labour Party; we will point out to them that their old voting habits are against their own interests. You, the Labour Party, will in return make the enfranchisement of women a key point in your political programme. And just to flex our muscles a little and to show you what we are capable of we will attend all your meetings and propose resolutions at the drop of a hat – and if even that fails to impress you, here is a petition to Parliament seeking Women's Suffrage which has been signed by 67,000 textile workers. Work with us and they could vote for you.

But this classic type of back-scratching failed to work. Labour was starting on its course to power; it could not afford to nail its proud red flag to the slender mast of Women's Suffrage. Talk about it in general terms by all means; let platitude follow platitude; but for Marx's sake don't let's forget that the point of politics is power and the power won't come from the women – most of them would vote Tory anyway!

The irritation of the Labour leaders began to make itself plain. The disillusionment of the Manchester women's leaders became equally manifest. Some were for carrying on the connection; others were for breaking it. Those who carried on formed a Textile and Other Workers' Representation Committee which had a lasting effect on the attainment of Women's Suffrage; those who broke away included Mrs Pankhurst, whose husband, a Manchester solicitor, had been counsel for the women in a famous Mancunian case of 1868, Charlton *v.* Lings as it is known in the records, when 5,346 women householders unsuccessfully claimed the right to vote. Dr Richard Pankhurst had earlier, with John Stuart Mill, drafted the amendment to the Reform Bill of 1867 which Mill had moved, and the year after his failure in the Charlton *v.* Lings case he was largely responsible for the restoration of the municipal vote to women. It was he who drafted Jacob Bright's Bill of 1870 and in 1882 he was the legal brain behind the Married Women's Property Act which allowed a wife to retain for herself her inheritance and her earnings. Over the years he had been the legal 'think-tank' in the furtherance of women's rights and especially Women's Suffrage. Both he and his wife had been active Liberals until Gladstone threw the women 'overboard' in 1884. But after this betrayal they left the party and Dr Pankhurst became one of the leading promoters in Manchester of the Independent Labour Party.

The Pankhursts were married in 1879, when Richard was forty and his wife twenty. She was born Emmeline Goulden, the eldest of ten children whose father Robert was the director of a Lancashire cotton printing company and a dedicated

87

feminist. At the age of fourteen she was taken to Paris and became a pupil in the École Normale which at that time was one of the pioneer institutions for girls' higher education. She spent five years there and in the course of her growing-up discovered within herself a fiery concern for the poor and the distressed. The Pankhursts had five children: Christabel (1880–1958), Sylvia (1882–1960), Frank (1883–7), Adela (1885–1961), and Harry (1889–1910). Frank died of diphtheria, Harry of polio. As one studies the life of Emmeline Goulden, so famous under her married name, one is often reminded of another of those great flames of fire that burned their way across the injustices of their time. Between Emmeline Pankhurst and Josephine Butler there seem to be subtle parallels; and in both cases the courage of the implacable martyr played havoc with the accepted rules of stormy dissent, and in both was a fierce hatred of the Double Standard which had one lax moral law for the man and another Draconian one for the woman.

In 1898, Richard Pankhurst died. His wife, who subsequently became a Registrar of Births and Deaths and a Poor Law Inspector, carried on the work for radical reform in which both had been involved. The coolness of the Labour Party towards the women's vote, together with her own impulsive character, soon made her lose patience with her second political party as well as with the old-fashioned, fuddy-duddy attitudes of the Manchester Suffrage Society, and the whole inefficient paraphernalia of democracy.

Emmeline Pankhurst was beautiful, charming, a great orator and self-contained to a degree. She impressed by her quietude. She was an autocrat, not to say a dictator when she could get away with it. When the suffragette campaign was at its height she saw her followers as an army and herself as their undisputed commander-in-chief. 'Autocratic?' she asked rhetorically in response to criticism. 'Quite so. But, you may object, a suffragette organisation ought to be democratic. Well the members of the WSPU do not agree with you ... we don't want anybody to remain in it who does not ardently believe in the policy of the army.'* And many let it be said, including her own daughter Sylvia, did not choose to remain.

* Quoted in *Edwardian England 1901–15*, Donald Read (Harrap, 1972), p. 219.

Like all autocrats, she had a sense of fun – which can often reveal itself, though not in her case, in a gamut which goes from elementary relaxing horseplay to practical jokes which are not far short of disgusting bullying and even sadism. But like all autocrats she had no sense of humour. After all, if an autocrat does not take herself seriously who else will? She was also, it appears, without a great deal of business sense. Budgeting was something beyond her scale of values. If she had money, she spent it. In the true aristocratic tradition, where the land will always provide more, she knew that the charisma of the elite excuses them from paying their bills. Despite this, she was well acquainted at least altruistically with the horrors of poverty. Living in Manchester, working as a Poor Law Inspector, she had before her, hour by hour, the dreadful degradation of the urban poor, the unemployment, the hopelessness of destitution, the pitiable results of incest and the swarming sex of the slums.

In October 1903, Emmeline Pankhurst with her three daughters and a few other supporters formed the Women's Social and Political Union in the front room of her home in Manchester. Their object was straightforward, so were to be their methods, so was their slogan: Votes for Women. That was their slogan, that was their object. Their method was to be direct action. While including in their constitution the usual banalities of educating public opinion by meetings, debates, demonstrations, leaflets, letters to the papers, deputations, that slip so easily from the pen of those writing prospectuses, plus the determination to act independently of all political parties, to oppose any government until women got the vote, and even to sponsor independent candidates against all government candidates at parliamentary elections, there were some ominous words in the fourth article: 'Vigorous agitation upon lines justified by the position of outlawry to which women are at present condemned.' The social aspect of the name bore witness to their belief that social progress for women could only come through the political franchise.

Over the years the WSPU tenet to oppose all government candidates gave rise to peculiar situations. There were many good suffrage supporters in the Liberal Party – Sir Edward Grey, the Foreign Secretary for one – who, when they discovered that as a matter of WSPU principle they were to be harangued and abused at meetings by those whose cause they supported, found themselves in the position of that old cliché 'with friends like these who needs enemies'. In the opinion of J. B. Priestley the suffragettes made a fundamental mistake in attacking the Liberals. They would have been much more politically effective had they attacked the Conservative opposition. The Liberals believed – and possibly with justice – that the majority of women would vote Tory. For the women to attack the Liberal Government, even under the guise of 'action entirely independent of all political parties' was simply to confirm a suspicion of some Tory plot. At the time of the WSPU's formation the Conservatives were in power with Arthur Balfour as Prime Minister, and nothing drastic had happened until the Liberals took office. In the long run the Liberals may well have felt their earlier suspicions confirmed when both Mrs Pankhurst and her daughter Christabel joined the Conservative party and were adopted as candidates.

For the first two years of its existence the WSPU was unheard of and ineffectual. In May 1904 there had been a slight frisson of activity which proved to be the outset of militancy. Mrs Pankhurst – Mrs Pancake her enemies were to call her – went to London to hear the debate on the committee stage of Faithfull Begg's Bill. From behind the grille which had been put up to protect the Members from the extravagances of protesting women, she listened to 'Labby' chatting on about verminous persons until Begg's Bill foundered in the quagmire of parliamentary procedure. Livid at this patent, smiling insolence she and a few supporters gathered outside the House and tried to hold a meeting of protest. Ordered away by the police they moved just beyond the forbidden purlieus of Parliament where they were joined by Keir Hardie. Here they held their meeting and here the militant movement began. 'Patience and trust were abandoned, and indignation and bitterness took their place. The old ways led nowhere, the old friends did nothing, and it was time for fresh enterprise.'*

Militant action, mild as it was, began the following year. On 13 October, Sir Edward (later Viscount) Grey and Winston

---

* Ray Strachey, *op. cit.*, p. 292.

Churchill addressed a meeting in the Free Trade Hall, Manchester. Manchester was at that time the political hub of
England, a glory that had once been Birmingham's and one
which was to continue throughout the first quarter of the
twentieth century. Christabel Pankhurst, who was then reading
law at Owen's College, Manchester, attended the meeting at
the Free Trade Hall. It was an important political occasion.
Not only was it being held in Manchester but the resignation of
Balfour meant that the Liberals were on the point of taking
office after nine years in opposition. With Christabel was Annie
Kenney, a cotton mill worker, whom she had met six months
earlier, when she was addressing a meeting at Oldham. With
Annie had been her two sisters, Jessie and Jane – three girls with
shining eyes, Christabel called them later. During the summer
Christabel and the Kenneys toured the Lancashire towns talking to the factory girls. The textile workers of the North-west,
where Beatrice Potter (later Webb) had noticed as a young
woman that in the relationship between men and women there
was no assumption of masculine superiority – 'men and women
mixing together in a free and easy manner but without any
coarseness that I can see' – these textile workers were the first
and as far as can be determined the only group to put up a
Women's Suffrage candidate at the 1906 Election which returned the Liberals to power with such an overwhelming
majority. The candidate they put up was Thorley Smith, the
constituency was Wigan, but the Liberal got in.

The WSPU deputed Christabel Pankhurst and Annie
Kenney to press the putative Liberal Government into accepting women's suffrage as a firm plank in their official programme. That Grey and Churchill would be members of that
government was without question. The decision was therefore
taken to force the issue at the Free Trade Hall meeting. Hiding
little cotton banners inscribed VOTES FOR WOMEN, Pankhurst
and Kenney went up under the porticoed arches into the puri-
tanical rectangle of the Free Trade Hall. Their mission was in
many ways an apt one. As its name suggests, Manchester's Free
Trade Hall is the visible monument of Cobden's and Bright's
Anti-Corn Law League. Extra-parliamentary opposition was
thus a Manchester tradition and it was a tradition that inspired
the Pankhursts' tactics. But seeking to be above party politics

was to court disaster. Since the days of Cobden, rigidity had become an essential characteristic of party discipline. Professionalism was beginning to take over from amicable amateurism. For the Liberals it was a difficult time. They were in a way an anti-party. They stood for nothing positive. They were anti-this and anti-that. They would reform this and correct that. They would fight the brewers and hit the landlords. They would curtail the Lords and so on. But to inspire people you need change not correction. Initially reform is excellent. It gives a relieving feeling to the soul. Before long, however, the excitement of catharsis disappears with its own function. The question arises: what shall we do instead? The Liberal governments of 1906–16 never answered the question. Nor, unfortunately for a democratic government, is it a question that can ever be answered. To me *The Strange Death of Liberal England*, the title of George Dangerfield's classic, is explained by the fact that the Liberals were an anti-party. You might not like the Tories; you might be appalled at Labour; but they both wanted something positive. The Liberals were the ambulance, and while everyone cries out for an ambulance when they are hurt, the healthy cannot care less.

At the end of the Free Trade Hall meeting, when questions were asked for, Pankhurst and Kenney politely asked what the new government's policy was with regard to women's suffrage. There was no answer. Jumping on to a chair to make herself seen and heard – an action that became peculiarly characteristic of her as the years went on – Annie Kenney unfurled her little banner. Shouts of anger arose: stewards rushed to pull her down, one holding his hat over her mouth to stifle her words. As this happened, Christabel rose and repeated the question. For her there were no stewards, simply smiles from the platform. Stewards were for the recalcitrant working women; daughters of well-known Mancunian Radicals were treated in the reflected glory of their fathers – even though the daughters were causing trouble at college. In the end, after Annie Kenney had tried once more, the two of them were manhandled down the steps into Peter Street.

That was how it began. Bearing in mind his strong support for suffragism it is perhaps surprising that Grey was so inept in his handling of the WSPU questions, unless of course the possibility of office did not seem so secure to him as it did to his audience. Added to this clumsiness was the unnecessary violence of the stewards. By tradition, women were silent at political meetings. The unexpected experience of women asking questions seemed to make the stewards react as if they had heard new Tory monsters. It was a reaction that brought years of embarrassment to the Liberals. Nor did the altercation stop in the Free Trade Hall. When Pankhurst and Kenney tried to hold a protest meeting outside they were arrested. Next day they were convicted of causing an obstruction and chose imprisonment rather than a fine. Kenney got three days, Pankhurst seven – the extra four days for spitting at a policeman. The value of that imprisonment to the WSPU was priceless. Into their hands was thereby given the weapon of publicity. Immediately they saw its importance, immediately they began to base their tactics around it. The meeting at the Free Trade Hall 'fired a train of bitterness and anger which carried the New Society (the WSPU) forward; and it was the insincere attitude of the Liberals as much as the fighting spirit of the women which led to the uprising of the militant movement'.*

Among the crowd which met Kenney and Pankhurst on their release was Mrs Flora Drummond who was to become one of the bulwarks of the suffragette campaign. She had started her working life as a girl telegraphist on the Isle of Arran in the Firth of Clyde and had passed all the examinations necessary to become a postmistress. But she was one inch shorter than a newly prescribed height so her appointment was cancelled. Then she had married and come to Manchester where she was now managing the Oliver Typewriting office. Although they were complete strangers to each other she and Christabel became 'friends at sight'.

After the Free Trade Hall meeting came the 1906 General Election which put the Liberals into power with a resounding majority of 243 over the Conservatives and an overall majority of 130. It was during this election that Lord Northcliffe's *Daily Mail* coined the name 'Suffragettes'. Christabel Pankhurst said, 'Suffragists we had called ourselves till then, but that name lacked the positive note implied by "suffragette". Just "want the

* Ray Strachey, *op. cit.*, p. 294.

vote" was the notion conveyed by the older appellation but, as a famous anecdote had it, "the suffragettes (hardening the 'g') mean to get it."'

Early in the new year (1906) Annie Kenney was sent to 'rouse London'. Important as Manchester was it could not hold a candle to London as a centre for conducting the sort of campaign the Pankhursts had in mind. Government, Parliament, press were all concentrated in London. What happened in Manchester was not necessarily news in London, but what happened in London was news throughout the world. But London initially proved a difficult nut to crack. The millions making their way to and from offices and shops had too many interests and problems of their own to saddle themselves with the enthusiasms and plans of the suffragettes. Nonetheless the WSPU's London campaign opened with some éclat. Caxton Hall was hired for a women's meeting to take place on 19 February 1906, simultaneously with the opening of Parliament a few hundred yards away. When it was learnt that there was no reference to votes for women in the King's Speech, Mrs Pankhurst led her cohorts through the rain to the Houses of Parliament. Here they were refused admission and waited angrily outside until at length a few dozen were admitted to lobby individual members. For Mrs Pankhurst it was a day of triumph. 'Those women had followed me to the House of Commons. They had defied the police. They were awake at last. . . . Our militant movement was established.'

Chapter 6

TEN SHILLINGS A WEEK

❧

At Bow Street police court in 1908, where Christabel Pankhurst was appearing on a charge of inciting a crowd to 'rush' the House of Commons, her mother recounted the work that she (Mrs Pankhurst) had done as a public servant and as a constitutional suffragist. Their campaign of militancy, she said, had not been undertaken lightly.

'We are driven to this . . . Just as it was the duty of our forefathers to do it for you, it is our duty to make this world a better place for women. We believe that if we get the vote it will mean changed conditions for our less fortunate sisters. The average pay of women wage-earners is only seven shillings and sixpence a week. There are women who have been driven to live an immoral life because they cannot earn enough to live decently.'

She had seen plenty of these when she was a registrar in Manchester and had been shocked by the number of young girls who came to record the births of illegitimate babies.

The average wage of 7s 6d a week is probably on the low side. In their study of *Sweating* published in April 1907* Edward Cadbury and George Shann stated that an unskilled woman's wage was about 10s a week. With Cécile Matheson they had made an extensive enquiry into women's work and wages in Birmingham which was published in 1906.† They

* *Social Services Handbooks No. V* (Headley).

† *Women's Work and Wages* (T. Fisher Unwin). But Mary R. Macarthur, the Women's Trade Union organiser in *Women in Industry* (Duckworth, 1908), wrote that although there were no reliable statistics as to the average wages earned by women workers 'speaking from a large experience' she estimated that 'the average wage of the manual woman worker,

found that 'wherever women replaced men the former always received a much lower wage and one that was not proportional to the skill or intelligence required by the work, but approximated to a certain fixed level – about 10s to 12s per week, the majority of women getting the lower amount'.*

Agitation about 'sweating' was very much a concern of late Victorian and Edwardian reformers. Half a century earlier humanitarians and moralists in the top part of the nation had been horrified at the disclosures about women and children working underground in the mines. The horror arose as much from the fact that men and women were working together in a semi- or totally-naked state as from the physical conditions under which they were working. Nonetheless, the concern resulted in legislation which excluded women and children from the pits.† Now in the Edwardian decade 'sweating' had become the equivalent topic for industrial and social reformers.

In 1890 a House of Lords Committee under the Chairmanship of Lord Dunraven found it difficult to define 'sweating' exactly but said that the evils known by that name were work that involved insanitary conditions, excessive hours, and an unduly low rate of pay; but at the turn of the century sweating, by common usage, was still identified with subcontracting and particularly with the women outworkers who slaved in their own homes to make clothes for manufacturers at starvation wages. Thus to limit it, however, did not give anything like a broad enough picture of the extent to which sweating existed. Sweating also existed where there was no subcontracting; and on the other hand in some trades such as the building trade, sub-contracting was allowed but union rates of wages had to be paid. Again, sweating was not necessarily synonymous with outwork, although it was generally true that the worst cases occurred amongst home-workers. In Birming-

* *Sweating*, p. 21.
† See Duncan Crow, *The Victorian Woman*, pp. 80–2.

taking into account slackness, sickness, etc, is certainly not more than 7s 6d weekly all the year round. The comparatively high average of the textile trades of Lancashire, owing to the unexampled organisation which has resulted in a membership of over 96,000 women trade unionists is included in my estimate, as is also the wage of the East End homeworker (which may sometimes drop as low as 2s 6d)'. No doubt it was Miss Macarthur's estimated figure that Mrs Pankhurst quoted.

ham, for example, there were women working on their own at home in trades like jewellery and electro-plate burnishing, who were making 16s a week. But there were trades wholly carried out in factories and workshops which certainly seemed to justify the name of sweated industries despite the amelioration of conditions created by factory legislation and enforced by factory inspectors. One witness before the Dunraven Committee said that the broadest definition he could give to the term sweating was that it was the process of grinding the faces of the poor. Gertrude Tuckwell pointed out in 1908 that 'sweating survives where [parliamentary] protection is incomplete, where the trade is not strong enough to organise and protect its wages, and where the State, as yet, has not safeguarded conditions of work'.* One example she gave was the girl clerk working for 10s a week in a crowded basement office late into the night. 'Yet this profession never figures in the popular imagination as an instance of sweating – the gentility of the occupation appears to lift it out of the category and to form its own reward.'

But sweating as it was popularly understood was epitomised by some figures given by Gertrude Tuckwell: a comparison of the prices as agreed between the Amalgamated Society of Tailors and Tailoresses and the London Master Tailors' Association, and the sweated rates for similar work. The union rate for making a dress coat was £1 5s 6d to £1 7s 6d; the non-union rate was 10s to 16s. Dress vest 8s to 9s 3d (union), 2s 6d (non-union). Dress trousers 7s 3d to 8s 5d (union) 2s to 4s (non-union). Ladies' costume 30s (union) 1s 7¼d (non-union). Ladies' jacket 23s (union), 9¾d (non-union). Ninepence three-farthings as against twenty-three shillings!

Clementina Black in her book on *Sweated Industry and the Minimum Wage*† gave some vivid and detailed descriptions of what sweating actually meant. Possibly the poorest trade of all was match-box making.

'The women fetch out from the factory or the middlewoman's, strips of notched wood, packets of coloured paper and sandpaper, and printed wrappers; they carry back large but light bundles

---

* 'The Regulation of Women's Work' in *Women in Industry From Seven Points of View* (Duckworth, 1908), p. 15.

† Duckworth, 1907.

of boxes, tied up in packets of two dozen. Inside their rooms the boxes, made and unmade and half-made, cover the floor and fill up the lack of furniture. I have seen a room containing only an old bedstead in the very last stage of dirt and dilapidation, a table, and two deal boxes for seats. The floor and the window-sill were rosy with magenta match-boxes, while everything else, including the boards of the floor, the woodwork of the room and the coverings of the bed, was of the dark grey of ingrained dust and dirt. At first sight it is a pretty enough spectacle to see a match-box made; one motion of the hands bends into shape the notched frame of the case, another surrounds it with the ready-pasted strip of printed wrapper, which, by long practice, is fitted instantly without a wrinkle, then the sand-paper or the phosphorus-paper, pasted ready before-hand, is applied and pressed on so that it sticks fast. A pretty high average of neatness and finish is demanded by most employers, and readers who will pass their match-boxes in review will seldom find a wrinkle or a loose corner of paper. The finished case is thrown upon the floor; the long narrow strip which is to form the frame of the drawer is laid upon the bright strip of ready-pasted paper, then bent together and joined by an overlapping bit of the paper; the edges of the paper below are bent flat, the ready-cut bottom is dropped in and pressed down, and before the fingers are withdrawn they fold over the upper edges of the paper inside the top. Now the drawer, too, is cast on the floor to dry. All this, besides the preliminary pasting of wrapper, coloured paper and sandpaper, had to be done 144 times for 2¼d.; and even this is not all, for every drawer and case have to be fitted together and the packets tied up with hemp. Nor is the work done then, for paste has to be made before it can be used, and boxes, when they are ready, have to be carried to the factory . . .

'The conditions of life secured in return for this continuous and monotonous toil are such as might as well make death appear preferable. The poor dwelling – already probably over-crowded – is yet further crowded with match-boxes, a couple of gross of which, in separated pieces, occupy a considerable space. If the weather be at all damp, as English weather often is, even in summer, there must be a fire kept up, or the paste will not dry; and fire, paste and hemp must all be paid for out of the worker's pocket. From her working time, too, or from that of her child messenger, must be deducted the time lost in fetching and carrying back work, and, too often, in being kept waiting for it before it is given out.'

Nor was shirt-making much better. The wages were often extremely low and were yet further reduced by the fact that the home-worker provided her own cotton. Clementina Black had seen a young deserted wife who was trying to support herself and her two young children by making shirts.

'These were flannel shirts of a fair quality, and were handed to her cut out. She did not sew on buttons nor make button holes; but except for these items made the shirt throughout, by machine, and put in a square of lining at the back of the neck. She was paid 1s 2d a dozen, and bought the cotton herself. She could make in a week "five dozen all but one"; for which payment would be five shillings, eightpence and a fraction of a penny, less the cost of cotton, machine needles, oil, and perhaps hire of machine.'

The Factory Inspector's Report for 1905 included a description of paper-bag making in Glasgow, a trade largely carried on by home-workers:

'. . . and no trade is more disturbing to the home. The paste seems to find its way everywhere, and many more things than the bags are found firmly pasted together. I visited two women, who, working usually in workshops, were, during the enforced period of absence owing to the birth of a child, given employment as outworkers. Nothing could exceed the misery and squalor amongst which the work was done. In both cases the workroom was also the living room and bedroom, and the whole of the available furniture, including the bed, was covered with damp bags, some hundreds of which had to be removed in one home before I could be shown the baby. The surroundings were unpleasant ones for making bags destined to hold pastry. . . . This work is poorly paid. Bags, by no means of the smallest size, are made for 3d to 5d a thousand, so that it is indeed a heavy weight which has to be carried for the daily shilling.'

The examples could be multiplied to tedium: toothbrush

makers, racquet ball makers, blouse makers, makers of underclothing, of baby clothes, of boot boxes, of artificial flowers,
cappers of safety pins (at 3s a 100 gross – 14,400 safety pins),
carders of buttons, umbrella coverers – all busy from minute to
minute, being paid a wage from ¾d to 2d an hour. 'Their work,
in some shape or form,' wrote Clementina Black, 'comes into
every house in this country.'

Ill-health was the chronic state of the woman home-worker.
Even though the journey was taken through the mires of city
back-streets, the factory worker did at least leave her home and
take a modicum of air and exercise on her way to her work-
place. Not so for the home-worker. Dragging herself out of bed
into the nightmare of a room crawling with bags or match-boxes
or the stacks of shirts she was making, smelling of paste, littered
with cotton strands of a myriad inanimate spiders, never a
change of scene, never the passing glance of a new face glimpsed.
Factory work, too, had its own enervating drabness, its own
forms of sweated labour and in many cases the workers were
financially little better off than the poorer sort of home-workers.
Most of the paid factory workers were engaged in packaging
rather than in actual manufacture.

'No foreman in the world can drive so hard as her own low
wage drives the piece-worker who has to support relatives. The
most worn-out girl whom I remember ever to have seen,' wrote
Clementina Black,

'was engaged upon no harder task than packing cocoa. . . .
She may have been eighteen or nineteen; she was absolutely
colourless, and, although there was no sign about her of any
specific illness, seemed exhausted literally almost to death.
She sat day after day pouring powdered cocoa into ready-
made square paper packets, of which she then folded down
the top and pasted on wrappers. She received a halfpenny
a gross. In the week previous to that in which I saw her she had
earned 7s. She had therefore filled, folded and pasted in the
week, 21,792 packets'.

A Sweating Exhibition was organised by the *Daily News* in
the West End of London in May 1906 and was opened by Princess Henry of Battenburg, the King's youngest sister Beatrice.

It lasted six weeks and was visited by thirty thousand people including the Princess of Wales (later Queen Mary). 'What can we do?' she asked as she went round the stalls where the workers were engaged at their various forms of slavery. 'What can we do?' others echoed. But most of the visitors no doubt went away glad to forget this sight of a forlorn world which was such a sinister challenge to the comfort and elegance of their own lives. 'The visit', as Clementina Black wrote, was 'a painful interlude between a visit to the shops in the morning and a visit to the theatre in the evening.'* But the feeling of concern stuck sufficiently for a National Anti-Sweating League to be formed to secure a minimum wage, and later in 1906 a three-day conference representing two million organised workers was opened by the Lord Mayor at the City of London Guildhall. Among the speakers were Clementina Black herself, Sir Charles Dilke, Lord Dunraven, Sidney Webb and Pember Reeves. All were agreed that voluntary action was ineffective. Consumers' leagues in Britain and the United States, designed to dissuade people from buying the products of sweated labour, had achieved little. Legislative action was the only answer. Trade unionism could regulate wages in the great industries like cotton and thus benefit the community as a whole. But by itself trade unionism was unable to destroy sweating in those industries like the garment trades, where sub-contracting and outwork took the origin of the product into thousands of one-room slum dwellings where fear of starvation and utter destitution was the goad to the acceptance of slavery and where the victims had neither the heart nor the opportunity to defend themselves by joint effort.

Nor was Protection the answer. As Bernard Shaw said in one of the lectures at the Sweating Exhibition, the operation of Protection would be wholly in the interest of the sweater. Sweating was even more rampant in protected countries than in Free Trade England. The *Daily News* exhibition had been suggested by an exhibition in Berlin and was followed by a similar one in Philadelphia. Sweating in Paris was as bad as anywhere. Octave Uzanne records† that exceedingly skilled needlewomen earned 4 francs a day for a twelve hour day while

* *Op. cit.*, p. xv.
† *The Modern Parisienne* (Heinemann, 1912).

less experienced needlewomen working in their own homes or scattered through the large workrooms of the 'Kingdom of Fashion' earned only 2 francs, about 1s 7½d. There were some 135,000 workwomen of all trades in Paris, the greater number being *ouvrières du dehors*, that is those who worked away from their own homes either for the State or for companies or for private individuals. The average wage of the 135,000 was 2.25 francs (about 1s 9¾d) for about ten hours work.

Nevertheless it was three of the British Protectionist Colonies (Victoria, New South Wales and New Zealand) which, wrote Clementina Black, had indicated the true path of reform by introducing either, as in Victoria, a wages board to determine a minimum wage, or, as in New South Wales and New Zealand, an arbitration system which also included the principle of the minimum wage. A bill was presented to the Imperial Parliament in 1907 on the lines of Victoria's wages board system and became law in 1909 as the Trade Boards Act to secure a minimum wage in certain sweated industries, (tailoring, dressmaking and shirt-making were specified), with the option of including further industries.

There were several trades, undoubtedly sweated, for which there was no likelihood of a Trade Board ever being appointed. Waitresses and barmaids were two, shop assistants were a third. The chaotic conditions of such trades where there were few, if any, regulations which would make for the workers' efficiency and comfort, could probably be explained, suggested Gertrude Tuckwell, 'by scruples as to interfering with the convenience of the public'.*

Despite the fact that shop assistants were considered to be among 'the aristocracy of Labour' a study of their conditions made it obvious that here, if anywhere, there really was sweating. 'Board and lodging is often provided, under the hated living-in system, by the employer, and the inadequate remuneration which is not paid in kind is often heavily taxed to supplement the poor food.'

Assistants, both men and women, were subject to fines for every petty error and their 'standing orders' covered almost every detail of their life and work. Clementina Black examined

* *Op. cit.*, p. 20.

several of these codes of rules. One, which was in force at White-
ley's, the big emporium in London's Bayswater, contained 159
rules; the code at another shop in the same district had 198.
For 'appearing in business in an untidy manner, fine 3d', the
wearer, of course, having to pay for the washing of the immacu-
late collars and cuffs which were essential to a tidy manner.
'Gossiping, standing in groups, or lounging about in an unbusinesslike manner, fine 3d.' 'Assistants must introduce at
least two articles to each customer, fine for not doing so 2d.'
'Unnecessary talking and noise in bedrooms is strictly prohibited, fine 6d.' 'For unbusinesslike conduct, fine 6d.' 'For losing
copy of the rules, fine 2d.' As far as the bedrooms or dormitories
were concerned these were generally bleak and regimented:
'No pictures, photos, etc., allowed to disfigure the walls. Any
one so doing will be charged with the repairs.'

'Brushes, bottles, etc., must not be left in the room, but put
away in the drawers. Anything so left will be considered done
for.'*

From the bedroom, with hair carefully dressed but body
usually inadequately washed because of the shortage of baths
and hot water, the young lady shop assistant hurried down to
the dining-room to take her breakfast of bread and butter and
weak tea among a crowd of companions. Twenty minutes later
she was in the shop, where she remained until dinner-time at
midday, working in the narrow space behind the counter,
being jostled and jostling, lifting down boxes, laying out goods
before the customer, putting them away, making out bills,
filling up forms, on her feet the whole time.

This was one of the two great drawbacks to being a shop
assistant – the long hours of standing. In 1899 the 1st Duke of
Westminster made his last parliamentary appearance to advo-
cate 'a step in the direction of prevention of cruelty to women';
this was a bill to make shops provide seats for their assistants. If
soldiers of the line were called upon to undergo the long periods
of enforced sentry duty imposed on shop girls they would certainly mutiny, he said, and he recommended a seat that had
been introduced by a Peckham draper which swung under the
counter when not in use. The bill became law on 9 August 1899.

---

* *Op. cit.*, pp. 49, 54–5.

It stated that in all retail shops where women assistants were employed seats must be provided behind the counter for their use in the proportion of not less than one seat for every three women working in that room. There was opposition, but as the Act was to apply only to women it did not encounter the full antagonism of those who were against all legislation which interfered with men's hours or conditions.

Half-an-hour for the shop assistant's midday meal, which if not inadequate was usually monotonous, then back to the counter; fifteen to twenty minutes break for tea at about five o'clock; and then back to the counter once again until closing-time which might be any time from seven, in the West End of London, until 9.30 in the less fashionable districts. On Saturdays some shops in the poorer quarters stayed open until midnight. After the customers had gone the shop had to be tidied and the goods covered over for the night. Then supper – usually a Spartan meal; and then freedom until 11 p.m., or 12 on Saturdays. Fifteen minutes after that the gas was turned out and no private lights were allowed. 'Anyone having a light after time will be discharged.' In lower-class shops the young lady assistant did not always have a bed to herself but had to share it with some other young lady without benefit of choice.

The harassing and nagging pettiness of the rules and restrictions contributed to the breakdown of health and nervous disorders which were so frequent among women shop assistants. The close confinement, the sameness, the lack of leisure, the niggling annoyances – all made the 'living-in' system the second great drawback to the occupation of shop assistant. If the system were abolished, Clementina Black maintained, it would lead to a marked improvement in the health of the whole class of shop assistants.

The hours worked by shop assistants in London varied between $50\frac{1}{2}$ and $79\frac{1}{2}$ a week, including meals, and in the provinces between $51\frac{1}{2}$ and $67\frac{1}{2}$, although they were sometimes as high as 70 or 74, exclusive of meals. The longest hours were worked in tobacconists, fruiterers, confectioners, and newspaper shops.* For this the London salaries (not 'wages') were from

* Under the Shops Act of 1886, which was to run until the last day of 1888, no young person was to be employed more than 74 hours including

£10 a year to £60, including premiums, with board and lodgings. Occasionally assistants who were not living in were paid £100 a year. In the provinces assistants sometimes received no pay for their first year and only £5 to £7 during the second. There were great variations in salaries depending upon the kind of shop and the locality, some assistants after eight years service getting only £15 a year, others £45 and up to £75. Showroom hands earned considerably more, sometimes as much as £200 or £300 annually. The *Dictionary of Employments Open to Women* (1898), from which the figures in this paragraph are taken, gave the average general wage as from 5s to 15s a week for ordinary shop assistants and from 15s to 20s and 22s for charge hands. Clementina Black reckoned that on average £35 a year was high pay for an ordinary saleswoman. 'Out of this income the assistant has to keep up the required standard of appearance, providing black gowns and spotless starched linen.'

These salaries were supposed to be supplemented by 'premiums'. Certain goods which the management particularly wanted to sell for reasons of their own were 'premiumed', and assistants selling them were given a small commission. 'The existence of premiums explains in great measure the annoyance to which all of us have been subjected by the endeavours of an assistant to force upon us goods for which we have not asked – goods known behind the counter as "intro" (or

---

mealtimes, in one week. This did not apply to a shop run solely by the members of one family. The Act was made permanent by the Shops Act of 1892. The next legislation affecting shop hours was the Shops Act of 1904 which provided that a local authority might make an order (which had to be confirmed by the government) fixing a closing hour for shops not earlier than 7 p.m. except on one day when it could not be earlier than 1 p.m. The order could define the shops or trades to which it applied.

None of these Acts, however, gave shop assistants a half-holiday. That did not come until the beginning of May 1912 when the Shop Act of 1911 came into force. As early closing was an issue that the Government felt was politically impossible to accede to it availed itself of the compulsory regulations about shop assistants' hours. Under the 1911 Act no assistant was to be employed after 1.30 p.m. on one day a week. Although there were limitations which spoilt the full effect of the Act, the half-holiday was finally achieved. (See also Wilfred B. Whitaker, *Victorian and Edwardian Shopworkers: The Struggle to Obtain Better Conditions and a Half-holiday* (David and Charles, 1973)).

introduced goods.'* Failure to introduce goods, as we have already seen, incurred a fine. Indeed the pennies that might be made by premiums were usually offset by the fines and the deductions to which the assistants were liable. All in all it was the better class shops that had the shorter hours and the higher pay.

Another pressure on the shop assistant was the 'book', that is the amount of goods which each assistant must sell in a week. Repeated failure to 'take her book' meant that the assistant lost her job.

With all these drawbacks why did the young lady shop assistants (many of them 'of refinement and of delicate feeling; some of them daughters of clergymen and of other professional men who have died leaving their girls unprovided for'), why did they not abandon the shop in a body and go into domestic service? The answer was simple.

'These girls, like the vast majority of their compatriots, will endure much hardship rather than lose caste; and, whatever may be the opinion of the wage-payers, there can be no doubt that among wage-earners domestic service ranks as a low-caste occupation. The middle-class mother who will not send her little girl to a public elementary school, the middle-class father who would rather see his son making a small income as a professional man than a large income as a tradesman, ought rather to applaud than to condemn the "young lady in business" who refuses to exchange her black uniform and her title of "Miss" for the cap and apron and the name without a handle of the domestic servant.'†

Commenting on 'an ordinary girl's choice of work' Cadbury, Matheson and Shann pointed out that her long-term career prospects were not a factor that entered into a girl's calculations. She expected to get married and therefore what mattered most to her when she looked for a job was the cleanliness and easiness of the work and, above all, nice company. That marriage would not remove her into a mode of life where she would no longer have to earn her living was demonstrated by the vast

* Clementina Black, *op. cit.*, p. 61.
† *Ibid.*

number of married women working in factories in any large town or city. Nonetheless, whatever the evidence to the contrary, few girls expected to be life workers. Usually a girl drifted into the first work suggested to her without any consideration of its possibilities. Economic pressure, too, had a telling effect on choice. In a poor household where every penny counted, no girl of working age could afford to spend months if not a year or more in training for a skilled job with good long-term prospects when her wages during the training period would be only pocket-money, 1s 6d to 3s 6d a week.

There was, however, one consideration which influenced all girls

'who have been awakened to any sense of self-respect and all mothers who have any thought for their children's welfare. This is the question of class distinction. . . . As soon as a girl takes any thought for herself at all, her desire is to "keep herself respectable", and when one realises the environment in which many of these girls live, their familiarity from their earliest years with the surroundings of vice and crime, one can understand how this desire, once awakened, becomes a ruling power in a girl's life and also why rigid class distinctions permeate the rank and file of manual workers. These distinctions are familiar to most social workers, but those who speak generally of the "working classes" or "the poor" can have no conception of their influence or their extent.'

For example, warehouse girls who did all the wrapping-up, sorting, boxing, weighing and packing in a factory – warehousing being the link between clerical and manual occupations open to girls – 'knew little or nothing about the work-girls in the factory, and many similar examples will be found in the work-rooms themselves'.*

In the metal trades burnishing had an excellent social standing. Even better was lacquering. One little girl who worked on a press said in answer to a question when she was being interviewed, 'Oh, the lacquering girls are ladies.' So marked were these social distinctions that in one factory in

* *Op. cit.*, pp. 47–8.

Birmingham the idea of providing a dining-room had to be
abandoned because the lacquerers would not eat in the same
room as the dippers. This was not simply snobbishness. 'These
girls know so well the lower strata of society, they are so well
aware how easily a girl or family is dragged down by the
pressure of want or ill-luck, that it is only natural that they
should make what seems to an onlooker to be a hard or unnecessary distinction and protest against being classed in any
way with the rougher women.'*

The over-riding importance of respectability had a crucial
effect on wage rates. Because one trade was more respectable
or, to use Charles Booth's word in his *Life and Labour of the
People*,† more 'fashionable' than another, there was competition
to enter it with a consequently depressing effect on wages. An
example cited in *Women's Work and Wages* were the Birmingham
warehouse girls who would probably have had better prospects
had not warehousing been 'the general refuge of the poorer
girls who make some determined attempt at refinement, just as
clerkships are sought by girls and boys alike who want to "rise"
into the ranks of business as distinguished from manual work'.‡
Another economic influence was that warehouse girls and clerks
came from better-class families and were therefore more frequently subsidised by their parents.

A final word about choice of employment comes from girls
in London Board schools who, in 1901, were asked to write an
essay on what they would like to be when they left school. In
most cases the choice was predictable. It was a question of
status: the better the status, the better the marriage prospects –
or even the better the chance of marriage at all in a country
where women outnumbered men by over one million in a total
population of 32·5 million. Those were the actual statistics,
but there was a popular belief, fostered by some of the popular
press, that the imbalance between the sexes was even greater.
'It is a common error,' said an article in the *Illustrated London
News* of 6 April 1901, 'to suppose that there are seven women
to every individual man – which would make the number of
odd women to every thousand men six thousand instead of the

* *Ibid.*, pp. 70–1.
† Volume IV, 'Women's Work'.
‡ p. 49.

true figure of about sixty.' With a common error like that who can be surprised that a girl wanted to increase her chances of marriage!

Top of the poll for the Board schoolgirls was 'housemaid' – a not unnatural choice considering that out of 4 million employed women in England and Wales no less than 1·7 million were domestic servants, and a housemaid's lot was the height of ambition for someone who was brought up to believe that God and her background intended her for a general 'slavey' or a 'tweeny', and for whom domestic service did at least promise board and lodging and the opportunity, as one put it, to 'learn to act and speak differently'. There were, however, a few more venturesome ones whose dreams of happiness were outside the common run. There were, for instance, a number who wanted to be a poet or a novelist, qualifying this excursion into fantasy lest it should incur the wrath of authority by its improvidence by adding, correctly, 'but it is a chance living'. However, the palm for the most original and subtly explained ambition, in which altruism was skilfully blended with personal advancement, must surely go to the girl who wrote that she hoped to become a Duchess so that she could be 'kind to little children and help them'. And why not? It was not only American heiresses who were becoming duchesses. Girls from the Gaiety were doing it too.

Chapter 7

THE COUNTESS OF GAIETY

Musical comedy is perhaps the form of entertainment most characteristic of the Edwardian age. The music hall was going strong, the legitimate stage had bright new playwrights in Galsworthy, Maugham, Hankin and Granville-Barker, as well as the established constellation of Jones, Pinero, Shaw and Barrie, the kinematograph had ceased to be merely a turn in a variety show and had become an entertainment of its own in an auditorium of its own – nonetheless it is musical comedy that seems to epitomise entertainment in Edwardian times.

The genre had established itself in England in 1892 with *In Town*, and over the next few years included *A Gaiety Girl*, *The Shop Girl* and *The Belle of New York*. The first musical comedy to be put on in London after the King's accession was *A Chinese Honeymoon* which, after being tried out in Hanley in 1899, opened at the Royal Strand Theatre on 5 October 1901. It ran for 1,075 performances and was the longest comedy run until *Chu Chin Chow* beat it during the First World War.

The Royal Strand Theatre was one of the eight London theatres controlled by Frank Curzon; another was the Prince of Wales. But though both were successful with their musical comedies neither quite captured the imagination as being the true home of the genre as did the Gaiety and Daly's under that magnifico of musical comedy, George Edwardes, whose genius seems mainly to have lain in collecting around him a highly professional team who could make the thing work.

The original Gaiety was closed on 4 July 1903 during the redevelopment of the eastern Strand area which cleared the

Drury Lane slums and created Kingsway, with its underground trams, running down from Southampton Row to Aldwych. On 26 October 1903 the new Gaiety, now lost in the entrails of a conglomerate office block, was opened on the western corner of the Aldwych. The show was *The Orchid* by Lionel Monckton and Ivan Caryll, and, to the wonder and disapproval of many, the opening night was attended by the King and Queen (though how they ever got to the theatre at all is a matter of wonder, considering Queen Alexandra's notorious unpunctuality). *The Orchid*, with Gertie Millar as a mill girl, made a star of the previously unknown Gabrielle Ray. It ran for 559 performances – 500 being par for an extremely good run in the musical comedy world. After *The Orchid* came *The Spring Chicken* (401 performances) adapted from the French by George Grossmith, the Gaiety's star comedian. After that came a burlesque, *The New Aladdin*, which was a flop although the music was by Monckton and Caryll – as its predecessors had been – and the principal boy was Lily Elsie whose first taste of fame had come in *A Chinese Honeymoon*. Nor was its successor, *The Girls of Gothenburg* (303 performances) a major success.

Meanwhile, at Daly's, George Edwardes had staged Monckton's *A Country Girl* (1902: 729 performances) and *The Cingalee* (1904), Messager's *The Little Michus* and *The Lady Dandies* by Hugo Felix. *The Little Michus* did well enough with 397 performances, but the killingly named *Lady Dandies* (an anglicisation of the even less box-office acceptably French title 'Les Merveilleuses' – called by London taxi-drivers 'The Marvellous 'Ouses') was a major disaster. But then came the most fantastic musical comedy phenomenon of all times. *Die Lustige Witwe*, which by a stroke of translator's genius kept its saucy sexy flavour in its English title of *The Merry Widow*, had played in 450 theatres on the Continent before it opened at Daly's on 8 June 1907 with Lily Elsie as the heroine. Apart from being translated, the piece was given a new look with more comedy and less music (although the music was Franz Lehar's), and there was a new Act Three.

As is so often the way with successes in the theatre – and indeed in other avenues of life – *The Merry Widow* was only put on by Edwardes as a stop-gap until *The Dollar Princess* became available. But it ran for two years (until 31 July 1909) and became the darling of the age. Not only did it sweep London with its performances and the whole country with its songs (there wasn't a girl alive with any pretension to a voice who didn't want to sing 'Vilia' in public and only those who were dumb didn't try it in private); not only did 'Vilia' keep the errand-boys bawling in the streets as Lottie Collins 'Ta-ra-ra-boom-de-ay' had done after she first presented it in 1891, but the *Merry Widow* became a cult; waltzes became the craze, there were sauces called after her, clubs in her name, and the whole paraphernalia of merchandising became linked to this *lustige* lady.

Curiously enough, although *The Merry Widow* had been seen often enough in Europe before it landed in England, the excitement that attended it at Daly's spread back across the Channel and at the height of its popularity 'it was being performed at over 400 theatres in Europe on the same evening'.*

With *The Merry Widow* waltzing her way round the country it was clear to musical comedy management that what the public wanted and would pay for was Viennese *Schmaltz* – and so they were given *The Chocolate Soldier* (1908) (based on Shaw's *Arms and the Man*, which had so infuriated Society when it was first produced by Emily Horniman in 1894 because it made fun of the Army – not that Society reckoned much to the Army as an instrument of national defence, but because every one took the Army seriously as an essential and therefore sacrosanct ornament of Society); they were given *The Count of Luxembourg* (1911); they were given *Gipsy Love*.

Musical comedy did not, however, get itself entirely bogged down in the Vienna woods with Parisian overtones. Contemporary English settings returned with Monckton and Caryll's *Our Miss Gibbs* in which Gertie Millar starred as a mill girl who went up in the world when she got a job in a West End store. It was analagous to their *The Shop Girl* of the 1890s, but had topical variations, including the theft of the Ascot Gold Cup (the centenary of the race had been run in 1907) and a set of the White City which had been the venue of the 1908 Franco–British Exhibition in Shepherd's Bush, London. For mill girls to become shop girls was part of the romantic dream of

* Ronald Pearsall, *Edwardian Popular Music* (David and Charles, 1975), p. 37.

1. 'When . . . waists were waists.'
A nurse-maid was obligatory in all
families with children where the
income was £500 a year and upwards (1906)

2. Sunday best (1906)

3. Summer holiday at Shering-
ham, Norfolk (1901)

4. Too hot for anything (1908)

5. Portrait of the Edwardian Woman – the subject and

6. the photographer (1905)

7. Two out of every five women were domestic servants. Annie pumping water. Yorkshire (1901)

8. 'Walking round the garden . . .'

9. '. . . while your husband wrestled with the motor,' in this case a De Dion Bouton (1908)

10. Anyone for tennis? (1908)

11. Autumn motoring (1909)

12. Lady driver (1908)

13. Washing the parrot (1906)

14. Everyone in the family had to work. The wife and eleven children of a Liverpool fish-hawker (1913)

15. Home workers: wood choppers in Birmingham (1906)

16. Dame Millicent Fawcett

17. Militant leaders: from left to right, Lady Constance Lytton, Annie Kenney, Mrs Pethick Lawrence, Christabel and Sylvia Pankhurst (1910)

18. Picnics for the motorist: Wisley, the Royal Horticultural Society's gardens (1905)

19. 'When hats were hats of startling size . . .' (1909)

20. Tea on the lawn in Buckinghamshire (1908)

21. 'Feast' for the local school-children at Farnley Hall, Yorkshire (1903)

23. Pierrots at Sandown, Isle of Wight. Note one small girl putting her fingers in her ears (1904)

22. Spring sunshine (1909)

working-class women; a girl's job affected her chances in the marriage stakes, and to be a shop girl immeasurably shortened the odds, for it was a job with much better status.

Other pieces with topical realism were *The Sunshine Girl* (1912), which had as its background Port Sunlight, and *The Girl on the Film* and *The Girl in a Taxi*. The latter, if it did nothing else, produced one of those catchphrases which seem destined to go on for ever: 'If you can't be good be careful'.

It was not only Curzon and Edwardes who gave London town what it wanted in the way of light after-dinner entertainment that demanded nothing in the way of concentration and allowed those who took boxes to arrive as late as they pleased, to gabble away to their companions, turn their backs to the stage and inspect the other boxes and the stalls without any possibility of their losing the thread of the piece or failing to understand the plot. Notable among the others was Robert Courtneidge who, after being in partnership with Edwardes at the Lyric theatre, where they produced a musical comedy (*The Duchess of Danzig*), a play and a pantomime, decided to chance his arm on his own. He took the Shaftesbury Theatre and opened there in 1909 with a musical comedy of which he was the part-author and which no other management would touch. His friends and even the members of the cast warned him against it because it was based on fantasy and the musical comedy world was dead against a plot based on fantasy – as if the whole genre itself was not based on fantasy. But Courtneidge believed in his idea and against all advice *The Arcadians* was produced with Phyllis Dare as the leading lady. It was the greatest hit of them all, *The Merry Widow* notwithstanding. From the very first night of *The Arcadians* the song of the injured jockey who had never won a race, 'I've got a motter – always merry and bright,' was acclaimed as a hit. And the overture has been constantly played over the years ever since. When the leading lady went on holiday after a year or more without missing a performance, her part was taken by her understudy, a young lady of seventeen called Cicely Courtneidge. *The Arcadians* ran in London for two and a half years and toured the provinces for ten years after that. And, according to Cicely Courtneidge, more than forty years after its first performance it was still earning huge royalties throughout the world.

When the plot of *A Gaiety Girl* had actresses marrying into the peerage in the 1890s it was not so far-fetched as later generations might think. Some two dozen Gaiety Girls over the years married lords of one rank or another from Dukes to mere barons. And as well as these ladies there were other 'theatrical Peeresses'. It was a process that had begun in the middle of the eighteenth century when the 3rd Duke of Bolton married the actress Lavinia Fenton, whose greatest stage success had been as Polly Peachum in Gay's *Beggar's Opera* and whose portrait in that role hangs in the National Gallery in London. It was continued in 1827 when the twenty-six-year-old 9th Duke of St Albans married the fifty-year-old widow of Thomas Coutts, the banker, who was one of the richest, if not the richest man of his day. The widow, *née* Harriet Mellon, had been an actress in her youth. It was not for her money that St Albans married her, for his fortune was considerable. The marriage was a happy one and lasted until Harriet's death in 1837, by which time she had doubled her capital, having retained control over her own wealth throughout. Most of her fortune was left to Thomas Coutts's granddaughter, Angela Burdett, better known as Baroness Burdett-Coutts, the famous Victorian philanthropist.

The Bolton family name was Powlett (later Poulett) and two of the 3rd Duke's descendants followed his example long afterwards by marrying actresses. Father and son, the 7th and 8th Earls Poulett, both married Gaiety Girls. The father married Sylvia Storey, whose own father Fred Storey was the Gaiety comedian and dancer; the son married Oriel Ross. Other theatrical peeresses from the Gaiety and other musical comedy stages were Denise Orme, *née* Jessie Smither, who became the Baroness Churston and later the Duchess of Leinster; Olive May, *née* Meatyard, who became the Countess of Drogeda; Rosie Boote, who became the Marchioness of Headfort; Connie Gilchrist, the Countess of Orkney; Gertie Millar, first married to Lionel Monckton and then, after his death in 1924, to the Earl of Dudley; Kitty Gordon; Eleanor Souray; Zena Dare; Delia Sinclair; Eva Carrington; Mimi Crawford (Countess of Suffolk and Berkshire, mother of that legendary Second World War hero, Jack Suffolk), and Tilly Losch, who died on Boxing Day 1975 (Countess of Caernarvon). Most of them seemed to marry earls, but there was an occasional duke – as for instance the 8th Duke of Newcastle who, as Lord Francis Hope, married May Yohé in 1894; and the 7th Duke of Leinster who, as Lord Edward FitzGerald, married May Etheridge, the lovely little London Pavilion star. After her death he married another lady and then for his third wife chose Denise Orme, who had been Baroness Churston.

Before these ladies there had been, among others, Belle Bilton (Countess of Clancarty) and Dolly Tester (Marchioness of Ailesbury). After them came others, including Marianne de Malkhazounny, who in 1933 married the 11th Duke of Leeds, and June Tripp, who married the 4th Lord Inverclyde. According to C. B. Cochran the only peeress who was a stage manager was Audrey Pointing, later the Countess of Doverdale.

Belle Bilton's marriage to Lord Dunlo, later 5th Earl of Clancarty, created a *cause célèbre*. Belle was one of the Sisters Bilton, a music-hall duo whose father was an army sergeant. Later they appeared in musical comedy. Florence, whose picture appears on page 209 of *The Victorian Woman*, had a truly beautiful pair of legs, and Belle, whom C. B. Cochran saw in *Venus* when he was a boy and whose opinion that she was the loveliest creature he had ever beheld was later confirmed by Sir Arthur Collins, the Drury Lane manager, who always maintained that the loveliest of all the lovelies of his time was Belle Bilton. But beauty, even of the essence, was not sufficient recommendation to Lord Dunlo's family. After he and Belle had been married in a registry office his outraged family sent him off on a long tour ending in Australia. In the meantime they had his wife watched.

Belle continued to live her cheerful Bohemian life, innocent enough to herself and her friends but having quite different implications to her in-laws who waited like spiders for her to blunder into their web. Eventually they thought they had a case. Dunlo was bludgeoned into being the petitioner, and a friend of his 'man-about-town' days, Isodore Wertheimer (son of Ascher Wertheimer the astute art-dealer and brother of Ena and Betty Wertheimer whose portrait by Sargent is a souvenir of their father's belief in the artist's genius), was named as co-respondent.

Three good things the case did: one, it brought Dunlo back to England – even his family could hardly run his divorce without his presence; second, Belle was appearing in the aptly-named *Venus* at the time and the case ensured that every seat was sold throughout the run; third, it gave Belle and Dunlo a tranquil married life, for the petition was dismissed and even the interfering relations had to confess themselves worsted. It is reported that the dismissal of the petition was celebrated by a happy dinner *à trois* at Romano's, the three being the unsuccessful petitioner, the successful respondent and the co-respondent.

Not all theatrical marriages into the peerage caused such a rumpus as the Bilton–Dunlo affair, but despite the comparative frequency with which they began to occur in Edwardian times they were still attended with social penalties in some quarters – as Pinero's comedy *The-Mind-the-Paint Girl* showed – even if the penalties were not quite as drastic as Belle's. When the Hon. Maurice Brett (second son of the second Viscount Esher) married Zena Dare, the Arcadian Phyllis's sister, in January 1911 – indeed when he became engaged to her – he had to resign his commission as a Captain in the Coldstream Guards, even though his father was a magnate in army politics and a close friend of the King's.* And the military hierarchy, especially of the Brigade of Guards, continued to look askance at actresses – as far as marriage was concerned at any rate – for many a long year. Shortly before the Second World War the then adjutant of the Life Guards married the film star Madeleine Carroll and as a matter of course had to give up his adjutancy and retire from the army.†

Musical comedy might well be the entertainment most characteristic of the Edwardian period but it was run a close second by the music-hall. To set against the Dares and the Gertie Millars were other stars just as popular who were on the music-hall stage. These were the days of Marie Lloyd (whom T. S. Eliot called 'the most perfect, in her own style, of British actresses'), of Nellie Wallace, Florrie Forde, Kate Carney, Marie Kendall, Vesta Tilley, Vesta Victoria, Ella Shields. The

* A few years later, under more strenuous circumstances, that great Scottish regiment, the Black Watch was delighted to have him as a Lieutenant-Colonel.

† He, too, like Captain Brett found his solecism excused by the exigencies of another World War.

songs that made these ladies famous are as well known today as they were when they broke out across the country in a storm of whistling errand-boys and sing-songs round thousands of pianos and pianolas.

Marie Lloyd, born in 1870, made her name with 'Oh Mr Porter'; she also made a feature of one of the best music-hall songs ever written and one which, after her own time, was a great favourite at the Player's Theatre in London during World War II and after – 'The Boy I Love is Up in the Gallery.' Marie Lloyd was not the first to sing this delightful song. It was 'created' (as they say of characters on the stage) by Jenny Hill and Nelly Power, both of whom died before Edward VII came to the throne, Hill in 1896, and Power nine years earlier. Nelly Power it was who started male impersonations. She was the first of the laddie-ladies, anticipating by several years those magnificent artistes Vesta Tilley and Ella Shields, who could wear a man's evening clothes better than a tailor's dummy, so much so indeed that Vesta Tilley (1864–1952) set men's fashions by what she wore on the stage in her impersonations. Vesta Tilley's great song was 'Algy'. Ella Shields, who was fifteen years younger than Miss Tilley, was that unforgettable lay-about 'Burlington Bertie From Bow', a character who, though clad somewhat differently, has long since moved off the stage in to the everyday life of the affluent society. As Ronald Pearsall wrote in his history of Edwardian popular music, these two ladies 'made the Edwardian hermaphrodite, the knut, an acceptable social figure'.

In terms of songs, the lady who had more famous songs under her stage corset than anyone else was probably Florrie Forde (1874–1941). For example: 'Down at the Old Bull and Bush', 'Oh, Oh, Antonio', 'Has Anybody Here Seen Kelly?', 'Hold Your Hand Out, Naughty Boy', 'She's a Lassie From Lancashire', and in 1912 in the Isle of Man she sang a song called 'It's a Long Way to Tipperary.' Despite this great personal repertoire, however, she seemed always, according to Pearsall, to live in the shadow of Marie Lloyd.

One of the most famous of all these stunning music-hall ladies had almost driven herself into the boards before the Edwardian years began. This was Miss 'Ta-ra-ra-boom-de-ay' herself, the fabulous Lottie Collins, who launched the song at the Tivoli in

1891 and who was soon making £150 a week for a quarter-of-an-hour spot nightly at the Gaiety. She danced and sang this frenetic number in a Gainsborough hat, a short red frock, and a gay frolic of white petticoat which was the 'turn-on' of the day. The popularity of 'Ta-ra-ra-boom-de-ay' made it a natural for risqué parodies, one of which went:

> 'Lottie Collins has no drawers,
> Will you kindly lend her yours?
> She is going far away
> To sing Ta-ra-ra-boom-de-ay!'

It was a version sung by youths at passing girls and, like the original song, was accompanied by pirouettes and high kicks. It was one of the greatest songs of the day and spread across the countryside like an epidemic. But in the end it destroyed Lottie Collins. The frantic exertions which its performance demanded killed her in 1910 when she was still a comparatively young woman.

As well as these great singing artists (and of course their male compeers) the leading music-halls also topped the bill with more unusual acts, many of them female. In May 1910 the Palace Theatre under the managing directorship of Alfred Butt, and with Herman Finck as the musical director, brought Pavlova to the English stage (with Michael Mordkin) at a fee of £750 a week.*

Another speciality act was the Australian swimmer Annette Kellerman, who had started swimming as a child in order to strengthen her legs which had been crippled by polio. She set several distance records in the early 1900s. In 1906 she did a 23-mile swim down the Danube in just over 13 hours and a 17-mile swim down the Thames. But she failed in three cross-Channel attempts. In 1907, when she was twenty, she was arrested on a beach at Boston, Massachusetts, for indecent exposure because she was wearing a brief one-piece swimming costume which she was 'promoting' for a manufacturer. Seaside

---

* One of the top music-hall money-spinners was Harry Lauder, who was at his peak in Edwardian days. When he appeared at the Glasgow Pavilion he was paid £1,000 a week. The equivalent today is almost impossible to calculate.

convention of the day demanded neck-to-knee shirt and bloomers. The publicity that resulted from the case which was brought against her led to a relaxation in the laws about women's swimwear.

To say that Miss Kellerman's swimming costume was brief is only by comparison with the practice of the time. In fact, when she appeared on the stage she wore stockings, short knickers, a blue jersey and a scarlet cap. But one look at that costume was enough to kill the knee-length costume overnight. The fame of the American court case and her long distance swims made Annette Kellerman a public attraction. Edward Moss booked her for the London Hippodrome which had been opened in 1900. The stage area was so designed that it could be used as an arena or it could be converted into a water tank for aquatic entertainments. Miss Kellerman disporting herself in her 'brief' costume was a great money-spinner. Indeed, so popular did her appearances become in London and in other cities round the world, especially in the United States, that she earned the nickname of The Million Dollar Mermaid. She became a star in Hollywood and appeared in silent films like *Neptune's Daughter* (1914) and *A Daughter of the Gods* (1916). In 1951 Hollywood made a film about her life in which she was played by another famous swimming star, Esther Williams. She died in Australia in 1975 at the age of eighty-nine.

By the end of the Edwardian era the special position of the music-hall as a mass entertainment was being challenged. The cinema had already made its presence felt. To begin with, after the first show in London in 1896, the kinematograph was a showman's novelty. Films were shown either in booths or fairgrounds, or as just another act in a music-hall programme, or by 'town-hall' showmen who travelled round the country booking local halls for as long as they could attract an audience. It was through these men that the first permanent shows came into existence. Gradually they found that they could retain public interest indefinitely, and in those places they stayed.

It was not only halls that were used as early cinemas. Shops too, were roughly converted into penny gaffs. In some the price of admission was only a ha'penny behind the screen because the titles appeared backwards! Theatres, music-halls, even skating rinks, were adapted for showing films, and the practice of including a film show as a turn in a music-hall bill continued for longer than some historians of the cinema realise. For example, when Pavlova appeared at the London Hippodrome in May 1910 she was the twelfth item on the bill and her 'act' lasted for thirty-five minutes. The thirteenth and final item was 'Kinemacolor' and the 'Urbanora' bioscope. 'Kinemacolor' consisted of two short films in colour: 'Paris, the Gay City' and 'Choosing the Wallpaper'. The 'Urbanora' bioscope was a newsreel showing the arrival of Lord Kitchener at Southampton (after a tour of Australasia and the United States), Mr Grahame-White's Great Aeroplane Flight (when he made the first recorded night flight in Great Britain during the course of the *Daily Mail* London–Manchester air race), and the Punchestown Races.

These makeshift screenings were not adequate however. The popularity of watching films was growing fast, and the next stage, which began about 1908, was to have a building specially designed and constructed to accommodate a film show, an 'all-picture house'. From then until the beginning of the war in 1914 there was tremendous activity in cinema building and conversion.

The popularity of the cinema was not far to seek. For a modest coin and, with continuous performances, the cinema-goer was able, whenever he wanted, to enter a new and glorious world where he could find excitement, adventure, romance and humour which had been created for his enjoyment at con-siderable cost. As the specially-built cinema arrived on the scene this new and glorious world, so far removed from the pains and pleasures of the everyday one, was available – still for that modest coin – in surroundings of warmth and comfort. For lovers it was a place to be alone, even though they were sur-rounded by several hundred other people. For the lonely it brought the solace of company. For the badgered it brought the relief of anonymity. And these were only the surroundings – which were improved and added to as the years went by. They were important, but they were peripheral. The film was the thing. The film was the story-teller of the people and 'it is the power of the film to tell a story in its own easily understood idiom which has made it so popular. The illusion of reality that is created through the artificial medium of the celluloid film paradoxically demands less from the audience for full enjoyment than the living actors and painted scenery of a stage play'.* Moreover, the vast majority of films – at least for the first fifty years of the cinema's history – told stories with a mass appeal. And, perhaps most of all, the cinema peopled the world once again with the gods of Olympus. The film star was born.

The man who invented the film star was Carl Laemmle. In the early days of the American industry an attempt was made by the Motion Picture Patents Company to form a monopoly. But this assumption of power did not go unchallenged. A number of independent producers defied the police raids and strong-arm tactics and went west to California, where they found a little Los Angeles suburb called Hollywood. Here they were far away from the Patents Company in New York, and even if its minions did chase after them from time to time to smash their equipment they were close enough to the Mexican border to take speedy refuge outside the United States until the coast was clear again. Carl Laemmle was one of these independent producers, and his company, until it changed its name in 1912 to Universal, was called the Independent Motion Picture Company. The practice of the Motion Picture Patents Company was not to mention the names of its actors and actresses on the screen. Their faces were familiar to millions, but their names were unknown except to a few. While Broadway shone with the names of Maude Adams, Maxine Elliott, Lillian Russell and Billie Burke, the name of the 'World's Sweetheart' was kept a secret. This was a great disadvantage to exhibitors because the public clamoured to know who she was. So the exhibitors invented a name for her. Anonymity may have helped the Patents Company to keep their actors and actresses from demanding higher salaries, but it proved inimical in another way. It gave Laemmle a chance to gain a striking advantage. Realising that if the public were allowed to identify themselves with the stars they would be drawn to the cinema as they were drawn to the theatre, he decided that the 'Imp Girl' should no longer be anonymous. As Florence Lawrence she became the first 'film star' in 1909, while Mary Pickford was still masquerading under the names the exhibitors gave her as the

* Duncan Crow, *The British Film Industry* (PEP, 1952), p. 17.

'World's Sweetheart'. As Laemmle had foreseen, the star system was an immediate attraction and before long anonymity had disappeared from the silver screen to be followed by escalating production costs as rival companies outbid each other for favourite stars. Named stars also meant that the pedestrian standardised type of film made by the Patents Company was swept away by the more attractive films of the independents. It was a change that was both artistically and commercially beneficial.

While the cinema blossomed into a world-wide entertainment and the music-hall continued to flourish, musical comedy went into a decline. Despite the delicious tunes it was frothy and forgettable. It was wallpaper theatre – a background to an evening out – with nothing depicted in its patterns that could upset the digestion by a sudden call on the intelligence. And as far as the matinée-goers were concerned the stimulation of the emotions was strictly within the limits of propriety and happy fantasy. There were, it is true, some odd exceptions in the musical field that suggested a possible future turn in popular taste and a tocsin for the genteel English musical comedy. First of these was *In Dahomey* at the Shaftesbury Theatre in 1903. *In Dahomey* was a negro opera. It had an all-negro cast and both words and music were written by two negroes, Spry and Cook. 'This musical,' reported *The Era*, 'with its wonderful vitality, its quaint comedians, its catchy music, and its unique environment, should be one of the dramatic sensations of the London season.'*
And indeed it was.

Seven years later came the first London appearance at the Palace Theatre of Pavlova with Mordkin, and in 1911, to celebrate George V's Coronation, London saw Diaghilev's production of *Scheherazade* with Leon Bakst's décor and costumes and the dancing of Nijinsky and Lydia Lopokova. Madame Lopokova later married the economist Maynard Keynes, a fringe member of what has since been dubbed the Bloomsbury Group but which was in origin a continuation with male and female appendages of one generation of Cambridge Apostles. As we shall see in the next chapter, Bakst's costumes with their Eastern design and hard acid colours had a profound effect

* Quoted in Ronald Pearsall, *op. cit.*, p. 34.

on fashion. Turbans, aigrettes, and harem dresses swept the town.

In 1913 came the *coup de grâce*. At the Hippodrome Albert de Courville staged a new American genre, the revue. This pioneer was *Hallo Ragtime*, which was in fact old-time burlesque, a combination of pantomime and variety with a new look. The star of the show was Ethel Levey, who could belt out the words of the syncopated music with a zest that left the audience breathless. 'Waiting for the Robert E. Lee', 'Row, Row, Row', and 'Hitchy Koo' were three of the numbers. The chorus line was altogether different from the genteel posturings and maidenly coyness at the Gaiety. Here at the Hippodrome it was led by Shirley Kellogg, who banged a drum and showed her legs as the saxophones and trumpets squealed out Irving Berlin's exciting rhythms. 400,000 people went to the Hippodrome to see the show. *Hullo Ragtime* was followed by a number of other shows of the same type. Its immediate successor was *Hullo Tango*, which included that ever-popular song, 'He'd Have to Get Under, Get Out and Get Under'.

Ragtime was music for the young, who were bored to tears with the *Schmaltz* of musical comedy and with the ballads that were such a popular entertainment for the Edwardians. By the end of Edward's reign dancing had become a widespread pastime – though to call it a pastime is to give it too uninspiring a name. Its popularity was tremendous. It was ceasing to be a formal social occasion encumbered by chaperones and had become an expression of the new and freer attitude between the sexes. The new generation wanted new dances and something new to dance to. A plethora of new dances were created or adapted from American sources: the cake-walk, the bunny hug, the turkey trot, the grizzly bear, the crab step, the kangaroo dip, the horse trot, and the Boston which appeared about 1909. In 1911 the first Chelsea Arts Ball was held and 'Alexander's Ragtime Band' hit London like a tidal wave. Then came the South American dances: the Brazilian maxixe and the sinuous tango, which despite its lack of rumbustiousness that caused middle-aged criticism of the ragtime dances, was nonetheless a highly exciting encounter – for those who were slim enough! The tango became so popular that clubs were opened and '*thé dansants*' held in restaurants and hotel lounges so that people could indulge their passion for the dance. The dancing craze was helped by a mechanical method of music-making which, like a number of other inventions that came to fruition in Edwardian times, had originally been invented in the 1870s. This was the phonograph or gramophone which was invented by Thomas Alva Edison in 1877 when he was thirty years old.

Despite the excitement that attended its birth the original phonograph was a short-lived novelty. Edison's own idea was that its main use would be as an office dictating machine, although he also saw that it would have other uses. In 1887, another American, Emile Berliner, invented the gramophone, which unlike the phonograph with its cylinder used a disc. Eventually the disc conquered the cylinder. In the United States the phonograph name remained, though the instrument that survived was the gramophone; but in Britain both cylinder and phonograph name disappeared. Another thing that disappeared was the idea that the phonograph gramophone would be mainly used as a piece of office dictating equipment. Its main use was as a music-maker.

From the very beginning there was a pop market and, in the United States, a concentration on opera singing. Symphonic recording flourished first in Europe – partly because one of the American companies had all the opera singers under exclusive contract. In millions of homes the gramophone or phonograph became a necessary piece of furniture, with people being encouraged to buy the machine by advertisements like this one in the *Illustrated London News:* 'What will you do in the long, cold, dark, shivery evenings, when your health and convenience compel you to stay indoors? Why!!! Have a Phonograph of course.' And as well as its other advantages the phonograph allowed you to practice the tango in private before venturing out to the *thé dansant.*

Before the turn of the century the opportunities for hearing music in Britain were not plentiful. Brass bands and bandstands were one popular source; musical evenings at home were another. Popular music was fairly available, the songs of the day making their way round the country through the music-halls, sheet music, plugging by piano in music shops, barrel-organs, whistling errand boys, and pianolas. But listening to serious music was a different thing altogether. It was the luxury of those who could go to the opera, to the Crystal Palace to hear the famous series of concerts conducted by Augustus Manns, to the Saturday and Monday Pops at the St James's Hall (which ended in 1898), to the Free Trade Hall in Manchester to hear the Hallé Orchestra, or, from 1895, to the Queen's Hall in London to listen to Henry Wood's Promenade Concerts, where Clara Butt, six feet two inches in height and du Maurier's model for *Trilby*, already famous for her singing of 'Abide With Me', was one of the first to sing Elgar's 'Land of Hope and Glory'; or of those who were invited to musical at-homes given by Arthur Balfour, Mrs Ronald, Mrs Blumenthal, Lady Barrington (where Paderewski and Joachim played) or Lady de Grey (where opera stars sang). If you were not eligible for an invitation to these gatherings, or if you lived too far from the halls where infrequent concerts were given, you had small chance of hearing a Beethoven symphony or a Mozart piano concerto let alone anything more unusual.

There were only two or three permanent orchestras in Britain. Sir William Walton, speaking on his sixtieth birthday said, 'We forget what a bad state music was in. I was born in 1902 and although I grew up in a musical family I was fifteen or sixteen before I ever heard an orchestra.' And there were few concert halls, scarcely half a dozen in London's West End – 'all absurdly inaccessible', wrote Thomas Burke in *Nights In Town*. Among them were the Aeolian Hall in Bond Street opened in 1904, the Queen's Hall in Langham Place opened in 1893, the St James's in Regent Street which closed in 1905, the Steinway Hall opened in 1875, and the Bechstein Hall, in 'the melancholic greyness of Wigmore Street', opened in 1901 and now called the Wigmore Hall. On the periphery were the Royal Albert Hall in Kensington Gore, opened in 1871, and the Royal Westminster Aquarium closed in 1903; and in the wilds of North London was the Alexandra Palace, which was opened in 1873 and which more than fifty years later became the home of Britain's latest excursion into mass entertainment – television.

Chapter 8

THE KINGDOM OF FASHION

One of the sensations of the musical comedy stage was Camille Clifford, who appeared in *The Catch of the Season* (1904) and *The Belle of Mayfair* (1906), the latter composed by Leslie Stuart, who also wrote the music for one of the most famous of musical comedies, *Floradora*. It was not Camille Clifford's acting ability that made her the rave of London – after all, few of those musical comedy ladies had any pretension to dramatic excellence. What captured the town was her hour-glass figure. She was one of the first 'Gibson Girls', a type created by the American illustrator Charles Dana Gibson (1867–1944); indeed, so superbly did she epitomise this type that she became known as 'The Gibson Girl'. However, if any one woman can lay claim to that soubriquet it was Gibson's wife Irene. Gibson had studied art in Paris and became famous in the United States for his black and white drawings (of which he was a master) and for his cartoons in which he satirised anything pretentious, especially foppishness and social climbing, which he also took apart in several books. His cartoons and drawings appeared in the leading American magazines – *Life, Scribner's, Century* and *Harper's*.

Irene was one of eleven children of whom eight survived their childhood, five girls and three boys. They were the children of Mr and Mrs Chiswell Dabney Langhorne of Mirador, near Charlottesville, Virginia. Irene was the second daughter. Her elder sister Lizzie married Moncure Perkins; her younger, Nancy, who was as pretty as Irene, married firstly at the age of seventeen a member of an old Boston family whom she divorced after two years, and secondly Waldorf Astor, later 2nd Viscount Astor. The fourth daughter, Phyllis, was also married twice, the second time to Robert Brand (later Lord Brand) who had been one of Milner's 'young men' in South Africa after the Boer War – others of whom included John Buchan, later Lord Tweedsmuir, and Philip Kerr, later Marquess of Lothian. The youngest of the Langhorne daughters was Norah, who married an Englishman, Paul Phipps, and had a son and a daughter. The daughter became famous on the stage as Joyce Grenfell. Norah, like most of her other sisters, subsequently married someone else.

'All the Langhorne sisters,' wrote one of Nancy's sons, 'whether they acknowledged it or not, attracted men like flies, different kinds of men for different kinds of reasons. They all had a great many admirers when they were young and continued to have admirers well into old age. Irene probably had more than any and did most to encourage them, being not only a famous beauty but also, in New York, the doyen of the Southern belles, exercising in that position the same rights and inspiring much the same feelings as Queen Mary exercised over the cadet branches of the Royal Family in London. She was, too, a great snob, in the grand manner, putatively admired by czars and emperors, and actually, if signed and framed photographs carry any meaning, the friend of contemporary czars on both sides of the Atlantic.'*

About his art Dana Gibson was modest to a degree; about his wife, whose gaiety entranced him, he was 'both loving and philosophical', and did not take her amatory interests too seriously, allowing her 'to indulge her fancy'. As he said, 'If you have a canary you must let it sing'.

The Gibson girl was a 'chocolate-box' beauty with a full rounded bottom that was matched in front, above a narrow waist, by an uncloven bosom made as large as nature and artifice would permit by the throwing back of the head and the extension of the neck to the limit of the upper vertebrae. While this voluptuous shape stimulated many, the staggered

* Michael Astor, *Tribal Feeling* (John Murray, 1963), p. 27.

hourglass curves did not entrance everybody. Indeed the gamut of female Edwardian fashion seemed horrendous to one commentator, Dion Clayton Calthrop, who wrote in his study of *English Dress from Victoria to George V*:

'The women were awful; there is no other single word for it. They seemed to have lost their heads, their bodies and their sense of proportion in colour. They defied Nature, they ignored Art. They adopted one Fashion more awful than the last. They were even, in their search for ugliness, worse than the women of a later day with platinum hair, chalked faces and purple lips. They looked like crazy housemaids.'*

Women's fashions were dictated by Paris. While Savile Row dressed the men, the Rue de la Paix dressed the women – men and women with money that is, for to be well turned out in the fierce competition of Society was an expensive business, and the quality magazines made sure that the latest information passed like lightning from one fashion centre to another. Paris had long since established itself as the world's capital of fashion. Only Vienna was beginning to compete with the style and cut of Parisian Haute Couture; indeed, since the Franco–Prussian War of 1870–1 the export of Parisian model dresses had increased so significantly that towards the end of La Belle Epoque some two-thirds of them were being bought by couturiers abroad.

Julius Meyer-Graefe, the German art historian who reported on the fashion section of the 1900 Paris Exhibition, wrote after seeing the exhibits that 'no foreign house dared to compete seriously with the Paris firms'. All the top Parisian couturiers showed their creations: there were dresses by the Worth brothers (Jean Phillipe and Gaston, sons of Charles Frederick Worth, the Englishman who had founded Parisian Haute Couture in the 1860s), by Paquin, Doucet, Callot Soeurs, Félix, Rouff, Chéruit and Redfern. Some displayed their wares in more theatrical fashion than others. The Worths designed tableaux of Longchamps and Deauville with wax figures dressed in the height of Worth fashion for the races and for the

---

* Chapman and Hall, 1934, p. 108.

pellucid northern light of the Normandy littoral where Proust's 'little band' sported themselves along the *digue* and ladies of fashion graced the front at Deauville and Trouville and gazed out from the stepped hotels of Villerville across the estuary to Le Havre. Madame Paquin, the first woman to reach the heights of Haute Couture, and who opened her salon in the Rue de la Paix in 1891, was equally theatrical in her display at the Exhibition. She had a wax model of herself placed in front of her own toilette table so that visitors to the exhibition could see her dressed in one of her own beautiful chic dresses. Other leading couturiers were less innovatory and stuck to the more traditional ways of showing their collections, a conservative approach which they later regretted when the Worths' tableaux, especially one they created of a Louis XVI salon, attracted so much attention that eventually the police had to be called in to control the crowds 'which never diminished during the next six months'.

The names of those grand couturiers who showed their creations at the 1900 Exhibition are famous to this day and the majority of their houses are still in business. Many others have joined them since – among them Dior, Fath, Chanel, Molyneux, Patou, Lelong, Heim, Alix, Piguet, Rochas, Schiaparelli, Vionnet. Some made their name before the First World War, others were stifled by the defeat of France in 1940, never to emerge again, others again still make the headlines in the latter part of the century. But none of these great names of fashion was the one that held the *gratin* of Edwardian women in thrall – and the phrase is not used loosely because thrall indeed it was. The couturier who was to be the Sultan of Fashion in Edwardian days was not represented at the 1900 Exhibition, except inasmuch as his genius as a designer was seen in the creations presented by Worth. Paul Poiret was his name and at the time of the exhibition he was working for the Worth brothers, protected by the business-like Gaston against the sensitive Jean Philippe who got artistic tremors at the young Poiret's bizarre brilliance of strident colours and simplified silhouettes. What Worth had been to fashion in the decades that had seen Napoleon III's Empire establish itself, burgeon ever more bloatedly, and then burst like an over-ripe medlar before the inauguration of the Third Republic, Poiret was to the Edwardians. Those long years during which Charles Frederick Worth was the dictator of fashion have been called 'the Age of Worth'. But in the opinion of one of the historians of Haute Couture, 'Poiret, with his artistic style, left his mark on his age infinitely more powerfully than did Worth and, with far more justification, the decade before the First World War can be called the "Age of Poiret". He made fashion so much a branch of art that the leading art magazines of the period . . . published articles on the art of fashion and fashion as an art.'*

Paul Poiret was the son of a Parisian cloth dealer. He was brought up in a bourgeois milieu which he hated. A world of dreary civil servants, big buyers from *Les Halles*, wholesale grocers, a grandmother who took snuff, girl cousins with ring-lets, hair slides and long dark woollen dresses, a house stuffed with dark Renaissance type furniture. 'The drab confines of my surroundings drove me into a land of dreams,' he wrote. His land of dreams was populated by the smart dresses he saw on elegant ladies in the streets of Paris. His passport to the land was his ability to draw. He took refuge from the style of life he found so dreary by sketching the fashions around him. And he went further down the paths of freedom by forming a musical trio, playing the violin himself and joining up with another boy who played the guitar and a third who sang. They were spare-time wandering minstrels, performing in courtyards and getting their payment in sous thrown down from surrounding windows. Paul was entranced by Jarry's *Ubu Roi*, a play which mercilessly caricatured the narrow-minded bourgeois attitude to life and flayed that attitude with whips of scatalogical venom.

Sketches of fashion, *Ubi Roi*, truant minstrelsy, even a Gibus that he bought and which his father destroyed – none of these was talisman enough to ward off the onslaught of bourgeois tenets. Although Paul had passed his baccalaureate and could have gone on to the university or could have been allowed to develop his considerable sketching ability and become an artist, his father would have none of it. 'If one wants to achieve any-thing in life,' he told his son, 'one must begin at the bottom of the ladder.' Suiting his actions to this portentous Victorian humbug he found Paul a menial job in an umbrella and walking-stick shop where he washed the windows and swept the

---

* Anny Latour, *Kings of Fashion* (Weidenfeld and Nicolson, 1958), p. 176. Translated from the German by Mervyn Savill.

floors and ran the errands. It was on these errands that he found the opportunities to break out of the stifling pedestrianism of the life his father had chosen for him and find once again those draperies of glamour that so allured him. As he carried messages and made deliveries he would make lightning sketches of passing ladies and on his return home in the evening would modify the sketches and turn them into dresses for a doll which he got from his sisters. Then he would sketch the dressed doll. Soon he had built up a collection of fashion drawings which he showed to leading couturiers like Doucet and Worth. Doucet bought some and in 1896 engaged Poiret as a designer. From the start he was a success; indeed his first model sold four hundred copies.

But Paul Poiret was not born to be a subordinate and before long he was causing Doucet a great deal of annoyance. Poiret had a girl friend, beautiful even among the beauties of the Bois. He dressed her in his own designs which he had made up for him by a small dressmaker. He himself aped Doucet, whom he much admired. He went to Doucet's tailor and shoe-maker and turned himself out in the dark-blue suits and patent leather shoes that Doucet favoured. With his girl friend wearing his own creations and with himself dressed to the nines in imitation of Doucet, Poiret and his lady took their place in the parade of elegance. Though imitation may be the proverb-maker's sincerest form of flattery, Doucet failed to see it that way. Poiret was sacked.

The parting would have happened in any case because Poiret was now of an age to do his military service. When he returned he was taken on by Worth, who knew his capabilities as a designer and who also knew of his cock-crowing on Doucet's own dung-heap. When he hired him Jean Philippe Worth said to him: 'You are here as in a restaurant where they make delicious *omelettes aux truffes*, but we have engaged you to produce ordinary roast potatoes.'

Nonetheless Poiret's originality was not submerged in roast potatoes. His respect for Jean Philippe's work was enormous but with his own great sensibility to the *Zeitgeist* of the new century he knew that Worth's style was outmoded. Instead of seeking his inspiration in the eighteenth century as Worth had been doing he turned to the Orient, to Polynesia, to fierce colours, and the rough-hewn intensity of negro carvings. Poiret's style mirrored the other arts, a breaking-away from the elaborately ornate, from sentimentality, from the fevered shadows of *fin de siècle*. These were the years when Isadora Duncan in a loose flowing robe pioneered free dancing; when Matisse and the other *fauves* were seeking to simplify painting, to revolutionise colour, to get a maximum of expression with a minimum of means; when Diaghilev brought Russian art, music and ballet to Western Europe; when Fokine, much influenced by Isadora Duncan's free movement and use of symphonic music, reformed choreography; when Bakst brought the glowing colours of Russian icons into the costumes and décor he designed for Diaghilev's Ballets Russes. It was part of the breaking-up of Victorianism, the revolt of the arts, rejection of the old leaders.

Not one whit of this artistic revolution affected the Haute Couture. But Poiret was part of it; indeed his whole attitude to life was part of it. In 1904 he left Worth's and opened a small maison of his own in the Rue Auber, near the Opera. Here he made dress design one of the arts. Elsa Schiaparelli who first met him some years later and who greatly admired him regarded him as the greatest couturier of his time. Certainly he was the most flamboyant. Over the years he gave a number of fantastic costume balls. At the first of these all the guests had to wear authentic 'Arabian Nights' costume and make obeisance to the Sultan as he sat in his garden surrounded by his concubines, while negroes and negresses burnt frankincense and myrrh, ballerinas danced on the lawn, music sounded from the bushes, ibises strutted, apes and parrots chattered, fakirs and soothsayers abounded, and an actor sat on a huge pile of cushions telling Eastern fairy tales. At another, in 1912, when he had just moved from the Rue Auber to the Rue St Honoré, he adopted an Olympian theme. All the 300 guests had to come as gods, goddesses, heroes, or dryads. Poiret himself was Zeus, with a golden beard and golden curls, and the arriving guests were brought before him by nymphs with torches.

'This Olympian fete soon developed into a bacchanal. Wine was drunk in horns which could be replenished from amphorae. During the night the three hundred guests drank nine hundred litres of champagne. As the sun's first rays burst through the wood, supper was served – three hundred lobsters, three hundred pâtés de foie gras, three hundred melons and three hundred portions of ice-cream.'*

By this time Poiret was the King of Fashion. The leg-of-mutton sleeves which were the mark of the early 1890s and were a fashion symbol of women's aggressive attitude by their emphasis on muscular strength had given place by the end of the century to a more feminine style. Sweet-pea colours became the vogue: mauves, pale blues and pinks – delicate colours and feminine shades. Poiret took control and from 1904 to 1914 it was his style that set the fashion. It began with a sack-like straight skirt, usually in a single colour – a *fauve* colour, red, green, violet, orange or lemon-yellow – worn below a tunic that sometimes reached as low as the hem of the skirt. This tunic was embroidered with arabesques and caught round by a belt in a contrasting colour. In 1906 the waist moved up, almost to Directoire and Empire levels. The corset went – a Poiret sensation – but with this freedom of the upper part of the body came a constriction of the lower, for Poiret brought in long, narrow hobble skirts that rose to a high waist. 'I have freed the bust from its prison,' wrote Poiret, 'but I have put chains on the legs.' The hour-glass figure was out and the long, lean look was the fashionable one. By the time war broke out in 1914 this long, lean look had produced the 'vamp' type in a tight caught-up dress, split in front so that its wearer could reach her legs out for the steps of the tango which had swept across from South America like a fever, a kimono blouse and a turban with an aigrette pulled down to the eyebrows.

Mid-way through the war the hour-glass figure returned in a modified form to produce the sort of feminine shape that absent soldiers were said to long for, although it is interesting to note that Raphaël Kirchner (1876–1917), an Austrian by birth but a Parisian by up-bringing and training, who drew for *La Vie Parisienne* and created the first internationally famous pin-up girl in Western popular art and for whose drawings of girls the Allied armies in France were an insatiable market, did not draw the bosomy figure that was considered to be fashionable but featured a 'slender, immature girl, partly undressed' having

* Anny Latour, *op. cit.*, p. 181.

'a tender, frank, erotic quality with origins in Viennese rather than French graphic art'.* This set the slinking fashion of the vampire or 'vamp'. After the war the long, lean look returned but this time with the waist as low as it had been high before.

To publicise his fashion creations Poiret made tours round all the capitals of Europe, his entourage consisting of two cars, a secretary and nine mannequins dressed, when not modelling the creations, in blue serge dress, beige-coloured cloth coat, and an oilcloth hat with the letter P embroidered on it. Poiret was a strict guardian of his mannequins' virtue, no easy task especially in St Petersburg, where he had to keep them under lock and key. In the United States, where he went with only one mannequin, he ran into trouble. A film showing his collection in Paris was banned because exception was taken to the skirts which allowed feet to be seen. Even so, no-one objected to the fact that the mannequin clad in her modest underwear stood beside him on the platform while he improvised – cutting, draping and pinning up a dress as the audience watched.

Poiret kept the link between art and fashion close. He gave Dufy a studio and used the artist's motifs in his fabrics. A number of other artists worked for and around him. Among them Bernard Naudin, Marty, Martin, Boutet de Monvel, Bakst, Paul Iribe and Georges Lepape. Iribe produced a book of water-colours of Poiret's creations in 1908. This was the book, with its personal dedication to every Queen and Princess in Europe, which caused the displeasure of Queen Alexandra. In 1911 Lepape produced an album called *Les Choses de Paul Poiret*. It brought him immediate fame. In 1912 Poiret founded a Craft School which he named after his daughter Martine. After his second daughter Rosine he named a new scent. This was the original *parfum de couturier*.

Schiaparelli's first visit to a *Maison de couture* was to Poiret's in the Rue St Honoré where she went with a rich American friend. While her friend chose dresses Schiaparelli tried on a coat made of black upholstery velvet with vivid stripes and lined with bright blue *crêpe de Chine*. Suddenly she saw Poiret watching her. 'Why don't you buy it?' he asked. 'It might have been made for you.' She told him she couldn't afford it, and anyway when

* J. E. Boswell in *1,000 Makers of the Twentieth Century (Sunday Times)*.

could she wear it. 'You could wear anything, anywhere,' he told her, and gave her the coat. That was the first of many gifts. 'Soon I had a whole wardrobe,' she recalled in her autobiography, 'for he kept on giving me wonderful clothes whenever I needed them – and also when I did not need them. . . . Sometimes I led fashion. At other times, wearing my ordinary clothes, I appeared like my own ugly sister.'*

Schiaparelli went to the midnight party when Poiret moved from the Rue St Honoré to the Rond Point des Champs Elysées in 1924. 'Each guest walked from one house to the other carrying a blazing torch. The new house was magnificent, but as sometimes happens when projects are too ambitious, the change did not bring him luck.' His star began to wane. He himself, though he would not believe it, became old-fashioned. Oriental robes and strident colours were a mode of the past. Nobody wanted gold embroidery and Persian motifs. He railed against the democratisation of fashion and the simplicity of the new styles, and died in destitution in 1943 after a long illness. By then the Edwardian years were far away.

Poiret was an autocrat and would brook no competition. His sister Nicole, married to an interior decorator, refused to work for Poiret, and set up on her own. Poiret was infuriated, especially as she was successful. Years later, when driving with friends in the Champs Elysées, he had a slight collision with another car driven by a woman. He looked at her frigidly and drove on. 'That lady was once my sister,' he announced casually to his passengers.

'The twentieth century,' wrote Octave Uzanne in *The Modern Parisienne*, 'is distinguished by the sobriety of costume worn in the street, worn over incomparably luxurious underclothing.' He quoted Balzac's phrases that, *'toute notre société est dans la jupe; ôtez la jupe à la femme, adieu la coquetterie! plus de passions. Dans la jupe est la toute-puissance; là où il n'y a que des pagnes, il n'y a pas d'amour'*.

How wrong he was, said Uzanne:

'If his words have any truth as a general proposition, it is certain that in the restricted sense of dress they are sheer heresy.

* *Shocking Life* (J. M. Dent, 1945), p. 43.

We recognise the tone of the moralist of a past epoch who grew faint with rapture at the sight of a white stocking with green clocks. How far we have travelled from our good ancestors! *"Là ou il n'y a que des pagnes, il n'y a pas d'amour."* Just think of that! . . . It is precisely on the sight of the "underneath" that love flourishes, and this present century can boast of having invented an exquisite, subtle, adorable art, the last mythological expression of woman. I mean the art of filmy, beautiful underclothing. . . . Up till now woman had not brought her refinement to bear upon her most intimate apparel. . . . Everything was for the outside.'

But as the severity and simplicity of the outer garments increased, as the English tailor-made style came into fashion, producing a levelling effect on the exterior clothing, so was the beauty and elegance of the 'underneath' developed in proportion – the one was a corollary of the other.

'The modern woman is in some degree like a book bound à la Janséniste, that is, with a plain undecorated cover, but inside the cover, delicately tooled with lovely or curious designs. The art of women's dress,' he claimed in contradiction to Calthrop's judgement, 'has never reached so high a standard, has never been so ingeniously conceived or so practically expressed as at the present moment. . . . Bad taste reigned supreme during most of the last century. . . . Now, thanks to the sober good taste of women's street costumes and the exquisite refinement of their lingerie, one may hope that the future reserves for us some even more delightfully decadent surprises in the combination of outer and inner garments.'*

It did! Until the general adoption of tights towards the end of the 1960s spoilt the whole thing.

Fashion in Edwardian days is neatly summed up in a couplet by Herbert Farjeon,

'Hats were hats of startling size,
And waists were waists and thighs were thighs!'

* *The Modern Parisienne*, pp. 23–6.

Chapter 9

ONE IN EVERY FOUR

In 1901, when the first and only census of Edward VII's reign was taken, the percentage of women and girls in employment in Great Britain was 24·9. Out of a total female population of 19 million, 4·75 million were employed: one in every four. This percentage was down from 1891 (26·4) and indeed had been steadily dropping since 1861 when 29·5 per cent of the female population was employed. In the course of Edward's reign (to 1911) it rose slightly to 25·7 per cent out of a total female population of just over 21 million. Ten years later after the First World War, the percentage had fallen marginally to 25·5 out of nearly 22·5 million.

The working women of Edward's reign were employed in some 400 different trades and occupations. *A Dictionary of Employment Open to Women* published by the Women's Institute of 15 Grosvenor Crescent, London, in 1898 gave a complete review of every occupation (bar the one mentioned by Mrs Pankhurst) open to women at the end of Victoria's reign; its researches are basically valid for the ensuing decade. The employment openings ran from accountants and actresses to worsted workers and writers, taking in a remarkable range on the way. Accountancy was one of the many professions that were closed to women, although in 1887 and 1891 a qualified lady, Miss Mary Harris Smith, basing her claims on the ground that she had the necessary knowledge having been in practice since 1879, presented herself for membership of the Institute of Chartered Accountants, but was refused. Indeed chartered accountants were not allowed to take girls as articled pupils. But, said the *Dictionary*, as women would undoubtedly take their places in this profession, as in others, they should remember that girlhood was the best time to commence training. A girl with talent in this direction and with a London Matriculation or some equivalent diploma was advised to become articled to a Lady Public Accountant of whom there were a few. Women were not finally admitted to the Institute of Chartered Accountants until 1920 when, appropriately enough, Miss Mary Harris Smith was the first woman to be admitted. Because of her long experience in the profession she was not asked to take the examination. The first woman to be admitted by examination was Miss Ethel Watts in February, 1924.

The struggle to enter the professions had begun with Elizabeth Blackwell, Sophia Jex-Blake and the other pioneer woman doctors. By the 1870s they were accepted, even though subject to difficulties in qualifying. Excluding the traditional women's professions of nursing and teaching,* few others accepted women willingly in the early years of the twentieth century. There were a handful of architects, several dentists, and a few engineers, the first woman being admitted to the Institute of Electrical Engineers in 1899. Horticulture too was coming in as a profession for ladies. But there were no women lawyers in Britain although in January 1901 Miss Margaret Hall of Kirn, Argyllshire, applied unsuccessfully to become the first woman solicitor. Women were not admitted to the legal profession in Britain until after the First World War, whereas in the United States there were a large number practising by the turn of the century and a lady had been admitted as a barrister and solicitor of the Supreme Court of New Zealand in 1897. The church was closed to English women except as deaconesses; in the United States, on the other hand, certain Protestant churches allowed them to be ministers. The army and navy too were closed to women, unless they belonged to Queen Alexandra's Imperial Nursing Service or to Miss Haldane's Territorial Nursing Service. Thus a girl choosing a career in Edwardian Britain did so by elimination rather than by selection. Instead of asking herself, 'What shall I do?' she had to ask 'Where are women accepted?'

One of the major changes that occurred in the pattern of

* 4·1 per cent (173,000) of the 4·2 million women employed in England and Wales in 1901 were teachers compared with 6·1 per cent (325,000) of the 5·3 million women employed in the United States.

women's employment in Britain in the nineteenth century was
the great drop in the numbers employed in agriculture. The
cause of this decline was the combined effect of raising men's
wages, which made the woman's contribution less essential to
the family wage, and the introduction of machinery, which
lessened the need for labour. Machines took the place of
women, but whereas in industry the machine-minders were
often women, in agriculture they were invariably men. Women
were employed in hay-making and in harvest fields, in picking
stones off fields and weeding, in setting and picking potatoes, in
hoeing corn, singling turnips, spreading manure, pulling and
clearing roots. In some districts – St Neots in Huntingdonshire,
for example – they had regular employment all the year round
in market gardens. In Kent and other parts of England they
were employed in picking fruit, tying and picking hops, milking
cattle and tending sheep. In Essex they were employed in pea-
picking.

Glendale in Northumberland was another part of the country
where women were regularly employed in agriculture; here they
received 1s 6d a day in summer, 1s 4d to 1s 6d in winter, and 3s
a day for twenty days at harvest-time. Pea-picking districts paid
1s 4d to 2s a day; for setting and picking potatoes, and for hop
and fruit picking, wages varied from 1s 6d to 3s a day.

At St Neots women were paid 10s to 15s a week in the
summer. In Wales they received 1s a day for all work except
hay-making and harvesting for which they were paid 1s 6d.
Hiring Fairs were held in Wales, in Scotland, and in the north
of England, which were occasions for meeting old friends and
merry-making as well as for seeking employment and finding
workers. The number of women employed in agriculture,
forestry and fisheries in Great Britain fell from 119,000 in
1881 to 81,000 in 1891 and then rose slightly to 86,000 in
1901.* Fifty years earlier it had been 230,000. During the
Edwardian decade, however, there was an increase to 117,000.
In Ireland over the sixty years the number fell from 167,000 to
59,000.

In Great Britain in 1901 there were as many women employed

* 1·8 per cent of the total number of women employed. In the United
States in 1900 13·2 per cent (700,000) of the female working population
were employed in agriculture.

as barmaids as there were in agriculture. By law, barmaids had
to be over eighteen and by custom married women were rarely
employed. Their hours were from 14½ to 18½ a day and 7 to 9
hours on Sundays. Sometimes there was no Sunday work at all,
even so a hundred hours work a week was not unusual. In Scotland and Wales, and in the case of six day licences in England,
the pubs were closed all day on Sunday. Wages over the
country as a whole were from 8s to 15s a week, with manageresses
getting from 15s to 20s. In hotels, pubs, large restaurants and
railway bars contracted for by large firms, barmaids usually
received board and lodging. 'The temptations of the life,'
warned the *Dictionary*, 'especially to drink, are great, and it
requires a strong, self-respecting character and power of will to
resist them.'

Among a number of employments for women which might
not immediately spring to mind were card leavers (ladies who
were paid 5s a day and travelling expenses to leave visiting
cards and thus save their employers the tedium of the tournée),
callers or knocker-uppers (who went round waking workpeople
in the early morning), doorstep cleaners (girls who went round
in very poor districts cleaning doorsteps for a ha'penny a step),
fire goyas (poor Christian girls in London who helped East End
Jews by going to their houses to tend their fires during the Sab-
bath at tuppence a family, a service that continued long after
Edwardian times), caddies (for carrying golf-clubs), dog-walkers
(ladies who were paid 2s 6d an hour to look after dogs or take
them for walks), fly-tiers (for fishing tackle – a well paid job
earning from 20s to 30s a week), lady couriers and guides (there
was a Lady Guide Association), and lighthouse keepers (they
had to be strong, trustworthy, and not very young).

Advice was given to those who had a literary bent and wanted
to earn their living as authors, journalists or poets. By the turn
of the century there were several hundred women actively
engaged in writing for a living, a few of them editors of successful magazines like Mrs Winifrid Ruth ('Biddy') Johnson of
Harmsworth's *Forget-Me-Not* and Miss Rita Shell of *The Lady*.
Those who wanted to be novelists were warned that although
George Eliot received £8,000 for *Middlemarch*, 'and it has been
stated that £18,000 have been paid in recent times for a work
from the hand of a well-known woman novelist', they would be

lucky to get £100 for a novel and 'even so small a sum as £10 to £15' would be nearer the mark. As for those who wanted to be poets the *Dictionary* informed them sternly that to study the techniques was not enough. 'We have one famous historic instance of a person trained from childhood for a poet's career, that of Jean Chapelain (born 1594), whose best-known work, the epic *La Pucelle*, is one of the greatest literary failures on record.' Poets be warned!

By far the greater number of those 4·75 million women employed in 1901 lived and worked in England and Wales – 4·2 millions out of a total female population of 16·9 millions. In 1891 the comparable figures had been 3·9 millions out of 15 millions. An analysis of the four million females employed in England and Wales in 1901 gives a good picture of the main occupations available to women at the beginning of the century. The chief one, as it always had been, was domestic service. Two out of every five women in employment were domestic servants,* which was, to put it another way, one in every ten of the female population of England and Wales – a proportion that was exactly the same as it had been sixty years earlier when the first census of Victoria's reign was taken. In the United States in 1900 women in domestic occupations (that is, working for families other than their own) and in service industries (cleaning, laundering, etc.) accounted for one-third of the 5·3 million women gainfully employed.

Second in importance as an occupation for women was dress manufacture (a term that included every article of apparel), which employed 710,961 (17 per cent), and the production of textile fabrics (including mill and factory hands of all descriptions), which employed 623,222 (14·9 per cent) – a combined total of one and a third million, almost a third of the total women employed. Taken together, domestic service and textile and dress manufacture gave employment to 72·5 per cent of the women and girls at work in England and Wales.

In the United States in 1900 the clothing and garment trades (comparable with dress manufacture) employed 671,000 (12·6 per cent), and cotton, silk, knit-goods and other manufacturing plant employed 261,000 (4·9 per cent). Together

* 1·7 million; the figure in 1891 was 1·4 million.

with domestic occupations these gave employment to 51·4 per cent of those women employed.

From 1891 to 1911 the percentage of employed women in Great Britain who earned their living in manufactures was almost constant: decennially the percentages were 43·4, 44·7, and 44·9. The actual numbers were (in thousands)

1891	*1901*	*1911*
1,948	2,123	2,430

But by 1921 the percentage had fallen to 38·4 and the number to 2,187,000. Factory work and domestic service had lost ground as occupations for women. Although Gertrude Tuckwell might see the girl clerk working for 10s a week in a basement as evidence of a sweated industry, not all those who worked in those conditions would have agreed with her. By the time she was writing, the 'office' had already become the location for a new major employment for women in the twentieth century. Both in the United States and in Great Britain was this true – it was less so in Continental Europe.* In the United States women had first gone into government offices at the time of the War between the States (1861–5). In Britain it had been somewhat later. Whereas, in the latter part of the nineteenth century it was only the occasional woman like Arnold Bennett's Hilda Lessways who worked in an office, by the middle of the Edwardian decade an office was the Mecca of most young ladies who were going out to work. The office had a social cachet that was lacking in factory work or domestic service or even in being a shop assistant and no doubt it also gave greater opportunities for casting around in the marriage market. Not until the 1921 census, however, did the trend to office-work fully reveal itself. From 1881 to 1911 the number of women working in offices in Britain went up decennially from 11,000 to 26,000 to 76,000 to 157,000. In 1921 it reached 862,000. In percentage of women employed this was an increase from 1·6 (1901) to 15·1 (1921) in twenty years.

* In Belgium, for example, as late as 1913 there were 514,914 women employed in agriculture (out of 1,204,810 of both sexes) compared with 327,725 women working in industry and 385,236 in commerce.

There were four inventions of the nineteenth century which had an enormous effect on women's employment. One of them, the sewing machine, brought additional efficiency (in the sense of greater speed) to an already traditional occupation for women, but the other three created entirely new work and through them women became the communications operators of the new age. These three were the telegraph, the telephone and the typewriter. The typewriter was invented in 1867 by Scholes and Gliddon and the first practical machine was manufactured by Remington and Son in 1873. From then on it was continually improved and by 1888 there were 60,000 typewriters in use in the United States. In 1893 the first light portable machines were brought on to the market. By 1900 there were 100,000 (1·9 per cent of the total number of women employed) stenographers, typists and secretaries.* France took much longer to accept the machines.

Linked to the skill of the typist were the hieroglyphs of shorthand. Shorthand had a long history, stretching back for a hundred years before one of its most famous seventeenth-century writers, Samuel Pepys, but it was not until 1873 – curiously enough the same year in which the first practical typewriter was produced – that Isaac Pitman published his world-famous system. *Stenographic Sound-Hand* the book was called and it sold for 4d a copy.

The Women's Institute *Dictionary of Employment* differentiated between three grades of typewriters – the substitution of the word 'typist' for 'typewriter' as applying to the individual operating the machine took place about 1906 or 1907, the change being instigated by the popular press. In the first class of typewriters were well-educated women who probably knew one or more foreign languages. 'These are employed in better houses, where the shorter hours are worked and the higher salaries given.' The second class of typists formed the staff of the better typing offices and were the 'superior type' in a commercial house earning up to 30s a week. And below them in the third class were the 'girls whose work is inferior and who are content to earn 10s to 15s a week'.

The third seminal invention for women's employment, the

* There were 74,000 (1·5 per cent) employed as bookkeepers, accountants and cashiers.

telegraph, came earlier than the typewriter. Already, by 1854, women clerks, suitably chaperoned, were employed by the Electric Telegraph Company in Manchester. But the telephone was contemporaneous with it. It was in 1876 that Alexander Graham Bell, a Scotsman from Edinburgh then living in the United States, and Elisha Gray of Chicago filed their patents in Washington – on the very same day, as it happened. In 1878 the first telephone company in the United Kingdom was registered and in August 1879 it opened its first exchange, in London, with seven or eight subscribers. In 1888 the British Post Office opened its first telephone exchange at Swansea in Wales. Eight years later the chief telephone companies merged in the National Telephone Company. In 1896 the Post Office took over all trunk lines and in 1902 opened the first of several large London exchanges, the Central, with 14,000 lines. Ten years later it took over the whole of the National Telephone Company with the exception of the systems in Portsmouth and Hull which operated independently for many years. By the end of the First World War the Post Office operated 819,000 exchanges. Not until 1927 was the first automatic exchange in England opened at Holborn, in London. Thus until then the manual operators, most of them women, were indispensable in an ever-expanding service.

In Edwardian England the age of the typewriter and the telephone truly arrived. As W. J. Reader percipiently says in his study of the middle classes: 'along with telephone exchanges, typing pools greatly widened the opportunities of earning an independent living which were open to middle-class women. The typewriter has done more for women's liberation than it is usually given credit for, and much more than any other mechanical invention, except perhaps the bicycle.'*

The bicycle, as well as contributing enormously to the liberation of women, and young women especially, by enlarging the radius of their world and relaxing the social formality between themselves and men (because a woman on a bicycle could no longer be under the close vigilance of a chaperon), also provided another possible small-scale employment for women.†

* *The Middle Classes* (B. T. Batsford, 1972), p. 57.
† The freedom afforded by a bicycle had its dangers too. In Sybil Spottiswoode's *Marcia in Germany* one of the young ladies causes her own

The Dictionary of Employment suggested that there was an opening for Cyclists' Rests in country villages or on country roads which were much used by cyclists. To be the owner or manager of such a Rest was an excellent job for a woman.

'An attractive site should be chosen at from ten to fifteen miles from a town, or from some well-known point of interest. The rooms should be comfortably and cheerfully furnished, and luncheons, teas and light refreshments of good quality provided at moderate charges. There should be two or more bedrooms, where lady cyclists can rest or be accommodated for the night, and a large shady garden, where tea etc. can be served in summer, is an advantage. . . . A small capital (from £150 to £300) is required, and an aptitude for housekeeping, with taste in decorating, and tact in welcoming guests.'

The precession from a rural to an urban economy in Britain created a new employment pattern, not only in the obvious way that agriculture employed less people and factories and offices employed more, but in a far more complex domino sequence. All sorts of jobs and services that no one ever previously thought of or considered essential arose when a multitude of people began to live and work in towns. A great deal of what occurred was occasioned by women. For example, when women in any number started to work in offices one concomitant of this development was that sanitary arrangements had to be provided if not improved, so that, as one factory girl put it, 'you can come out respectable when you were done'.* Another example was that they had to have somewhere to eat their midday meal. Tens of thousands of women could not eat sandwiches for ever, nor always bring snacks with them from their own homes. They could not and would not go into public houses, and the

* Cadbury, Shann and Matheson, *op. cit.*, p. 116.

ruin and the downfall of her family because her bicycle is seen parked with another against a shooting-box in a lonely part of the woods near her home in Waldberg. Neither owner of the bicycles is anywhere to be seen. Because of the disgrace that ensues when it is discovered what she has been up to, her brother has to resign his commission, her sister's engagement is broken off, and the whole family has to exile itself to the wilds of Eastern Pomerania.

basement eating houses that existed in most cities were far from attractive.

In her reminiscences of Edinburgh in her young days before the turn of the century, Elizabeth Haldane recalled that tea-shops hardly existed:

'One could go to one or two shops in Edinburgh for a luncheon of a kind. I think soup was provided and possibly some other mild eatables. But I remember the excitement when a cafe was first set on foot in Edinburgh on a semi-charitable basis, as a sort of antidote to public houses, and how popular it instantly became.'*

In the country districts it was almost impossible to get any form of light refreshment until the age of the bicycle began in the 1880s. Until then one had to go into the commercial room of a hotel and order a fairly expensive solid meal.

In the early 1890s the first Aerated Bread Company's tea-shop was opened in London, and in 1894 the first Lyons, which was in Piccadilly. The ABCs and Lyons's were a real boon to women, and to several generations of male students and office-workers as well. The tea-shops provided the answer to the office woman's problem of where to eat. To begin with they really were tea-shops, providing only tea and buns. It was not until some years later that the menu was widened to include full meals and snacks. On a somewhat grander level the big London and Provincial stores also reacted to modern needs by opening restaurants to provide reasonably priced luncheons and teas for ladies who had come to town for a day's shopping or to meet their friends. The first store to do this was Debenham and Freebody's in Wigmore Street, London, in 1907. Its quiet elegant restaurant was hailed as a great innovation. Others soon followed, for the Edwardian years were a boom time for department stores with their attractive combination of grandeur and personal service.

In filling the need for cheap, respectable places where a woman could eat on her own, the tea-shops created more jobs for women. Girls who worked in ABC shops at the end of the

* *Op. cit.*, p. 32.

century were taken on between the ages of sixteen and eighteen. Before they were engaged they had to be certified as being in good health and they were required to live with relations. Their hours were nine a day, six days a week. For the first month they were on probation and worked without wages. After that they began at 9s a week, then 10s a week, finally becoming counter hands or desk hands, when they earned 12s to 25s a week, and as visiting lady superintendents 25s to 30s a week. All staff had paid holidays. Another leading chain of tea-shops, Lockhart's, was comparable in its terms of pay and employment except that there was no restriction as to the person with whom the girls lived, and all the food was provided for them at half-price.

By now the attitude to middle-class women working had greatly changed. If we go back to the beginning of Victoria's reign we find that women in what may be called the Top Nation did no work, not even in their own homes if they could possibly avoid it, or if they did they took good care to hide the signs of that work when anyone called. *Punch* had many jokes about this convention, showing mother and daughters preparing the food and making arrangements for a party in the morning and then, similarly grouped, receiving the guests in the evening as if they had been doing nothing all day except sketching, singing, and dabbling with fancy work. If financial catastrophe hit a middle-class family, the girls had only the occupations of governess or possibly part-time sewing open to them if they were not to fall into destitution or descend into the Lower Nation as prostitutes.

'As civilisation has increased during the last century,' wrote the feminist Bessie Rayner Parkes in 1865, 'a number of women have been uplifted by the labours of men into a sphere where considerable cultivation and a total abnegation of household work have become a custom and a creed, but no corresponding provision has been made for them of occupation in the higher and more intellectual fields of work. They share, through their male relatives, in all the vicissitudes to which individual members of the middle class are subject – and they are helplessly dependent on these turns of the tide, having been trained to no method of self-help. All that seems to me to be wanted is that women of the middle classes, belonging to the professional or commercial classes should heartily accept the life of those classes, instead of apeing the life of the aristocracy.'*

It turned out to be more complex than that, but there was one element in the apeing which developed into an occupation for many middle-class women. This was visiting the poor which, from being a social convention, developed into active rescue and reform work and provided a cause into which the 'maiden aunts' especially could pour their intelligence, their education (when at last they got it), their compassion, and their ambition. Philanthropy and social reform, while giving the women themselves intellectual and emotional satisfaction, also gave Britain – and the United States too for that matter – a new social structure, a new concept of the rights and duties within society. Linked with philanthropy, but also exercising a compulsion of its own, was religion, which was an important occupation for a great number of women – an occupation, that is, in the sense that to it they devoted a large amount of their time.

As opposed to the comfortable and cosseted life of the ladies in the Top Nation – comfortable, that is, when the tide of financial fortune did not turn against them and they were left with 'no method of self help' – the women of the Lower Nation worked extensively and under grievous conditions, though the grievousness was nothing new. The harsh conditions and tedium of work had always been there, but those who did the work and suffered the conditions never had voices that carried far enough for others to hear – not indeed that there were more than a handful who were prepared to listen. The eighteenth century saw nothing unusual in long hours, insanitary conditions, starvation wages, and the exploitation of little children. Nothing, indeed, shows the measure of the move away from the abyss of barbarism so clearly as the horror of public opinion – Top Nation public opinion – at the conditions revealed by the Blue Books of the 1840s.

When reformers from the Top Nation sought to improve conditions for Lower Nation working women they not infrequently met with opposition from the women themselves,

* *Essays on Women's Work*; Bessie Rayner Parkes later became Madame Belloc and the mother of the writers Hilaire Belloc and Mrs Belloc Lowndes.

whose attitude was that it was less bad to earn a pittance in slave labour than to starve in idleness. Nevertheless, where the Top Nation reformers did succeed and did make Lower Nation women have more time for their domestic chores, the results were, almost invariably, an improvement in living conditions. The motive of these reformers may have been purely humanitarian – and indeed the suffering in town and country was amply great enough to rouse this instinct. But consciously or subconsciously there was another motive too. The Top Nation, through wealth and the comforts that wealth brought, had achieved a pleasanter life. The existence of a completely barbarous Lower Nation was a continual threat to that style of life. The riots of the 1820s and 1830s, and the Chartist movement that lasted until 1848, showed that the threat was real enough. The wise among the Top Nation perceived that this threat could not be kept under control indefinitely by force. The long-term, but effective, way to disperse it was to de-barbarise the Lower Nation. To do this the key move was to de-barbarise the women. It was – and still is – women who determine the state of society. To de-barbarise them they had, if possible, to be removed from the rough arena of work and put into hutches. If this were not possible, as clearly it was not, then they should at least be removed, by law if necessary, from the more uncouth and dangerous sorts of occupation. The trouble was, of course, that Top Nation mental furniture did not allow the reformers to suggest, nor did the climate of the time make it even entertainable, that loss of employment needed compensation.

To some extent the economic aspect of the compensation came by adjustment of men's wages aided by trade union activity – and of course trade unions were at one with the de-barbarising reformers in not wanting women to do work outside domestic chores, because this depressed the union's bargaining power by creating a reserve of labour. But there was another aspect of compensation that escaped their notice – compensation for 'nothing to do'. After a generation or two of 'nothing to do', some Top Nation ladies were being driven literally mad by idleness. In the upper class the easy access to personal acquaintance with leaders of thought gave women of that class a continuing education and training which would have made a university training, had one been available, an amusing episode rather than a necessity. But in the middle classes the situation was different. After marriage, maternal and domestic duties combined with a limited income set a term to any further social education. As Clara Collet, social worker and Fellow of University College, London, put it in an essay on *The Age Limit for Women*, written in December 1899, it was difficult for any married middle-class woman 'to resist the tendency to become absorbed in her purely personal worries and cares; brain atrophy sets in, and with it old age, the closing up of the mental avenues to new impressions and feelings'.

Sometimes, it is true, as in the case of Florence Nightingale, it was the upper-class women who led the way for the young ladies of the Top Nation towards work and education, both of which were the only way of exorcising present idleness and the future closing up of mental avenues. Mostly, however, it was the middle-class women themselves who, sometimes by their individual example, sometimes by their organised campaigns, attacked the enforced idleness of women which brought brain atrophy and consequent old age when women were still young in years. This was the fight that went on during the second half of the nineteenth century, at the same time as the endeavour of the de-barbarisers and the unions to drive the Lower Nation women away from work. Both succeeded in some respects. On the one hand, for example, women were admitted to universities* and forced their way into the medical profession, while the opportunities for middle-class women's employment, limited as they were, expanded somewhat beyond being a governess, and by the end of the century it even became socially acceptable to keep a shop provided it dealt in something decorous like hats or gowns or flowers.

'It was the early days of the lady shop-keeper. All over the west end of London the amateur tradeswoman was making her feeble, half-frightened first appearance before the gross public

---

* They were not always welcome there even as late as 1913. The professor of Latin at Glasgow University at that time refused to teach women or allow them to attend his lectures as he saw no possible reason why women should learn Latin even though the University regulations made it essential to pass an examination in Latin if they were to take a Master of Arts degree.

of the pavements. Trivial little tea-shops, flower shops and bonnet shops – in which gentility and commerce danced a brief breakdown and then put up the shutters – were to be seen in every street. . . . . A peeress was making a game fight in Bond Street; and Mrs Marchant and her daughters and cousins were, it was said, running their much-advertised tea-rooms into a substantial success.'*

On the other hand women were forced out of the mines and were subject to various special restrictions under the Factory Acts. In this respect Great Britain was in advance of many other western countries. In France, for example, underground labour by females in mines and quarries was not prohibited until 1874, and the Ten Hour Day was not introduced until 1900. Childbirth regulations similar to the British ones passed in 1891, which made it illegal knowingly to employ a woman in a workshop or factory within four weeks of her confinement, were not made until 1913.

Industrial legislation in Great Britain, as the Webbs pointed out, had from its inception followed the line of least resistance. By doing this it had left many gaps in the network of protective laws. With efficiency as the only guarantee of success, the labour market at the beginning of the twentieth century was still crowded with little children who should have been at school or at play, and with married women who worked too long into pregnancy and returned to work too soon after childbirth, whatever the regulations, and thus kept up the terrible rate of infant mortality that still obtained. There were those who held that this mortality was caused by putting babies out to be cared for and by mothers not breast-feeding their infants. May Tennant, writing in *Women In Industry* in 1905, claimed that there was plenty of evidence to show that the level of infantile mortality and the industrial employment of mothers were directly related. The law as it stood was a difficult one to enforce, but she wanted it to go further. It was, she claimed, a law for the mother and not for the child.

When the bill which resulted in the 1891 Factory and Workshops Act had been before Parliament the women's movement were much against it. To prevent a woman from working was

* W. B. Maxwell, *Vivien* (Methuen & Co, 1905), p. 61.

to condemn her to starvation or prostitution they claimed.*
May Tennant took the opposite attitude: 'the mother would
serve her children and her husband by her presence in the
home, and not by her presence in the factory'. It was the old
mid-Victorian attitude. Furthermore there was the nation to
consider. It is interesting to see that in the introduction to
Maternity, a collection of letters from working-women to the
Women's Co-operative Guild published in 1915, the Liberal
Cabinet Minister and Chairman of the Local Government
Board, Herbert Samuel (later Viscount Samuel) emphasised the
importance of the State stepping in to reduce the level of infant
mortality. Admittedly it was wartime and the need for manpower was a dominant issue in governmental minds. The waste
of children in the cradle was something the nation could not
afford. It was something the Germans had been insisting on for
years.

Those who were trying to improve women's working conditions and wages by organising them into trade unions encountered many difficulties. In the first place the women themselves
were on the whole apathetic and the limited opportunities open
to them created such a large reservoir of labour that they were
unwilling to risk the sack by upsetting their employers. Furthermore, class distinction had a retarding effect. In the essay on
Trade Unionism which she contributed to the *Women in Industry*
symposium, Mary Reid Macarthur, a leading women's labour
organiser, wrote that among the higher grades it was 'a narrow
class prejudice' which caused 'the semi-professional class of
workers to look askance upon anything in the nature of trade
unionism'. It was this same feeling which made 'the telephone
girl employed in the Government service inclined to look down
upon her sister who is not a Civil Servant but is doing precisely
the same work for the National Telephone Company, or, as
inside the Civil Service itself, makes the clerk in the Savings
Bank or Money Order Department of the Post Office consider
herself on a different plane to the Telegraph clerk in another
department of the same office'.†

As well as the social divisions and distinctions existing
amongst them, other difficulties in the way of women success-

* See *The Victorian Woman*, pp. 320–1.
† *Op. cit.*, pp. 75–6.

fully combining were listed in the fifth and final report of the Royal Commission on Labour published in 1894: 'that un-married women frequently consider their employment as one which will be terminated by marriage, and not as a life affair'; that women had an 'hereditary incapacity for transacting busi-ness in common'; that there were great difficulties in the way of their meeting because of domestic duties; and that employers felt a special dislike to them organising, regarding it as nothing less than an impertinence that women should question the work and wages offered to them. The Royal Commission might also have added that their male fellow-workers had as rooted a dislike to them joining unions as had the employers, for they saw them as competitors who inevitably cut wages and they took refuge for their attitude in the comforting belief that women's place was in the home; or if they did not regard them as competitors this was because the work they did was so masked off from that done by men that the men had no interest in the conditions and wages of women's work.

Although there had been attempts to recruit women into unions in the early 1830s it was not until the 1870s that women's trade unionism in Britain really began. In 1872 the Edinburgh Upholsterers Sewers Society was formed and in 1875 the Women's Protective and Provident League (WPPL) was organised by Mrs Emma Patterson, who also organised the National Union of Working Women in Bristol. Mrs Patterson was then aged twenty-seven, married to a cabinet-maker, and had been apprenticed as a girl to a book-binder. She had worked for a time with Miss Emily Faithfull who ran the Victoria Press, the first printing company to be staffed entirely by women. She was also secretary to a working-men's club and to a women's suffrage society. In 1874 she visited the United States and there came in contact with some women's unions. Struggling as these were, they inspired her with the desire to create something similar in England. With the encouragement of Harriet Martineau, Charles Kingsley, and some active trades unionists she started the WPPL. This became, in fact, a collective title for a number of little struggling unions which arose among

'women dressmakers, upholsterers, bookbinders, artificial flower-makers, feather-dressers, brick-s lace-, paper-box and bag-makers, glass, tobacco, jam and pickle and small metal-workers, rag-pickers, shop-assistants and typists. These little societies were exceedingly unstable; they sprang up and melted away with great rapidity, and Mrs Patterson and her friends soon realised that the task they had set before themselves was one which was appallingly hard'.*

Nor were their problems made any easier by the attitude of the men's unions. Not until 1889, three years after Mrs Patterson's death, did the Trades Union Congress agree to lend support to the organisation of women. That same year the WPPL was turned into the Women's Trade Union League and women members of a number of other unions were transferred to it. As Ray Strachey records in *The Cause*,

'the motives of the men were perhaps a little discouraging to the women. "Please send an organiser to this town", was the sort of message that arrived, "as we have decided that if the women here cannot be organised they must be exterminated". Yet even so it was better than the uncompromising hostility which had gone before.'

After her death Mrs Patterson's work was continued by a number of women including Mrs Margaret MacDonald, wife of Ramsay MacDonald, who was later to be the first Labour Prime Minister, Lady Dilke, who was Chairman of the League until her death in 1904 (by which time it had been re-named the National Federation of Women Workers), her niece Gertrude Tuckwell, who had been honorary secretary of the League since 1892 and who succeeded her aunt, and Mary Macarthur, who took over as secretary from Miss Tuckwell.

Mary Macarthur believed that the difficulties in the way of women combining were much exaggerated. 'If the time and ability spent in explaining obstacles in the way of organising women had been devoted to overcoming the difficulties which do exist, the percentage of unorganised women's labour would be considerably less than it is to-day,' she wrote in 1908.† Nonetheless, the advance that had been made in bringing

* Ray Strachey, *op. cit.*, p. 241.
† *Op. cit.*, pp. 72–3.

women into trade unionism was far from insignificant. There were more women trade unionists in Britain in 1908 than there had been men represented at the first Trades Union Congress which was held at Sheffield in 1868. Out of some five million women workers in Great Britain in 1908 there were 150,000 trade unionists (3 per cent) as against two million male trade unionists out of a possible eleven million (18·2 per cent). Miss Macarthur's comment on these figures was that she was less impressed by the percentage of women unorganised than by the amount of organisation that remained to be done among male workers.

She did not deny that there were real difficulties in organising women, especially the low standard of living which was

'at once the cause and consequence of women's lack of organisation. This sounds paradoxical, but it is nevertheless true that while women are badly paid because of their unorganised condition they may be unorganised mainly because they are badly paid. ... The very lowest class of women's labour can never be efficiently organised until the workers are raised to the standard at which intelligent contemplation of their position becomes possible.'

But Trades Boards would be a great help in overcoming this difficulty. Much could also be done to raise the lower grades of women's labour through the organisation of the higher grades. 'This can be seen in Lancashire, where the strong organisation of the women textile workers had undoubtedly raised the wages paid to many other classes of unorganised women in the same district.'*

In the United States similar problems obtained, although statistically the organisation of women was much lower. Out of the seven and a half million women gainfully employed the best estimate is that only 77,000 (1·5 per cent) were members of unions. The natural place for women's unions to originate was in the garment trades, where a large proportion of the workforce were women. The earliest branches (or locals) of what is now the International Ladies' Garment Workers' Union began

* *Ibid.*

in 1900. Before then, however, there had been the same short-lived attempts in other trades to organise as there had been in Great Britain. It was in fact the example of the Female Umbrella Makers Union in the United States that gave Emma Patterson her idea for forming the Women's Protective and Provident League.

The problem of getting young women to join a union, even though it was their own exclusively women's union, was summed up by an experience of Mary Macarthur. Soon after she had become secretary of the National Federation of Women Workers she addressed a number of girls at a street corner meeting. The girls were impressed by her eloquence and the promises that trade unions seemed to offer. They gave their names to join the union. 'Ten days afterwards the girls looked more inclined to mob me than anything else and I asked them what was the matter. "Oh! we've been ten days in the union and our wages haven't gone up."'*

* Quoted in Gladys Bourne, *The Women's Trade Union League* (New York 1942), p. 30.

Chapter 10

CHIEF COOKS
AND LADY HELPS

❦

Looking down from the leads of Chevron where he habitually hid from his mother's week-end guests, Sebastian, the nineteen-year-old Duke of Chevron could tell the time by the procession in the small courtyard far below him. It emerged from one door and made its way to another door opposite. The procession meant that at a precise moment in the servant's dinner, 'the flock of housemaids had risen from their seats in the servants' hall, and, carrying their plates of pudding in their hands, were retiring to their own sitting-room to complete their meal. . . . The servants' dinner began at half-past twelve, and the punctuality of the house was reliable as the sun himself. It must therefore be a quarter to one.'*

Daphne Fielding, formerly Marchioness of Bath, has recorded that a similar ritual obtained at Longleat, but Consuelo Vanderbilt Balsan, formerly Duchess of Marlborough, recalled in her autobiography that nothing of that nature occurred at Blenheim when she was chatelaine there. The upper servants sat tight in their own room and never mixed at meals with the rest of the servants even for a single course.

Chevron, the creation of Vita Sackville-West in *The Edwardians*, was as big as a palace and was no doubt based on Knole Castle, the Sackville family seat. It employed fifty servants and was organised like a regiment. Generation after generation sent its sons and daughters into the Chevron regiment and the regiment provided its own pensions for its old soldiers. Occasionally

* V. Sackville-West, *op. cit.*, pp. 11–12.

the chain was broken and someone refused to follow the tradition. Sebastian's sister was one of the commissioned ranks who went off on her own. Even more upsetting to the 'regimental tradition' was a son of one of the senior NCOs who threw up all this and went into a garage – a most Edwardian thing to do!

The servants at Blenheim in Madame Balsan's time were a butler (or house steward), a groom of the chambers, a valet, an under-butler, three or four footmen, a number of odd men to do the butler's bidding (washing windows, carrying coals, and so on), two electricians (whose status because of the scientific nature of their calling was equal to the butler's and who were treated as such by him); and on the female side – a housekeeper, six housemaids (far too few for an establishment the size of Blenheim), five laundresses, and a still-room maid who cooked breakfasts and made cakes and scones for teas. There was a French chef with a staff of four. A head nurse, a second nurse, and the Duchess's maid completed the list of the servants. A total of thirty-one plus the odd men.

There were few establishments in the country which were run on such lavish lines – not more than a few hundred among the seven million households. Like an Adjutant-General of Domestic Regulations, Mrs Beeton laid down the establishment for personnel in different sorts of households. The criterion was the level of income. There were some 600,000 people with an income between £160 and £400 a year, and 400,000 with an income over that amount. Starting at the lowest – and below that even a shabby-genteel household could not pretend to keep a servant – an income of £150–£200 a year should warrant a general servant or girl to do the rough work. At £300 a year there should be a cook and a housemaid. At £500 there should be a foot-boy as well. At £750 the foot-boy should be replaced by a man servant; and at £1,000 there should be four servants – cook, upper housemaid, under housemaid, and man servant. These establishments did not include a nurse-maid whose presence, provided there were children, was obligatory certainly from £500 a year upwards.

By the time Edward came to the throne, Mrs Beeton was long since dead. Her book of household management, however, was still very much to the fore. As the years passed there were fewer and fewer ladies of any social pretension whatever who could afford to avoid the rules that she had laid down and which later editions continually adjusted to the changing customs of the time.

It has become a standing, though kindly joke against her – demonstrating the affection in which she has for so long been held – that Mrs Beeton's main cooking instruction was 'Take a dozen eggs'. The fact is that such an edict for the building of a superb, or even a plebeian dish, never appeared in her original edition. Nor, so far as one can see, in any subsequent ones. The cook who really deserved the soubriquet of 'Take a dozen eggs' was Rosa Lewis, famous in her middle age and later as the proprietor and matriarch of the Alice-in-Wonderland Cavendish Hotel in Jermyn Street, London, where she died in 1952 aged eighty-five. Escoffier called her The Queen of Cooks and her culinary extravagance was legendary. The Cavendish under Rosa was in its hey-day in the Edwardian era. Later, when the First World War had aged her and killed the Sakiesque characters who drifted through the champagne bubbles of her parties (for which only the richest footed the bill), the dim corridors and dusty furniture harboured a sense of hectic hopelessness that was not exorcised until the decimating re-play of Europe's long suicide began in September 1939.

Rosa Lewis was born in the village of Leyton, Essex, in 1867. She was the fifth of nine children born to Eliza and William Ovenden. Her father was a watch-maker and undertaker, her mother, the daughter of a retired jeweller. At the age of twelve, after four years at a Board School, Rosa went out to work as a general servant. Four years later she had had enough of humping coals, cleaning floors and blacking grates from 5.30 in the morning to nine at night. All these and other chores fell to her because she was the only servant. In a large establishment with its platoons of servants there was a demarcation of duties and a chance of promotion. Rosa decided to join such an establishment. Through the good offices of an uncle who was a friend of the exiled Comtesse de Paris's chef at Sheen House, Mortlake, she got a job there as an under-kitchen-maid at 12s 6d a week. On the face of it she was little better off than she had been as a general servant. For months she did nothing but scrub floors. Nevertheless, there was a vital difference; instead of the drab household of Mr and Mrs Musgrave where she had first worked, she was now a part, however humble and subservient a part, of the dazzling world whose elegant and exciting life was reported in the *Morning Post* and magazines like *Modern Society* which she avidly read.

From scrubbing floors Rosa progressed to washing up, and from washing up to gutting poultry and game, and from gutting to making coffee and tea, and from that to making toast and from toast-making to preparing vegetables. It was a pilgrim's progress and the goal was to make herself one of the finest cooks in Europe if not in the world. As she worked at her own particular task Rosa kept her mind open to the other tasks that were going on in the kitchen, and whatever she was told to do she did with assiduity and with little special touches of her own – as when she used to sew up the gutted game with as careful stitches as if she had been doing embroidery. Once she was complimented by the Prince of Wales (later Edward VII) on the ptarmigan pie, a dish as essential to Society menus of those days and throughout the Edwardian era as chips were to less august menus in a later age.* 'The chef makes the pies, sir,' she said. 'I just takes the innards out of the birds, sir.' At the age of twenty she was promoted to head kitchen-maid.

The great advantage of being at Sheen House for Rosa's culinary ambition was that the Comte de Paris entertained the *gratin* of French and English Society. Sooner or later everyone who was anyone came to dine at the house. Her name got about. She was lent by the Comte de Paris to his uncle the Duc d'Aumale and spent some time at Chantilly. Others begged that they be allowed to borrow her. Before long she gave in her notice in order to work as a free-lance cook for the swells in London. She started with a temporary job and then went to an agency which sent her as an occasional cook to Lady Randolph Churchill, who already knew of her from dining at Sheen House. Her reputation grew, she was continually dotting from one place to another to produce dinners of mouth-watering excellence. Although she had no need of the security, when Lady Randolph offered a permanent job she accepted it. But the permanence was only temporary. Before long she was back to 'cooking around' and bringing *acclame* to different hostesses,

* Pinero or Granville Barker should have written a play called 'Ptarmigan Pie With Everything'.

although as the guest lists were habitually drawn from the same catchment area the gastronomic joy was not spread over a very wide area. As her biographer Daphne Fielding, who knew her well has summed it up: 'her presence in the kitchen was the best bait with which to hook a royal fish'.*

Rosa was a feminist and marriage was not particularly to her taste. At the age of twenty-five, however, in an off-moment she succumbed to the pressures of her parents and the entreaties of a suitor called Excelsior Lewis. Excelsior was one of two illegitimate children (the other was his sister Laura) of Miss Mary Cubitt Siely Chiney Lewis of Horsham St Faith, Norwich, and was the butler to Sir Andrew Clarke, the well-known engineer and colonial administrator who had served in New Zealand, Australia, the Straits Settlements (where he suppressed piracy), and India. In the course of his service Excelsior had put away a substantial nest-egg which he wanted to invest in a high-class boarding-house. He needed someone to run it with him. He wanted Rosa.

One 3 June 1893 she took him on at Holy Trinity Church, St Marylebone, where Robert Browning and Elizabeth Barratt among many others had been married. If 'took him on' seems an impolite way of describing the marriage it is justified by Rosa's attitude to the whole business. No white wedding dress or orange blossom for her. She would have preferred a registry office. Nor was there any honeymoon. She married him and went into business with him at 55 Eaton Terrace, SW1. There was not much joy. Excelsior was a weak character and passed his time drinking – not that the two characteristics are necessarily yoked together or that one cannot exist without the other! Rosa bought a bicycle and rode off to unknown destinations; Excelsior continued to drink; his sister Laura came to stay. Eventually, both for her own satisfaction and to keep them solvent Rosa left Laura in charge of Excelsior and went back to her peripatetic cooking. The peak of her catering career came in 1902, the year of Edward VII's belated Coronation, when she provided twenty-nine suppers for balls in a single week. 'When people said, "Rosa Lewis is going to do the supper", it was the accurate forecast of a "good party".'†

* *The Duchess of Jermyn Street* (Eyre & Spottiswoode, 1964), p. 39.
† Daphne Fielding, *op. cit.*, p. 47.

By this time Rosa had got to know Jackson, the Piccadilly grocer, and in order to augment her income she began to sell him Virginia peach-cured hams cooked by herself. From hams to chutney and preserves, all prepared in the kitchen at 55 Eaton Terrace, as were the foundations of the meals which she cooked for her outside clients. When the foundations were ready she and her assistants would descend on the client's kitchen, often to the anger and chagrin of its regular inhabitants, take it over and add the finishing touches to the dinner or supper. In order to relieve the strain on her ankles from long hours of standing Rosa invariably wore what she called her cooking-boots, a pair of which lasted her only a month. Shod in these she would marshal her dinner, shouting away her tensions by swearing like the proverbial trooper.

By this time Jackson had become her friend and it was he who told her of the place that was to become as linked with her name as Clive with Plassey or Wellington with Waterloo. There was, said Jackson, a small hotel for sale just round the corner at 81 Jermyn Street. Its name was the Cavendish. It would just suit her talents.

To Rosa it seemed a brilliant idea and one which would lighten the burden of Excelsior. He could sell 55 Eaton Terrace, invest the money in the Cavendish, and run the hotel as he wanted – with Laura's help. All Rosa required from it was the use of the big kitchen in which she could carry on her catering and cooking activities. Excelsior was agreeable and in 1902 Rosa Lewis moved into the Cavendish Hotel. But the arrangement did not work out as planned. Once again Excelsior proved himself to be a disappointment. He was lazy, unmethodical and extravagant: he began to ape the well-heeled clientele and splash his money around. Before long there were nasty rumours emanating from the tradesmen who supplied the Cavendish. Rosa investigated and found that Excelsior was keeping no accounts and paying no bills.

She had had enough. One day, having secured the cash-box and hidden it in the oven, she physically drove Excelsior and Laura from the Cavendish. Then she instituted divorce proceedings. When they were concluded (for she had plenty of evidence against Excelsior) she preferred 'never to speak or think of him again, for he was the only person in her life of

whom she was ashamed: her only failure'.* Left with debts of
£5,000, she paid them off in sixteen months by doing all the
purchasing and cooking herself.

Rid of Excelsior the Cavendish under Rosa began to become
a legend. She developed and expanded it, making it into suites
with private dining-rooms rather than a communal hotel with
a table d'hôte. As well as running the Cavendish she continued
to be an 'outside caterer', being one of the first to manage the
catering for White's Club (unusual in itself; unknown for a
woman). She also, on Edward VII's recommendation, cooked
for the Kaiser when he stayed at Highcliffe Castle on a private
visit in 1907.

Edward VII was a regular visitor to the Cavendish. Sometimes he came incognito, either as Mr White or Mr Jackson –
two pseudonyms whose origin is not far to seek in the context of
Rosa: Jackson the grocer, and White the club. When he was
thus masquerading the King, it seems, had a penchant for a
simple, nursery diet. What he wanted was not quail pudding,
which was one of Rosa's *pièces de resistance*, nor was it the ubi-
quitous ptarmigan pie. His favourite menu was bacon in parsley
sauce with broad beans.

Interestingly enough the King and Rosa had a close mutual
friend in Sister Agnes Keyser, daughter of a rich stockbroker,
who started what was later to become the King Edward VII
Hospital for Officers. Sister Agnes ran a nursing home at 17
Grosvenor Place, opposite the back gate into the grounds of
Buckingham Palace. Frequently the King would slip out to see
Sister Agnes and relax from the gastronomic rigours of regal
banqueting by eating the invalid diet that she gave her patients.
Whether Edward was simply seeking a brief respite from his
nickname of Tum-Tum, or whether a psychiatrist should see in
this sporadic addiction to the simpler life as purveyed by
'nanny' figures some compensation for the Spartan upbringing
he had undergone at the hands of his tutors is an open question.

That anyone should ever desire a change from Rosa's quail
pudding is hard to believe. Try one!

'Take your quail and truss for braising, and leave in marinade
for a few hours. Make an ordinary suet paste, line a basin with

* Daphne Fielding, *op. cit.*, p. 50.

it, then place your quail, one for each person, in slices of beef as thin as paper, which when cooked dissolve into the sauce; add some fine chopped mushrooms, parsley, shallots and good stock, and put a paste top and boil for one hour; serve rice or barley with it.'

Or try one of Rosa's dinners. This gastronomic dinner she prepared for that great gourmet W. W. Astor (later the first Viscount Astor), at his home Hever Castle on 10 July 1909:

Melon glacée   Consommé Princesse   Bisque d'Écrevisses
Blanchailles   Suprême de Volaille à la Maréchale
Selle d'Agneau à la Chivry   Foie Gras à la Gelée
Salade Nantaise   Cailles rotis sur canapés
Pêches Rose de Mai   Caroline Glacées   Croûtes de Merluche*

After reading that menu one learns with surprise that dinners were becoming much shorter in Edwardian Society than they had been in Victorian days. Sometimes this shortening was achieved by Draconian means. Consuelo Duchess of Marlborough – perhaps because she was so exasperated by the Duke's eating habits when not in company, which involved his pushing back his chair, crossing his legs and staring at his plate for three-quarters of an hour without touching his food while he mused silently on the problems of being a duke – Consuelo insisted that her dinners when she had guests should be served in one hour flat, and they were eight course dinners! Two soups, one hot and one cold served simultaneously; two fish, one hot and one cold with sauces; entrée; meat dish; sometimes a sorbet; game; sweet; savoury; peaches and other fruit. It must have been something of a strain for slow eaters or for those who would have liked a second helping of a favourite dish!

Despite these examples to the contrary, the trend in Edwardian days was certainly towards shorter and simpler menus, chiefly, it has been suggested, owing to the lack of domestic help which made entertaining on a lavish scale both more difficult and too expensive for all but the 'yellow rich'. The complications of entertaining at home also brought into vogue the habit of

* This menu is printed in Daphne Fielding, *op. cit.*

dining-out with one's friends at restaurants. The habit had been given the royal seal of approval in the 1890s when Edward and Alexandra, then Prince and Princess of Wales, had regularly appeared for Sunday supper at the new Savoy run by Cesar Ritz. Escoffier was the chef and the music came from Johann Strauss. It was at the Savoy in 1896 that a lady was first seen to smoke a cigarette in the public dining-room of a London hotel. She was the Duchesse de Clermont-Tonnerre, a friend of the Wales's. Alexandra would not have disapproved. She, like other ladies at Marlborough House, was an inveterate smoker even when pillars of the Church were present.

Among the many habits of the English that Sybil Spottiswoode's heroine Hedwig von Klausdorff found difficult to understand was one at least which seemed to her incredible. One day Mrs Ilford's daughter, Beatrice, dressed in a 'delicate Doucet creation', took her to her club, the Olympian. Not only was it Hedwig's first visit to a ladies' club – ladies' clubs were sprouting like mushrooms at this period – it was her first visit to a club of any description. At the Olympian she met two of Bee's friends, Daphne and Frances Selkirk-Forbes. Their father was the youngest son of Lord Rellington, 'a real bad hat' who had practically killed his wife and then died leaving his three daughters 'absolutely penniless'. What, wondered Hedwig, was the fate of penurious girls of the English nobility? In Germany they would, quite naturally, have been looked after by their relations; presumably the same happened in England. When Bee told her what the Selkirk-Forbes girls had done she could not believe her ears. 'They declined to live on the charity of relations, and were too sensible to attempt to become governesses or companions.' So Daphne, who was good at drawing, did fashion plates for a ladies' paper, and Frances made use of her good figure by going into the mantle department of Marshall and Allen's, one of the smartest London shops.

Serving in a shop! That was bad enough. But what did the third one do? 'Oh, Betty said straight out that she hadn't the brains or the appearance to do anything ambitious, and her only marketable attribute was a magnificently healthy, strong constitution, so she secured an excellent post as parlourmaid.'

It must be a joke! A young girl of good family working as a servant! Bee assured her it was true, and by no means unusual.

'Lots of people I know only keep lady servants, and they are infinitely better treated and paid three times as much as governesses. Servants are so valuable and sought after now that you treat them with the utmost consideration.' Governesses and companions were two a penny and could be 'snubbed and underpaid with impunity'.

Even so, Hedwig protested, there were some things a young girl of good family simply could not do. No doubt the three Misses Selkirk-Forbes were cut by everybody. Not a bit of it, Bee told her. 'Perhaps some common, snobbish people might object, but decent people only admire them.'

In casting Betty Selkirk-Forbes as a parlourmaid Sybil Spottiswoode was not giving way to fantasy. In fact she was noting an interesting social phenomenon of the day, although the general experience of most lady helps was not as satisfactory as Bee was made to imply. The term 'lady help' was coined by Mrs Rose Mary Crawshay in 1874 in a paper on 'Domestic Service for Gentlewomen' that she read to the Social Science Congress. The paper, which was subsequently published, aroused considerable interest for two reasons. Firstly, because at a time when the supply of domestic servants from the traditional Lower Nation sources seemed to be falling off dangerously it offered a new source; and secondly, because it apparently offered a means of employment to impoverished ladies which they could undertake without loss of dignity. Some of those who became lady helps were energetic and capable women, but the only qualifications of many was their dire need for remunerative work and in their case their gentility in no way made up for their incompetence. Increasing opportunities for education and employment in other fields led to a falling-off in the supply of lady helps; the demand for them too decreased greatly, except for the care of young children.

Twenty-five years later, at the end of the century, there was a revival of the lady help idea – but with a difference. The thought now was that domestic service as a career for gentlewomen should not be the last resort for the untrained but a recognised profession for which a thorough practical and scientific training was required. Courses of hygiene and domestic service started by the London School Board, County Councils and various Polytechnics for 'traditional' servants indicated the lines on which training schools and classes should be arranged.* Three establishments ran courses exclusively for training lady helps as cooks, parlourmaids and housemaids, while a fourth included the training of ladies in domestic duties as part of their preparation for emigration. The first three were the Residential School for Household and Domestic Training at Camp End near Malvern, the Grove Institute at Ashover near Chesterfield, and the portentously named Guild of Household Dames at Cheltenham; the fourth was the Guild in Aid of Home Duties at Zeals near Bath. Not only were the training schools for lady helps something of a novelty at the end of the nineteenth century in England; domestic science classes of any description were still somewhat unusual, unlike in Germany where most young girls learnt domestic science at school.

Commenting on the resurrection of lady helps the Women's Institute's *Dictionary of Employments Open to Women* thought that the question might perhaps be asked whether it was

'fair that cultured women should enter into the ranks of those who have not had their advantages. The answer is, that those ranks are at present by no means full, as the supply of highly qualified servants, cooks and parlourmaids especially, is not equal to demand. Also, it may be pointed out that the very restrictions which are causing a host of workers to prefer the factory or the workshop to domestic service may not be so irksome to women whose lives have been spent in strictly ordered

* *The Dictionary of Employments Open to Women* published by the Women's Institute in 1898 listed training schools for cookery (and in some cases laundry as well) in London, Chester, Edinburgh, Glasgow, Manchester, Norwich, Newcastle-on-Tyne, Northampton, Leicester, Nottingham, Salisbury and Cardiff, which were run by the National Union for the Technical Education of Women in Domestic Service. The County Councils of Devon, East Suffolk and Staffordshire also ran cookery training schools. There was a School of Housewifery and Training College for Teachers of Domestic Science at Stamford Hill, North London; a Training School for Domestic Economy in Deansgate, Manchester; and three other cookery schools in London – the Kensington School of Cookery, the National School of Cookery in Buckingham Palace Road, and at the Battersea Polytechnic. The last two as well as all the County Council schools and the schools of the National Union were recognised by the Education Department.

homes, and who might value comfort and security above the freedom of more precarious employments.'

There were many arguments in favour of properly trained gentlewomen taking up domestic service as a career, the *Dictionary* continued, not the least that in raising the standard of work they would also raise the status of servants as a whole because employers would have to improve the conditions under which at present servants had to live and work, 'and such an advance would prove a gain to the community generally'. Furthermore, from trained lady helps might be expected 'forethought, accuracy, and skill in the use of labour-saving appliances, the demand for which would, as a consequence, greatly increase'.

Despite these laudable sentiments, however, a pamphlet called *Lady Servants*, published in 1906, showed that the lot of a lady help was not always as Betty Selkirk-Forbes's. Like the governess some lady helps, even with training, found themselves in limbo: they belonged neither 'upstairs' nor 'downstairs', humiliated by the other servants and spoken to like a dog by those of her own class who employed her. But others were more fortunate and were treated as the professionals they were and not as a more exotic form of household drudge.

Chapter 11

THE MARRIAGE QUESTION

❧

'No book describing the occupations open to women would be complete without some remark on the duties of a wife, in view of the fact that in England, Wales, and Scotland alone, five millions of the nineteen millions of women in the United Kingdom are married women, and that although many of these are engaged in businesses and professions, a very large number are fully and solely occupied in the management of their own households and the care of their children.'

Thus the *Dictionary of Employments*. But in fact the duties explained were simply the legal duties of a wife, 'so that it may be understood how far, according to the present laws, a man is bound to maintain his wife, what her legal duties are, and what her position with regard to property'.

The basic fact was that despite the legislation of the past half-century the legal position of a wife was merged in that of her husband. 'My wife and I are one, and I am he.' The law imposed no duties on her as a wife. A Court might order her to live with her husband, but could not force her to do so: all it could do, if she refused, was to decree a separation. Neither had the husband any right to compel his wife to live with him by force, nor was there any legal means of compelling her to perform her household duties.

The case which determined that a husband could not compel his wife to live with him by force is an interesting one. It occurred in 1891 when a man called Jackson seized his wife as she was leaving church and forcibly carried her off because she had refused to return to live with him. She was kept incommunicado at Jackson's house in Blackburn, Lancashire, until her relations applied for a writ of *Habeas Corpus* and she was brought before a court. It was contended by counsel for the husband that a husband had a right to restrain the liberty of his wife. The Court refused to accept this view of the law and decided that legally no wife was bound to stay with her husband, nor could a husband use force to prevent her leaving him. Mrs Jackson was to go free. This case gave married women a further step towards decency in marriage which had been begun by the Divorce Act of 1857 and continued in 1884 when Parliament abolished imprisonment as the penalty for denying a spouse's conjugal rights. 'Prostitution within the marriage bond' the extreme feminists had called it. Only easy divorce would entirely protect a wife sexually they felt.

A wife, on the other hand, had certain legal rights and privileges. She was presumed to have authority to pledge her husband's credit with tradesmen for the supply of household and personal necessaries unless he specifically deprived her of that authority, in which case he had either to provide the necessaries himself or supply her with an adequate allowance for the purpose. If he failed to do either, the law gave the wife an authority to order the necessaries on his credit. In fact a wife was entitled to maintenance by her husband unless she forfeited it by her own misconduct. The Married Women (Maintenance in case of Desertion) Act of 1886 allowed justices or a police magistrate to make a maintenance order up to £2 a week.

As far as children were concerned, under the Infants' Custody Act of 1873, if a husband and wife were living apart the wife could apply to the Court for an order giving her custody of any children of the marriage until they were sixteen, and if the Court considered that such a course would be for the children's benefit it would make such an order. In any divorce action the Divorce Act, 1857, gave the Court an absolute discretion as to the custody of the children of the marriage. Generally, the custody of the children was given to the innocent party.

In the case of property, if a husband died intestate his widow had a right to one-third of his personal property if he left children surviving, or to one-half if he left no children. By the Married Women's Property Act, 1882, all a woman's property acquired by her since the Act in the case of those married before the Act, and all her property, in the case of those married since the Act, belonged to her free from any right or control of her husband. The husband, however, still remained liable in respect of his wife's torts, i.e. civil wrongs in respect of which damages might be recovered against her. In such a case he was entitled to recoup himself out of his wife's separate property, if she had any.

Almost without exception a woman who was divorced or separated from her husband, whatever the cause, was a woman with a 'lost reputation' – an Edwardian invitation to lust if ever there was one. But John Galsworthy put into the head of Mrs Audrey Noel, the heroine of his novel *The Patrician*, who is separated from her husband, 'the conviction that to a woman the preciousness of her reputation was a fiction invented by men entirely for men's benefit; a second-hand fetish insidiously, inevitably set up by men for worship, in novels, plays, and law courts. Her instinct told her that men could not feel secure in the possession of their women unless they could believe that women set tremendous store by sexual reputation.'*

Public attitudes to sex in the Edwardian decade were little different from what they had been in Victorian England – which is hardly surprising, because the change of a century or the death of a statute does not necessarily invoke a whole new personality in the psyche of a nation. Nonetheless, behind the frontal platitudes a revolution was gaining ground. The old shibboleths and taboos were being nudged into oblivion. It was to be a long process.

Edward Carpenter and Havelock Ellis were two writers who pioneered the way. Carpenter's *Love's Coming-of-Age*, published in 1896, and Havelock Ellis's *Studies in the Psychology of Sex*, published in six volumes from 1897 to 1910, were books which had a fundamental effect in changing the American and especially the English attitude to sex. 'To Havelock Ellis belongs the honour of producing the first considerable English treatise on sex, at a time when that vital subject was a matter for shameful evasion or giggling facetiousness, and when the mere mention of it seriously in print exposed the writer to ignorant and unscrupulous misrepresentation.'† For a long time his volumes had to be procured furtively. Any work 'that discussed sex

* Heinemann, 1911, p. 111.

† George Sampson, *The Concise Cambridge History of English Literature* (CUP 1949), p. 1045.

seriously was instantly supposed to be encouraging lechery by people who would never have supposed that a treatise on nutrition was an encouragement to gluttony'.*

Although Carpenter and Ellis are the two authors who are known as the pioneer psychiatrists of sex writing in England, there were other writers who were expressing the same ideas in novels and on the stage and are equally deserving of recognition in this connection: George Gissing who was the first important English novelist to consider seriously the psychology of sex, George Meredith with at least four novels on the subject, George Bernard Shaw, John Galsworthy, H. G. Wells, Henry Arthur Jones, Sir Arthur Pinero, and Henrik Ibsen among them. Ibsen's *The Doll's House*, translated by William Archer, was first performed in London on 7 June 1889 and led the attack on the old conventions. But it was Jones, in his play *The Case of Rebellious Susan* (1897), who produced the neatest aphorism about the double standard: 'Admittedly, what is sauce for the goose is sauce for the gander. Unfortunately for the goose there is no gander sauce.'

For many women the outset of marriage was a misery as no doubt it was too for many men. There were no handbooks on sex which a young woman would know about, let alone be able to get her hands on. That they could have read Ellis is unlikely in the extreme, for his books could not be bought openly in Great Britain until 1935, and Carpenter's idyllics were not of much practical use to the uninitiated. Marriage brought a painful disclosure. When Nerina Shute's Edwardian mother was married she spent her first night in the Charing Cross Hotel, London, on her way to France. Her husband, a kindly enough fellow, appeared before her in the bedroom, told her she looked pretty, and shortly afterwards said, 'You know what has to be done, so don't make a fuss'. But she had literally no idea what had to be done – nor did millions like her. All she had learnt was from one of her married sisters who had said, without further explanation, 'When the time comes, dear, try to think about something else. It's the only thing to do.' Too late on her wedding night Nerina's mother remembered the sound advice of her sister.†

---

* *Ibid.*

† *Come Into the Sunlight* (Jarrold, 1958), p. 65.

But not all women would have thought the advice sound at all. A new attitude was appearing, along with the militancy of suffragettism and the anger of the sex war that it brought with it. Why should the idea of sex without parenthood be only a dream? Why should it be men only who got the pleasure from sexual intercourse? The Almighty had not limited orgasms to men; let women enjoy themselves too.

After 'the horrors of the honeymoon', as it was for most of those like Nerina's mother, and the onset of a family another problem arose for those women who wished to avoid unending pregnancies. How to stop them? Or could they be stopped at all without the denial of conjugal rights? Writing to one of her daughters after that daughter had had her first child the Edwardian novelist Elizabeth von Arnim, cousin of Katherine Mansfield: 'No wonder you say the next one shall be adopted – and you have a proper decent husband who won't force you, as I was forced instantly before I had even bodily recovered let alone spiritually, to have another.' Countess von Arnim had had one child after another – five in all – and she hated it. As far as one can gather her method of stopping the flow, as no doubt it was the method of other women, was to refuse to sleep with her husband.

Although contraception had a long history and its methods were increasingly being used, it was still far from being accepted as a practice that should be used by 'decent people' – that, at least, was the Church's attitude and the Lambeth Conference of Bishops in 1908 regarded 'with alarm the growing practice of the artificial restriction of the family, and earnestly' called upon 'all Christian people to discountenance the use of all artificial means of restriction as demoralising to character and hostile to national welfare'. And apart from this moral disapproval there was the practical difficulty of knowing what to do. The Malthusian League, which Charles Bradlaugh had started in the 1860s to spread contraceptive knowledge and which had been fading away until revived in 1877, as a result of the publicity about the Bradlaugh–Besant trial over *The Fruits of Philosophy*, was increasingly active. Nevertheless, the problem still remained of how to spread knowledge about contraceptive methods. Nothing could be done by the enemies of contraception to gag word of mouth dissemination, but the use of printed information was jumped on. The Post Office refused to handle it and in 1911 a bookseller in Durham chose to go to prison (where he died) rather than pay a fine for selling a book containing an illustrated list of contraceptives. The League's 'tradition was strongly against practical propaganda which its leaders feared would arouse prejudice'.* But in 1913 the League both conducted a series of open-air meetings in working-class districts of London and issued *Hygienic Methods of Family Limitation* after the Council had been empowered at an annual general meeting to give married persons the necessary information. 'We want the poor to be taught to limit their families by the same contraceptive methods which most married couples in the richer classes are employing,' wrote *The Malthusian. Hygienic Methods* was a practical leaflet. Its circulation was restricted and it was only available to those who were over twenty-one, married or about to be married, and who signed a declaration that they would hold themselves responsible for keeping it out of the hands of young persons. Despite these restrictions, 1,203 copies were issued within six months, one in ten to medical practitioners. The war confirmed the change in attitudes to contraception. By 1922 all organised opposition to birth control was dead, except that of the Roman Catholic Church.

Looming over all in the Marriage Question, as Shaw called it in a Fabian pamphlet, were the impossible straits in which both men and women could find themselves when they were shackled for life to partners from whom only death could them part. The pioneer for the new release was Lord Russell. Francis Russell and his younger brother Bertrand were grandsons of Lord John Russell, afterwards Earl Russell who was Prime Minister from 1846 to 1852 and from 1865 to 1866. Their father was John Russell, Viscount Amberley, who was called Vice-Count A-B Lie by his Tory opponents in the South Devon parliamentary election of 1868 on account of his known sympathies for contraception. Their mother Kate Louisa was the fourth daughter of Lord Stanley of Alderley and Lady Stanley, one of the founders of the Girls' Public Day School Trust. In 1876 their father died when Francis was eleven years old. His mother and a younger sister had died of diphtheria twenty

* Peter Fryer, *The Birth Controllers* (Secker and Warburg, 1965), p. 235.

months earlier. In 1878, on the death of his grandfather he became the second Earl Russell.

The orphans were taken to live at the Russell home, Pembroke Lodge in Richmond Park, a milieu which did not suit them at all. 'Religion might occasionally be spoken of with bated breath and in a hushed curate sort of voice, but sex, birth, swearing, trade, money, passion were subjects I never heard mentioned.' Twice he ran away and was then sent to a preparatory school, from there to Winchester, and then, in 1883, he went up to Balliol. But towards the end of his second year he lost his temper with the Master of his college, the redoubtable Benjamin Jowett, and what was to have been a one month's rustication turned into his being permanently sent down. He set up house at Teddington on the Thames, first living a happy-go-lucky existence with Robert Louis Stevenson's cousin Graham Balfour as his companion, with whom he travelled extensively in the United States and elsewhere, and then with a Lady Scott and her daughter Mabel Edith. According to the Countess von Arnim's pseudonymous biographer Leslie de Charms (and the involvement of Elizabeth of the German Garden in this brief biography of Russell's life will appear shortly), Lady Scott and Mabel Edith were 'adventuresses of a pronounced type and already notorious'. Within a few months, in 1890, Russell married Mabel Edith. But he had married the wrong woman. It was the mother he was in love with – not surprisingly: he was in his early twenties, he had lost his mother when he was nine, Lady Scott was middling aged and attractive; indeed the fact that his mother had died when he was a child is irrelevant!

His friend, the great philosopher and poet George Santayana, described the tender trap that had been set for Russell: 'Lady Scott persuaded Russell that the way to make him and her friends for life, and guardians of each other's happiness, was for him to marry Mabel Edith. Mabel Edith was insignificant, but she was not less attractive than others who could so easily seduce him.'* The marriage was not a success. The Scotts, mama and daughter, soon found they had caught a Tartar. Russell and Mabel Edith lived together for three months:

---

* *The Middle Span* (Constable, 1947), p. 80.

'Russell as a husband, Russell in the domestic sphere, was simply impossible: excessively virtuous and incredibly tyrannical. He didn't allow her enough money or enough liberty. He was punctilious and unforgiving about hours, about truth-telling, about debts. He objected to her friends, her clothes, her borrowed jewels. Moreover, in their intimate relations he was exacting and annoying. She soon hated and feared him. One day she couldn't endure him any longer and ran home to her mother, crying like a frightened child. Her mother clasped her to her bosom, patted her, soothed her; and they began to consider, with their solicitors, how best to get money out of Russell.'*

They started a campaign against him that lasted for several years, bringing one lawsuit after another against him. In 1891 he faced an action for divorce, Mabel Edith charging cruelty and 'heinous crimes'. The action was dismissed. Three years later she brought an action for restitution of conjugal rights. Then in 1895, Russell obtained a decree of judicial separation, but the decree was successfully appealed.

Russell, in the interim, did not let his bed grow cold. He popped around, in the intervals of being what *Webster's Biographical Dictionary* classified as electrical engineer, barrister and agnostic. One lady he pursued as far as San Francisco. But in 1895 he settled for Mollie Somerville, described by Santayana as 'a fat, florid, coarse Irishwoman of forty, with black curls, friendly manners and emotional opinions'. That Russell had something that appealed to women is undoubted. Perhaps before he became exacting and annoying his dominance was compelling. At any rate Mollie, who had been twice married, left two young sons and went off to live with Russell. Russell was determined to marry her. So he took her to the United States and established legal residence in Nevada by spending six months at Lake Tahoe. Then they were married by a local judge.

In May 1900 they returned to England. According to American law they were married; according to English law he was a bigamist. In the spring of 1901 he was presented with a warrant for his arrest and cost in damages of £1,500 for adultery; he was

* Santayana, *op. cit.*, pp. 80–1.

tried, as was his privilege, by his peers in the House of Lords. He ultimately admitted that he knew Nevada divorce laws were invalid in England and was sentenced by their Lordships to three months in prison. In passing sentence the Lord Chancellor said:

'My Lords, for my own part, speaking with considerable knowledge of this unfortunate litigation which, as Earl Russell has explained, has led to this terrible catastrophe, while I think he was undoubtedly suffering under almost intolerable provocation, the circumstances of his domestic life being such as might lead him to do almost anything to get rid of the person who had poisoned the whole atmosphere in which he lived; on the other hand, of course, it is impossible for your Lordships to pass over that defiance of law which I cannot forbear from saying I think he exhibited. . . .'

He did not serve his time the hard way. In the maximum of comfort possible he spent his time reading the Bible from end to end and all of Shakespeare twice. He also wrote some religious essays which were later published as *Lay Sermons*. And he achieved his end. His marriage to Mabel Edith, with whom he had at last succeeded in arranging matters, was dissolved and his marriage to Mollie was made legal.

Russell now used his own unhappy experience to try and benefit others. It had taken eleven years and an infinite degree of sordidness and legal expense, let alone a few months in prison, for him to dissolve a marriage which was doomed from the outset. Others with a less secure social position (after all an Earl was an Earl whatever he did) and with less money would have had an infinitely harder and more soul-destroying time in achieving what Russell had eventually achieved. In the spring of 1902 he presented a bill in the Lords which proposed three kinds of modification to the existing law of 1857. The thesis of that law accurately reflected the opinion of the time as regards women. It stated, in effect, that a man might divorce his wife for adultery, although adultery alone was not a sufficient ground for a woman to obtain a divorce. But if a husband added cruelty or desertion or the crimes of sodomy, bestiality, or rape to his adultery then the wife had grounds for divorce. Adultery was the only grounds for divorce although desertion and cruelty without adultery were grounds for judicial separation. Collusion was rigorously disallowed: there could be no divorce if both parties were guilty of adultery, nor was a judicial separation permissible if husband and wife parted by mutual consent.

Russell's bill proposed to modify the law in three ways: the grounds for divorce should be extended to include cruelty, penal servitude for three years, lunacy, three years' separation or one year's separation if both parties concurred; the legal position of women and men should be equal; and divorce actions should be heard in County Courts, thus reducing the cost of a divorce suit and making divorce feasible for the poor.

Russell in his speech argued that English divorce law was the twisted rump of ecclesiastical law and was neither logical nor just; that by denying freedom to those who were genuinely ill-suited it encouraged immorality; that the law in Scotland which was somewhat less stringent had not caused greater moral laxity in that country; and that what he proposed could have no deleterious effect on those whose marriages were soundly footed. The seventy-eight-year-old Lord Chancellor, the Earl of Halsbury,* thought otherwise. Instead of the sympathy he had extended when passing sentence on Russell the previous year he now turned on him with venom and accused him of trying to destroy the institution of marriage. It was the clause about one year's separation if both parties concurred that particularly upset him. He moved that the bill be rejected – which was a calculated insult. Normally a bill was defeated by moving its postponement. To move for its rejection was unheard of in modern Parliamentary practice. The rejection was carried and Russell was both defeated and insulted.

In the next session he tried again, having removed the one year's concurrence clause. He concluded his speech: 'I submit this Bill to the House as an honest attempt to remedy an intolerable state of things. I ask whether among all the Members of this House there are none who recognise that the present marriage laws do inflict upon a vast number of men and women in this country great hardship; that the present marriage laws

* Halsbury presided over the digest of the *Laws of England* from 1905 to 1916 and led the diehards in the House of Lords against the Parliament Act in 1911. He died in 1921 aged ninety-eight.

lead in many cases to the contracting of immoral alliances between separated men and women, and that the granting of a judicial separation is really to throw upon the world two potential adulterers. It is easy to legislate for human nature, but it is less easy to control it after your legislation. The present law offers a divorce as a reward for immoral conduct.'*

Once again the bill was defeated, but at least Russell had succeeded in bringing the issue of divorce into the arena of public discussion. The discussion, kept before the public by the Divorce Law Reform Association, forced the Government to appoint a Royal Commission in 1909 to consider reforms in the laws of marriage and divorce. As mentioned in Chapter One the Commission's report did not result in any changes to the law, and it was left to the Independent member for Oxford University, A. P. Herbert, a quarter-of-a-century later to carry on the parliamentary work that Earl Russell had started. Alan Herbert's amendment of the law made cruelty, desertion and insanity grounds for divorce, so that, as he pointed out in his famous novel *Holy Deadlock*, those who wanted a divorce were no longer forced to commit adultery whether they wished to or not.

Lord Russell's matrimonial adventures were not concluded when his marriage to Mollie was legalised. At the end of 1913 he started to woo another lady whom he had met occasionally in England and who was now living in Switzerland. Santayana records that one day early in 1914 he found Mollie in deep distress.

'She confided to me that she was troubled about Russell. He was in love with somebody else. . . . "She wants to be his wife; she wants me to divorce him!" Why? Did the silly woman wish to be a countess? No: she wasn't silly, and was a countess already. She was the Countess von Arnim, author of *Elizabeth and Her German Garden*. Russell was very much in love with her.'†

On 25 February Russell left 'fat, friendly' Mollie. Two years later he obtained his divorce and on 11 February he married the English-born Elizabeth.

* Quoted in Samuel Hynes, *The Edwardian Turn of Mind* (OUP, 1968), p. 189.

† *My Host the World* (The Cresset Press, 1953), pp. 89–90.

Christened Mary Annette, she was called May by her family but eventually became known to all by her pseudonym of Elizabeth. She was the author of many popular semi-auto-biographical novels of the Edwardian period and after.

Elizabeth's first husband, who features in some of her books as the Man of Wrath and whose second wife she was, died in 1910. With this first husband Henning von Arnim-Schlagenthin Elizabeth had had monumental rows though their relations eventually improved after he had been imprisoned for ten months in 1899–1900 on false accusations of embezzlement. There are times in reading her biography when one feels that whatever anger the Man of Wrath gave vent to he had more than a little justice on his side. She could be a very difficult lady. According to Hugh Walpole, who was for a short time tutor to her three eldest children in Germany, she had three moods:

'(1) charming, like her books only more so (this does not appear often). (2) Ragging. Now she is unmerciful – attacks you on every side, goes at you until you are reduced to idiocy, and then drops you limp. (3) Silence. This is most terrible of all. She sits absolutely mute and if one tries to speak one gets snubbed. She was like that at lunch today, and we all made shots in turn and got "settled". You see she is not an easy person to live with, but I'm sure there's a key somewhere which I hope to find.'*

He never did and was asked to remove himself from the Arnims' home at Nassenheide after four months. At least one later tutor, with a greater innate ability to worship femininity, was more successful at Nassenheide. This was C. E. Stuart, a fellow of Trinity, Cambridge, who fell deeply in love with her. But it was an unrequited passion. In the end, according to her biographer, she came to be convinced that 'he alone, of the various men who professed devotion, had truly and unswervingly felt it'.† He was killed in 1917. Among the others was H. G. Wells, but he went away *unverrichterer dinge* – as did no doubt most of the others.

* Walpole's Journal quoted in Rupert Hart-Davis, *Hugh Walpole* (Macmillan, 1952).

† Leslie de Charms, *Elizabeth of the German Garden* (Heinemann, 1958), p. 108.

If Henning von Arnim was the Man of Wrath, Francis Russell turned out to have a temper which was even more ungovernable. Within two months of their marriage 'life with Francis had, in fact, become martyrdom pure and simple, redeemed only now and then, but less convincingly each time, by his sudden and astonishing transformations from tyrant into lover'.*

In her diary for 17 April 1916 she wrote, 'F. left early for London. . . . Came back at six a mixture of grossness and disagreeableness, then suddenly sweetness. I find this shattering, the insecurity of it, the jumpiness.'

And a month later: 'May 16. . . . I can't go on every day recording F's tempers but today was worse than usual.'†

In March 1919 she left having, as she wrote to one of her daughters, 'discovered behaviour of a secret nature that made it impossible for a decent woman to stay'.‡ He died in March 1931, she in February 1941.

* *Ibid.*, p. 178.
† Quoted in de Charms, *op. cit.*, p. 178.
‡ *Ibid.*, p. 201.

Chapter 12

THE ENGLISH MISS

If one is to believe Beatrice Ilford in Sybil Spottiswoode's *Hedwig in England*, the education of young ladies in Britain at the beginning of the twentieth century had changed little from that of their grandmothers. Governesses tried to 'drum speeches from Shakespeare into their heads, and although they saw the plays acted, with all the dull parts cut out, the end result seemed to be that they merely felt virtuous and cultured for having been to see something classical'. Poetry was just rubbish made to rhyme, the reading of which merely showed people's superiority; they would infinitely prefer an exciting novel. The useful things learnt were dancing and riding as a baby, then golf and tennis – finally cards; enough piano to play dance music and accompany a small repertoire of songs, as long as the room was not too big nor the audience too critical. They also learnt to put on their clothes and make the most of their appearance and to pick up bits of information and tags of criticism which got them along well enough and saved a tremendous amount of bother. The basis of their philosophy was that a good figure and quick wit would procure a woman most things, whereas the profoundest learning and broad hips would leave her in the lurch. Of cookery they were even more ignorant than of Shakespeare, and yet if they married a poor man they seemed to manage wonderfully, learning by instinct.

By contrast, the training received by Baroness Hedwig von Klausdorff: she attended the *Töchterschule* as there was a compulsory secondary education system in Germany long before there was one in England. She had classes in Shakespeare twice a week, where all the plays were classified and extensive notes made, which were later expanded into essays. She was equally knowledgeable about Schiller, Lessing and Goethe. Most young girls went to cooking schools, where they learnt cookery, house-keeping, fine laundry work and sewing. Hedwig was of the opinion that German men would not like dinners cooked by instinct.

Another view of the *Töchterschule* was given by the Countess von Arnim. Writing from their German home in Nassenheide in May 1907 to her eldest daughter Evi, who was at St Paul's School, London, she gave her all the local gossip. She had been to see the local pastor and his wife, one of whose daughters had been sent to school, but hated it so much that her father had brought her home and was now teaching her himself, while the other one was 'in a *Töchterschule* where the poor *Töchter* are not allowed to learn anything really useful in case it should spoil them for being proper *Hausfrau* later on and spending their lives in the kitchen'. As may be gathered from that comment, Elizabeth was only spasmodically a *Hausfrau* and then only under duress. She preferred to drive through the fir forests to the silver sands of the Baltic, or lie in her garden and meditate about the beauties of nature, or suddenly rush off to England or Italy. She had five children which was rather too many to please her – and the three eldest, all girls, after being taught initially by the village schoolmaster, had their education con-tinued by a succession of governesses and tutors, among them E. M. Forster as well as Hugh Walpole – two young gentlemen who were to become even better known in English literature than Elizabeth herself.

In case the dour Hedwig should take away too bad an opinion of English ladies, Beatrice's mother, who could see when her daughter was tending to pull the hidden Teutonic leg even on such a serious subject as education, gave a sharp reminder:

'You must not go back and say all Englishwomen are ignorant and uneducated. Some of us go to Newnham and Girton, and read Greek and Latin for pleasure, and have most cultured minds. And I will tell you one thing that will astonish you – I have actually met one woman who is a brilliant mathematician, and manages also to have a good figure and complexion and tasteful clothes.'

Although the Edwardian period was not one of any violent

change in post-primary education for girls in Britain, for Beatrice Ilford to say that the education of young ladies was much the same as it had been in their grandmothers' day was incorrect. What happened during the first fourteen years of the twentieth century was that the ideas and organisations established during the previous thirty years were developed over a wider field.

To see what those new ideas and organisations were we must go back to the Royal Commission on Endowed Schools, also known as the Schools Inquiry Commission or the Taunton Commission, which was appointed in 1864. Originally it had not been the intention for the Commission to inquire into girls' education, although the framers of the Commission's terms had not specifically limited the inquiry to boys' schools because, it has been said, they were too oblivious of the girls to exclude them. However, Emily Davies, leader of the movement to get higher education for women in Britain, appealed to the Commission to investigate the education of middle-class girls as well as of middle-class boys on the grounds that 'so long as they [the Commissioners] thrust aside female education it will not come before the nation as worthy of serious thought'.

The Commissioner's report appeared in 1868 and even as far as girls were concerned it had an important effect on their education in the future. The Commissioners found that in the upper classes the education of girls was a domestic industry carried on by the mother (who sometimes delegated routine work to a governess), and by visiting masters. Also educative was the whole environment of home life with its books, travel, seasons in London, and conversation. Next, for the middle-class girls, were the boarding-schools and ladies' seminaries, many providing a totally inadequate education, but others which were extremely good. Below these girls, socially, came those in 'that unfortunate situation just too high to make use of the Charity and National Schools. For them there was rarely anything better than a superior dame school in a parlour or a very inferior visiting governess.'*

Thirty years later the situation had been transformed. While there was still education at home there were now also the big

* G. M. Young's Summary of the Report in *Victorian England* (OUP, 1936).

public boarding schools, the equivalent of Eton, Winchester, Uppingham, Rugby and the host of others, for girls of the upper classes (and all of them just as expensive); and for the second and third classes mentioned above there had come into existence in 1873 the Girls' Public Day School Company (later Trust) which founded high schools for girls.

Great steps forward were made in the higher education of women during the last quarter of the nineteenth century with the foundation of Girton and Newnham Colleges at Cambridge, and Lady Margaret Hall, Somerville College, and St Hugh's at Oxford, and with other universities following the lead given by London University in 1878 and making all degrees, honours, and prizes accessible to both sexes on equal terms. 'But it is not only by its peak that a pyramid must be judged,' wrote Alicia C. Percival in *The English Miss Today and Yesterday*.

'To be perfect it must be solid and regular. . . . The most remarkable achievement was the foundation and growth of a system which aimed at putting a good secondary education within the reach of any girl whose father was willing and able to pay about £16 a year for it. It is true that the secondary schools were not the base of the educational system, and that this base also was being laid during the latter part of the century, from the time of the 1870 Act which began the process of making elementary education compulsory and free. But this great primary movement had to pass a hard test, and the era of overcrowded schools, of hard-worked pupil-teachers, and of payment by results, inevitable as these things may have been, can hardly be considered a time of educational success. It is the second course of the pyramid, to return to our metaphor, that was so well and truly laid at this period – those great high schools, founded up and down the country from Newcastle to Exeter, and from Ipswich to Swansea, where an ever-growing number of pupils was being given an education at the same time liberal and practical.'*

The Girls' Public Day School Trust came into being as a result of a meeting held in the Albert Hall. Its founders were

* Harrap, 1939, p. 187.

Mrs William (Maria Georgina) Grey, her sister Miss Emily
Shirreff, Mrs Russell (Mary) Gurney, and Lady Stanley of
Alderley, who had added her name to Emily Davies's appeal to
the Taunton Commission. The schools started by the GPDS
Trust took for their model Miss Frances Mary Buss's North
London Collegiate School which her mother had founded as a
private school and which had been re-organised with Miss Buss
as its headmistress in 1854. Miss Buss had been one of the first
students at Queen's College, London. The North London
Collegiate was a public trust financed by the Brewers' Company
which owned considerable property in that part of London
from which the school drew many of its pupils. In 1873 the
Privy Council Education Committee established it as a first-
grade public school. A few years later Manchester High School
came into existence and was soon established as a first-grade
public endowed school like the North London Collegiate. The
importance of Miss Buss's work is demonstrated in the constitution of the Manchester High School which said that 'The rules
and regulations of the Trust for carrying on the North London
Collegiate and Camden School for Girls shall be adopted as the
basis of the permanent constitution of the Manchester Public
Day School for Girls.' The name, incidentally, was changed
from Public Day School because the first headmistress was Miss
Day and it was thought there might be some confusion.

But Miss Buss's influence extended far beyond trust deeds.
The North London Collegiate was the only one of its kind and
had twenty years' experience behind it. Details of its organisation and of Miss Buss's ideals were bound to inform all the
public day schools that came later. And soon there were dozens
of them. Some were started by the GPDS Trust, others were
revived or newly formed from old endowments, others were
founded by newly created trusts: the Mary Datchelor, the
Haberdashers' Aske's, the Westminster Grey Coat, the Birmingham King Edward VI Foundation schools, the Harper Trust
school at Bedford, the Perse schools at Cambridge, schools at
Leamington, Warwick, Bradford and Leeds – 'up and down the
country from Newcastle to Exeter and from Ipswich to Swansea'.

By the opening of Edward VII's reign the high school was a
well-established part of English education. Its time-table and
arrangement of hours went back to Miss Buss. There was no

afternoon school, although there was preparation for the next day's lessons; Saturday was a whole holiday because she wanted the girls to have time with their families and to be able to help with the household chores on Saturday morning. There was a strong tradition of health – food, ventilation and sanitation were as good as could be managed. Hygiene was taught. Physical training was introduced. There were medical inspections by a woman doctor. Organised games were introduced – not always with the whole-hearted approval of the headmistresses. The curriculum too, reflected Miss Buss's outlook. It was linked to the boys' curriculum because she believed that girls must take the same public examination as boys – the London Matriculation, for example – so that they could prove by work under similar conditions that girls and women could compete on equal terms with boys and men.

Two fundamental differences between the girls' high schools and the girls' public schools which also came into existence at the same period were that the education given at the high schools, although just as good, was much cheaper than that at the public schools, and second, that there was no question of social class involved. At Cheltenham Ladies College, for example, the school's proprietors accepted girls only if their parents' status met the criterion that Cheltenham was a school 'for the daughters of gentlemen'. But at the North London Collegiate, recalled a pupil of the 1880s, 'no-one asked where you lived, how much pocket-money you had, or what your father was – he might be a bishop or a rat-catcher'. Nor was it a disgrace to be poor: 'girls would openly grumble at having to buy a new text-book, and it was an act of merit to make your clothes last a long time', instead of being looked at askance at a private school for appearing in a 'turned' dress.

The Cheltenham College for Young Ladies, later re-named Cheltenham Ladies' College, was founded, originally as a day school, in 1853. In 1858 Miss Dorothea Beale, the other great luminary of girls' secondary education in England in the second half of the nineteenth century, was appointed to its headship and under her it became the first girls' public school with boarders outnumbering day girls. The second girls' public school was St Leonard's at St Andrew's in Scotland. Founded in 1877, with Miss (later Dame) Louisa Lumsden as its first head, it too had day girls. But the next girls' public school which was started in 1884, was purely a boarding school. This was Roedean, run by the three Misses Lawrence, which was to be a school for the sisters of the boys who went to Eton and Winchester, just as Cheltenham Ladies' College was, on the whole, started for the sisters of the boys who went to the recently founded Cheltenham College. Other schools followed. Among them Godolphin at Salisbury in 1886, Wycombe Abbey started in 1896 by Miss Alice Dove who had been headmistress at St Leonard's, Sherborne in 1899 under Miss Mulliner, and in 1903 St Paul's Girls' School in London, endowed by the governors of St Paul's School for boys. St Paul's was unique in that it was both a public school and a day school. Evi von Arnim had to board out and travel to school daily. While Cheltenham was an important influence on these later schools they never modelled themselves so closely on it as had the high schools on Miss Buss's North London Collegiate. But what did have a profound effect on the pioneers was, naturally, the work of the great headmasters who had inspired the renaissance of boys' public schools – Arnold of Rugby and Thring of Uppingham among them. This resulted in the adoption by the new girls' schools of the whole public school plan; the house system, prefects, games, colours, the team spirit, stiff upper lip, 'good form' – the whole paraphernalia. It was not at all as it had been in grandmother's time! Nevertheless *The Lady* magazine in 1900 felt that the education of girls was 'still too much directed towards the matrimonial market and the facilities for trade training outside London leave much to desire'.

Games began to hold as important a place in the hierarchy of girls' public schools as it did in the boys'. The trend, however, had its opponents. Miss Beale was one of those who were highly suspicious of 'men's sport' for girls and it was not until 1890 that her prejudice was overcome and she allowed hockey to be played at Cheltenham. Earlier she had been equally stubborn at refusing to allow the introduction of lawn tennis – originally known as sphairistike or 'sticky'. It was Miss Lumsden, who was on the Cheltenham staff before she went to St Leonard's, who persuaded her. By then 'sticky' had become accepted, the first Wimbledon championships being played under the auspices of the All-England Croquet and Lawn Tennis Club in

1877, the year Miss Lumsden went to St Leonard's. Miss Lumsden was also responsible for the introduction of lacrosse to schools in Great Britain. She had seen it played by Red Indians on the Canadian prairies and despite its comparative difficulty it was immediately accepted, some schools giving up hockey for lacrosse. The other winter game adopted by girls' schools also came from North America. This was basket-ball, which was played under cover in America when snow prevented outdoor games. Adapted and re-named netball, the first mention of it in England was in 1895 when it was played at Miss Osterley's Physical Training College with wastepaper baskets as goals. The great advantage of netball was that it provided a great deal of exercise in a limited space. Swedish drill and musical gymnastics became very popular for girls in the 1890s.

Apart from Miss Lumsden another pioneer in games for girls was Miss Lawrence of Roedean. She had been educated partly in Germany and always had a love of outdoor exercise, particularly swimming, which was unusual at that period. All three Lawrence sisters, Penelope, Dorothy and Millicent, had a reputation for athleticism and one apocryphal story circulated in the neighbourhood of Roedean was that when one of the Miss Lawrences came to a gate she did not open it – 'Oh, no! She lays her hand on the top and lightly vaults over it.'

The argument about games continued long after Miss Beale. In 1907 the Headmistresses Association was complaining that games were 'overdone'. One of their number Miss Blanche Clough, disagreed. 'Games,' she said, 'occupy the vacant space, and they also produce an antiseptic atmosphere.' The rebuttal was that the atmosphere was not always antiseptic. This had been one of the worries about girls' higher education in mid-Victorian times. Away from home girls would be prey to immoral influences; that was why female boarding-schools were so 'unspeakably pernicious'.* That there were raves, *grandes passions*, and *Schwärmerei* in girls' public schools was not something to be denied. Indeed, wrote Alicia Percival in 1939:

'a girl of the Middle School age would probably be omitting one of the natural stages of growth if she did not feel a deep affection and a genuine admiration for both contemporary and

---

* *Essays in Defence of Women*, 1868.

senior members of her own sex. Those who throw about such psychological terms as "Lesbianism" need to study both in theory and in practice the development of the growing girl, and to realise how often and how naturally these friendships and enthusiasms pass into the next stage, and only serve to widen and deepen her character. Of course, there are unhealthy attachments – the most skilfully drawn is perhaps that in Clemence Dane's *Regiment of Women* – as there will always be human beings whose love of power or emotional gratification urges them to exploit the weakness and affection of others. And there are always people who through inexperience, lack of tact, selfishness, self-distrust, or some other cause, cannot successfully handle any emotional situation. But there is little reason, except the rather vague one that they are unmarried, to expect such folk to be in the majority among schoolmistresses, particularly as their position has improved and they have to attach more respect to their profession and to themselves as members of it.'*

While Beatrice Ilford and her governesses may have been the pattern for those girls of the British Top Nation who did not go to a public school or a high school, there were people who were trying to get official recognition for good educational thought by which to bring up the young children of the Lower Nation. In 1904 the Code for use in Elementary Schools was brought out. In this Sir Robert Morant, who became Permanent Secretary to the Board of Education, gave a statement of aims, which as late as 1937 was officially described in a Board of Education Handbook of suggestions for Teachers as being 'as finely conceived and as nobly expressed as any that can be found'.

The Introduction to the Code of 1904 gave the following basic purposes of elementary education: to form and strengthen character; to develop the intelligence of children; to make the best use of school years for both boys and girls according to their needs, to fit them practically and intellectually for the work of life. They could be taught some of the facts and laws of nature; some familiarity with the history and literature of their own country – remembering to make them conscious of the limitations of their knowledge, while developing such a taste for good reading and thoughtful study as would enable them to

* *Op. cit.*, pp. 223–4.

increase that knowledge in after years. Encouragement could be given in practical work and manual instruction, and the healthy development of their bodies by physical exercise and organised games and also by telling them some of the simpler rules of health education. Individual gifted children should be discovered and helped to pass on to secondary schools, 'so far as this can be done without sacrificing the interests of the majority of the children'.

The final two paragraphs of the Introduction are perhaps one of the reason why millions of young men went singing off to France between 1914 and 1918, and why millions of young women sent them there with waves and tears and sadly muted choruses. The ideas which had been propagated on the playing fields of Eton in the past were now being brought into the kitchens and living-rooms of the country.

'Though their opportunities are but brief, the teachers can yet do much to lay the foundations of conduct. They can endeavour, by example and influence, aided by the sense of discipline which should pervade the School to implant in the children habits of industry, self-control, and courageous perseverance in the face of difficulties; they can teach them to reverence what is noble, to be ready for self-sacrifice, and to strive their utmost after purity and truth; they can foster a strong sense of duty and instil in them that consideration and respect for others which must be the foundation of unselfishness and the true basis of all good manners; while the corporate life of the School, especially in the playground, should develop that instinct for fair-play and for loyalty to one another which is the germ of a wider sense of honour in later life.

'In all these endeavours the School should enlist, as far as possible, the interest and co-operation of the parents and the home in an united effort to enable the children not merely to reach their full development as individuals, but also to become upright and useful members of the community in which they live, and worthy sons and daughters of the country to which they belong.'

These high ideals found an echo in another code that was published a few years later. In 1908, the hero of Mafeking, Sir Robert Baden-Powell (who had just been promoted to lieutenant-general) started the Scout movement. To some extent it was spontaneous. Baden-Powell did not set out to organise a youth movement. In 1899 he had published *Aids to Scouting for Soldiers* and in 1907 he ran a trial camp. These stimuli resulted in the creation of scout patrols and groups in different parts of the country. When he learnt of this enthusiasm, B-P (as he was popularly known) wrote *Scouting for Boys*, which was published in 1908. Lieutenant-General or not, he wanted no cannon fodder. 'Military drill,' he wrote, 'tends to destroy individuality, whereas we want, in the scouts, to develop individual character.' Individual character was necessary to keep the country from decadence and to make sure that the flag continued to fly over the Empire on which the sun had learned, comparatively recently, never to set. Among the ways in which individual character was to be developed were by eschewing all unhealthy practices such as smoking and secret bad habits. In Ireland B-P's initiative was followed by the Countess Markiewicz (*née* Constance Gore-Booth), who founded Fianna nah-Eireann – the Irish National Boy Scouts – in 1909.

Popular as it immediately was with the young, the Scouting movement ran into initial difficulties. Despite the title of his book Baden-Powell did not limit the recruits to boys. Girls could join as well. This led to vociferous protest and dark accusations – which in view of Baden-Powell's position as a stout defender of conservative morality against any encroachment of sexual liberty, indeed of sexual knowledge, seems rather unfair. However, the powerful editor of *The Spectator*, St Loe Strachey, took the side of the protesters and urged Baden-Powell not to ruin a good idea by setting public opinion against the Scouts, 'as he most certainly will by insisting on this mad scheme of military co-education'.

Knowing when to conduct a tactical withdrawal, B-P with his sister Agnes immediately announced the forthcoming formation of the Girl Guides. Saving the nation from decadence, they wrote in their first prospectus, was not only a mission for boys. Girls, too, had a vital part to play. Three specific ways in which they could help the country and the Empire were by making themselves of practical use in case of invasion; by preparing themselves for a Colonial life in case their destiny should lead them to such; and, by making themselves more useful to others and to themselves by learning useful occupations and handi-work and yet retaining their womanliness.

In 1912, two years after the Girl Guides started, the first edition of *The Handbook for Girl Guides* was published. It was sub-titled 'or How Girls can Help build the Empire'. Written by Agnes Baden-Powell with her brother's collaboration, it was even more damning about adolescent sexual practices than the boys' book, threatening hysteria, lunatic asylums and serious illness as a result of transgression. Just what these practices were was left to the reader's imagination – or knowledge. Perhaps those who had been at a public school could have helped; or even those who had been nurtured in the swarming stews of the cities. Cold baths and exercise were recommended as a prophylactic.

One result of the introduction of State primary education which began with the 1870 Act and was continued by the 1876 Act (making education compulsory) and the 1891 Act (making it free to all) was a publishing boom. The publishing empires of Arthur Pearson, George Newnes and the Harmsworths were founded on the new readers turned out by the State education system. Other social changes contributed to the growth of those empires, especially the steadily growing emancipation of women which made them a market in their own right to be catered for separately. It was this that caused the great expansion of the women's press between 1885 and 1910. What facilitated it were technological advances that applied to the press as a whole. What made it financially possible was the growth of advertising.

In 1891, Alfred Harmsworth (later Lord Northcliffe) formed the Periodical Publishing Company, the parent of his famous Amalgamated Press, for the sole purpose of publishing women's magazines. His first publication was *Forget-Me-Not*, which was edited by Miss Winifred Ruth ('Biddy') Johnson. In 1894 Pearson started *Home Notes* and the following year Harmsworth countered with *Home Chat*. Catering for a higher class of reader-ship, as their names suggested, were *The Lady*, inspired by Thomas Gibson Bowles, which started in 1885, and *The Gentle-woman* (1890). With the appointment of Miss Rita Shell as editor in 1894 *The Lady* became an important and influential periodical. But it was *Home Notes* and *Home Chat* which led the way in the creation of the women's magazine industry. In 1910 came an important new periodical from D. C. Thomson's of Dundee. Called *My Weekly*, it was aimed at working-class women, a readership below that of *Home Notes* and *Home Chat*, and it quickly achieved a large circulation on the basic tenet of 'reader identification', which is the cornerstone of women's magazines to the present day. Not only had women as a whole become an important market for periodicals but within that broad market special groups, whether categorised by age, by education, by social class, or by activity (housewives and working-girls, for example) were increasingly being catered for.

The contents of the different magazines naturally reflected the interests and obsessions of their intended readership. As regards fiction, the higher the class of reader the less the amount of fiction. Middle-class journals were strong on ways of keeping up appearances on modest incomes that were being eroded by inflation and by increasing social expectations – as indeed their predecessors like Beeton's *Englishwomen's Domestic Magazine* had been doing in mid-Victorian times. But it was the home that was the main theme in most magazines, their articles giving advice and consolation to worried women, to the hard-pressed wife for whom, as *The Lady's Companion* wrote in one of its 1910 issues,

'there is no relief and no release, and where there is a large family and a small income, there is no limit to her anxieties nor her sphere of duty. She is Chancellor of the Exchequer, Officer of Health, food and clothes provider, charwoman and nurse, queen and slave, and expected to be the infallible guardian of the family fortune and honour and happiness'.*

However important the activities of the women's rights movement may have seemed to those concerned it seems reasonable to conclude from the evidence provided by the contents of women's magazines that the impact of the movement on the vast majority of women was minimal. Although the Edwardian women's press took more notice of feminist activities

* Quoted in Cynthia L. White, *Women's Magazines 1693–1968* (Michael Joseph, 1970), p. 85. For a full account of women's magazines in the Edwardian period see Chapter 2 of that book.

than it had in the past it remained non-commital. Lord Curzon and *The Queen* were at one in their attitude. Curzon proclaimed that political activity would 'tend to take away woman from her proper sphere and highest duty which is maternity, and the vote is not desired, so far as can be ascertained, by the large majority of women'.

The Queen (January 1900) suggested that 'the most adequate contribution to the welfare of the state must, speaking roughly, always be rendered by women, no matter what their social rank in their own homes'.

Chapter 13
NO VOTES FOR WOMEN . . .

The importance of the publicity lavished on the new Suffragettes was not lost on the keen political brains of the suffragists. In February 1907, three days before Parliament re-assembled, the National Union of Women's Suffrage Societies, the constitutionalists, held their first great demonstration. They marched in their thousands from London's Hyde Park to Exeter Hall at the far end of the Strand – and as they marched the rain poured down. Their long skirts trailed in the mud and filth of London streets, and this long quiet procession, dressed mostly in black, from which the militant suffragettes were noticeably absent, has gone down in history as the 'Mud March'. At Exeter Hall, famous as the fount of missionaries, the wet proud women – some of them pioneers from the early days with their grown-up daughters marching beside them – listened to speeches from an array of political and intellectual oratory. Some of the speeches caused an unexpected surprise when they praised the absent militants for bringing the movement to life again. Not unnaturally the Liberals on the platform were vehemently against any praise being given to those outrageous women who had been hounding the ministers and members of their party. They heckled speakers and even hissed Keir Hardie, their great Labour supporter, when he dared to say that while he still supported their cause, 'if it is advanced today, you have to thank the militant tactics of the fighting brigade'. Votes for women, he urged them, were more important than party considerations. Notably, one of the speakers who gave credit to the suffragettes for putting breath into the dying corpse of the women's movement was none other than the suffragists' own President, Mrs Millicent Fawcett.

With its establishment in London the character of the WSPU

began to change. It had been started as a working women's organisation and it was with this political alignment that it came to the capital. Annie Kenney lodged with Sylvia Pankhurst at her studio in Chelsea and it was from here that they made contact with Socialist groups and East End working women. To help them with the secretarial work Mrs Flora Drummond arrived from Manchester and borrowed a typewriter from Oliver's London branch. After the meeting at Caxton Hall on 19 February 1906 many new enthusiasts joined the WSPU, notable among them being Mr and Mrs Pethick Lawrence. The Pethick Lawrences had met and married when both were working in the East End of London. Emmeline Pethick was a Quaker, who with Mary Neal, a pioneer in the Folk Dance movement, had started the Esperance Girls' Club to lighten the lives of East End working girls. Frederick Lawrence, four years her junior, was an old Etonian, a Cambridge graduate, a barrister and a dedicated Socialist. He was also rich. When he first met his wife he was working in an East End settlement. Gradually the centre of the WSPU planning moved from Sylvia Pankhurst's studio to the Pethick Lawrences' flat in Clement's Inn. Here in September 1906 the official headquarters of the WSPU were opened. As Emmeline Pethick Lawrence through her efficiency and her connections began to raise substantial sums for the WSPU's fighting fund and her husband used his organising ability to put the whole thing on a business-like basis, the complexion of the Union began to change. Support came increasingly from upper- and middle-class sources. Membership was no longer preponderently working class. Mrs Pankhurst and Christabel encouraged this trend; Sylvia and Adela abhorred it.

The affairs of the WSPU came to rest in the hands of Mrs Pankhurst, Christabel Pankhurst and the Pethick Lawrences. These four decided what was to be done; 'the others,' wrote Ray Strachey, 'obeyed, and enjoyed the surrender of their judgement and the sensation of marching as an army under discipline'.* Mrs Pankhurst herself was so busy dashing round the country making speeches and taking part in by-election campaigns that the real power lay with the other three. Christabel too, did a great deal of speaking. She was a good speaker,

* *Op. cit.,* p. 310.

though she did not have the rhetorical flow of her mother. She had an incisive, well-modulated, upper-class voice without a trace of its northern origin, but with a partially guttural 'r'. She spoke with the clipped delivery of a colonel giving orders to his junior officers.

The autocratic conduct of affairs naturally led to schism. In September 1907, three prominent members of the WSPU broke away to form the Women's Freedom League, taking with them a sizeable following. Their leader was Mrs Charlotte Despard, an Irishwoman who was the sister of General Sir John French (later Field-Marshal the Earl of Ypres), who had distinguished himself in the Boer War as the cavalry commander and was to be the first Commander-in-Chief of the BEF in 1914. Mrs Depard was a staunch member of the ILP, a pacifist, and a loyal friend of the poor among whom she worked in South London and Dublin. She was one of a number of suffragettes who stood for Parliament in the Khaki Election of 1918, failing to get in for the London Borough of Battersea. In 1927 she was expelled from the Irish Free State as a dangerous character. The other two who broke away were Teresa Billington (later Mrs Billington Greig), the first woman ILP National Organiser and one of the earliest WSPU recruits, and Mrs Edith How Martyn who, with Charlotte Despard, had been on the WSPU Committee.

The suffragettes' strategy was to turn the Liberals out and to make themselves such a power in the land that whoever succeeded the present Liberal Government would be bound to grant them their demand for the vote. To make themselves such a power in the land was, on the face of it, impossible. Power implies force and as G. K. Chesterton wrote in the *Illustrated London News*, 'A woman putting up her fists at a man is a woman putting herself in the one position which does not frighten him.' But the suffragette praesidium brilliantly realised that force was not necessarily the 'putting up of fists'. Publicity was power. Northcliffe had given them their name. Northcliffe could give them their aim. Thus they embarked on exploits which, however disgraceful they seemed to those who regarded rowdy and extravagant behaviour by women as totally shocking, nonetheless provided the colourful basis for stories which would sell newspapers. Shouting at Members of Parliament from barges moored in the Thames off the Terrace, chaining themselves to railings, sporting their colours of purple, green and white (symbolising justice, hope and purity), in row upon row of banners and dresses, welcoming their released heroines from prison with brass bands and garish floats, 'bombing' London with leaflets, singing their superb marching song the 'Women's Marseillaise' and later the March specially written for them by Ethel (later Dame Ethel) Smyth; it all brought a little excitement to the hundreds who saw it and the tens of thousands who read about it.

For the leaders there was even greater excitement. They fed upon the excitement of their power, and the knowledge that they had power made them ever more aggressive, ever more headlong. Debate was not their way. Their work

'. . . resounded with charges of the treachery and ill faith of their opponents, and was sharpened by sarcasm, anger and excitement. Moreover, since they deliberately put themselves in the position of outlaws dogged by the police, they were always wrapped round with secrecy and mystification, and planned surprises alike for their followers and for the public'.*

Mrs Pankhurst herself revelled in it all. She enjoyed the sportingness, the scent of battle, the exploits conducted with cunning and contrivance; she would indeed have made a superb leader for one of those 'private armies' that flourished during World War II. It has been written of her that her ambition was to find her own niche in history and that she would do anything to get it.

But this was the path to ultimate disaster. With their followers, as in all totalitarian organisations, more loyal to the leaders themselves than to the cause they supported, the leaders of the WSPU had forever to stage bigger and more breathtaking surprises. Deputations, such as the one to the Prime Minister, Sir Henry Campbell-Bannerman, on 19 May 1906, when he talked to the 300 representatives of over 180,000 women led by Miss Emily Davies, the doyenne of higher education for women, and assured them that although he agreed with every word they said he would do nothing whatsoever about it because of divided opinions within the Cabinet

* Ray Strachey, *op. cit.*, p. 30.

and the Liberal Party, and advised them 'to go on pestering' but to exercise 'the virtue of patience', advice which made Annie Kenney jump up on to her chair and tell him loudly, 'Sir, we are not satisfied' – such deputations were clearly not enough.

Thus the suffragettes' campaign went from the jollity of pageants and colourful escapades to the more serious 'raids' on Parliament, when they would try to approach Westminster and would be met by cordons of police. Such confrontations would inevitably lead to derision, violence, arrests and imprisonment. From this they moved on to breaking windows, waylaying Cabinet Ministers, stoning them, beating them over the head, trying to horse-whip them, and then, when they reached prison, flouting the rules.

Apart from creating an uproar with their utensils before and after meals they took to organised insubordination. Punishment followed. The punishment was made a platform for martyrdom. Suffragette after suffragette took to hunger striking and going without sleep. Before long the point of imprisonment was nullified by hunger strikers. Rather than let the prisoners die on their hands the prison authorities were instructed to release them. By 1913 this bitter laughter at authority brought a riposte from the Government in the form of a law officially called The Prisoners' Temporary Discharge Act but popularly known as the Cat and Mouse Act, under which suffragette hunger strikers were temporarily released from prison when their health was in danger of breaking down but which allowed them to be put back in prison, ostensibly as soon as their health was sufficiently recovered, but in actual fact when they made a nuisance of themselves again. Mrs Pankhurst's score under this Act, starting with imprisonment on 3 April 1913, was nine releases and nine rearrests, the last on 16 July 1914.

Explaining the purpose of the Cat and Mouse Act, Reginald McKenna, the Home Secretary, told the House of Commons, 'We have to deal with a phenomenon which I believe is absolutely without precedence in our history. There are four alternative ways of dealing with it. The first is to let these women die in prison; the second is to deport them; the third is to treat them as lunatics; and the fourth to give them the vote!' And that, it would appear, the Government would *never* do though

McKenna was one of the many in the Cabinet who were in favour of it.

The pattern had now been set: frequent appearances in court, repeated terms of imprisonment, and, in counter to the hunger-strikes, the torture of forced feeding. For women of sheltered upbringing and gentle breeding their experiences in the streets (when the 'roughs' would set upon them, tearing their clothes off, dragging them into alleyways and assaulting them),* in the police cells, the courtrooms and the prisons were horrifying. Whatever the new class image of the WSPU, those who were arrested began to learn what life was like for the 'S's' of the WSPU. Suffragettes were initially classed as common criminals and had to serve their sentences in the Second Division – that is to say in prison clothes and on a prison diet – or in the Third Division with hard labour. This was another source of anger. Men who preached rebellion in Ireland were treated as political prisoners and served their sentences in the First Division – that is, they wore their own clothes and could send out for food. Suffragettes demanded to be treated as political prisoners, but for the majority this was refused until March 1910 when Winston Churchill who was then Home Secretary ruled that suffragettes would be treated as political prisoners unless their crimes involved 'moral turpitude'.

There were some exceptions before this – among them Lady Constance Lytton. Lady Constance joined the WSPU in February 1909 and immediately took part in her first demon-stration. She was arrested along with Mrs Despard from the WFL, Mrs Pethick Lawrence, and several others. They were tried, convicted and imprisoned. But their sentences were served in the First Division, a fact that aroused public comment and confirmed the widely held belief that there was one law for the rich and another for the poor. So upset was Lady Constance at this denial of martyrdom that on a subsequent occasion she disguised herself as a working woman, committed an offence by breaking the prison governor's windows at Walton Gaol, Liver-pool, was arrested, convicted and served her sentence in the Third Division at Walton. After four days of fasting she was forcibly fed, despite the fact that she had a chronic heart

* One of Douglas (later Field-Marshal Earl) Haig's sisters died as a result of such an assault.

condition and was practically asphyxiated each time she was fed. When Keir Hardie raised the matter of forced feeding in the Commons, the House roared with laughter. Writing to *The Times* he said: 'Had I not heard it, I could not have believed that a body of gentlemen could have found reason for mirth and applause in a scene which, I venture to say, has no parallel in the recent history of our country.'

Meanwhile bill after bill, resolution after resolution came before Parliament; and whether they were rejected, talked out, or even passed their Second Reading they all met the same fate: No votes for women.* The opposition was too well organised.

Male opposition was formalised in 1909 in a Men's League for Opposing Women's Suffrage under the presidency of Lord Curzon. Nor did the assault of the suffragettes and suffragists go unchallenged among their own sex. Many were not content to decry them airily like Mrs Ilford but in 1908 organised themselves into an Anti-Suffrage Society with Mrs Humphry Ward, the novelist and niece of Matthew Arnold and a strong anti-feminist for many years, as their President. In 1910 these two 'anti' organisations amalgamated under the title of the League for Opposing Women's Suffrage. Petitions were got up deploring both the actions of the suffragettes and the aims of those actions; no votes for women was their cry. When the author's mother was a schoolgirl in Glasgow at the end of Edward's reign she was asked to take a petition round the senior forms for the girls to sign, saying that a Glasgow Girls School was totally opposed to all that suffragettes, and by implication the suffragists, stood for. Most signed it, but some did not. Indeed, in view

---

* The bills introduced were:

1904 May 12: Faithfull Begg's bill talked out.

1905 May 12: Bamford Slack's bill talked out before introduction.

1906 April 25: Keir Hardie introduces a women's suffrage resolution, which is ridiculed.

1907 March 8: W. H. (later Sir Willoughby) Dickinson's Women's Suffrage Bill is rejected.

1908 February 28: H. Y. Stanger's Women's Enfranchisement Bill carried by a majority of 179. The Prime Minister, H. H. Asquith, subsequently refused to consider the next stage.

1909 March 19: Geoffrey Howard's Electoral Reform Bill, proposing votes for women, passes its Second Reading, but Asquith says that such a bill would have to be a Government measure to be acceptable.

of her later life it is something of a surprise that the bearer of the petition signed it herself, for while she did not approve of the suffragettes she was certainly a suffragist and had a hard fight against parental displeasure to get herself to Glasgow University. Once there she more than justified her determination by getting a first-class honours degree in mathematics.

The Men's League for Opposing Women's Suffrage was immediately countered by the formation of a Men's League for Women's Suffrage. Other pro-suffrage leagues and societies sprung up. In 1910 alone the NUWWS added sixty new branches. In 1903 it had had sixteen affiliated societies; by 1911 it had over 300.

In 1910 there came a break in the parliamentary clouds. The Liberals were returned to power in February but in a decimated state. They had a majority of only two over the Conservatives and were in an overall minority of 120. Women's suffrage had been a live issue in the election and as soon as it was over the Earl of Lytton, Lady Constance's brother, together with the radical journalist, H. N. Brailsford, formed an all-party conciliation committee to draft a bill that would give the vote to a limited number of women. To give it to all women was a political impossibility inasmuch as there was still a substantial proportion of the male population which was disenfranchised. The terms of the Conciliation Bill would give the vote to about one million women – those who occupied premises for which they were responsible. The effect of the bill was to give the WSPU and the WFL the opportunity to declare a truce. While the followers of Mrs Pankhurst might be happy to continue their sacrifice the cadre of the movement was exhausted. Like all guerrilla groups under stress a truce would give them the opportunity to rest their bodies and resuscitate their colandered organisation. Furthermore it would do something towards giving them a better public image. Their initial pleasanteries had entertained the public; their later challenges had seemed too like revolution.

During the period of the truce there was no cessation in the propaganda campaign: meetings, processions, handbills, bicycle parades, speeches, deputations – the war went on but with guarded foils.

In June the Conciliation Bill was introduced in Parliament

by D. J. Shackleton, the Labour member for Clitheroe. To show their support a suffragette demonstration estimated at 10,000 marched from the Embankment to the Albert Hall. Three days later, to show their disapproval of the methods the suffragettes had used, the suffragists of the NUWSS sent a deputation to the Prime Minister. He received them – as later the same day he received a deputation of anti-suffragists. The following month the Conciliation Bill passed its Second Reading with a majority of 139. But the excitement of success soon turned to dismay. The Government, preoccupied with the struggle between the Lords and Commons over Lloyd George's Budget, announced that no time could be allowed in the present session for the next stage of the bill to be taken. In November the struggle between Lords and Commons reached such a pitch that Parliament was dissolved.

The suffragettes were appalled. They were not concerned with the right of the Lords to amend financial bills that the Commons had passed. What they wanted to know was: would a new Liberal Government give the vote to women – at least to some women? On Friday, 18 November 1910, they demanded an answer. They tried to see the Prime Minister; he refused to meet them. They tried to reach the House of Commons; they were repulsed by the police, in uniform and in plain clothes. Several women were hurt. In all, 119 arrests were made – but the following day the Home Secretary, Winston Churchill (who had suffered much unpleasantness at the hands of the suffragettes) ordered that all charges be withdrawn, except in the case of those who had committed acts of violence. Several women were fined but chose to go to prison instead. One of these was Mrs Pankhurst's sister, Mrs Clarke. The prisoners were released one month later. Two days after that, on Christmas Day, Mrs Clarke, who was staying with the Pankhursts, went upstairs to lie down. When Mrs Pankhurst went up to see her some time later she was dead. The following week another of the imprisoned demonstrators died of heart failure. In suffragette history the 8 November confrontation went down as 'Black Friday'.

With the return of another Liberal Government at the second 1910 election the parliamentary battle for women's suffrage was rejoined, albeit a side-show to the main constitutional battle of the Parliament Bill which was to limit the powers of the House of Lords. But the physical battle on the streets was stopped once again as the suffragettes resumed the truce in deference to the fact that 1911 was the Coronation Year of the new King George V. Apart from such turbulent trade union groups as the dockers, miners and railwaymen – and a considerable number of other 'unpatriotic' dissidents – there was a spirit of national euphoria in the air and a feeling, even if it was not specifically stated in these terms, that just as a new reign in foreign parts was signalised by an amnesty of political prisoners, so the anointing of George V would be marked by giving the vote to women – to some women, that is. The arts added their encouragement with plays and films, and Dr Ethel Smyth composed a new song for the suffragettes called 'The March of the Women', which was intended to replace the popular 'Women's Marseillaise'. It was played for the first time at a social evening at the Suffolk Street Galleries in London on 21 January 1911 to welcome the release of the Black Friday prisoners.

Over and above the promise that was present in the euphoric spirit of the months that preceded the Coronation there seemed to exist another hopeful prospect that votes for women would be granted. Sir George Kemp headed the ballot for Private Members' bills in the House of Commons and announced that he would be presenting an amended version of the Conciliation Bill. On 5 May the bill passed its Second Reading with a large majority. Lord Lytton pressed the Prime Minister to make an unequivocal statement of the Government's position: would facilities be granted for the bill to go forward?* Possibly to avoid a new outbreak of violence so close to the Coronation if he refused, Asquith agreed that full facilities for the bill would be given in 1912.

To celebrate the Coronation in their own publicity-conscious way those in favour of votes for women staged a huge demonstration in London on 17 June a week before the ceremony. As well as the WSPU and the NUWSS, which had been getting a horde

* The rules of parliamentary procedure in the House of Commons make the passage of a Private Member's bill entirely dependent on the goodwill of the Government which can either make available or refuse the necessary parliamentary time for the bill to move through its various stages before enactment.

of new recruits in the early months of the year, representatives of many suffrage societies abroad who were in London for the Coronation also joined the procession.

Then, yet again, the hopes of summer were dashed by the cold chill of November. On the 7th Asquith announced that the Government would introduce a Manhood Suffrage Bill to abolish plural voting and extend male franchise. In so doing, as Lloyd George put it, he 'torpedoed' the amended Conciliation Bill which had been drawn up on existing franchise laws. The women were up in arms at this betrayal. After solemnly promising to give full facilities to the Conciliation Bill, Asquith had effectively gone back on his word. 'If it had been his object to enrage every woman suffragist to the point of frenzy,' said Mrs Fawcett, 'he could not have acted with greater perspicacity.'

Ten days later Asquith received a deputation from the suffrage societies and the WSPU, the five ladies from the WSPU (Mrs Pethick Lawrence, Lady Constance Lytton, Annie Kenney, and Christabel and Sylvia Pankhurst – their mother was away on a lecture tour in the United States giving her advice to the suffragist organisations there) making a late entrance to the sound of distant cheering from their supporters outside. It was a calm meeting, but at the end of it Asquith smilingly told the deputation that they had failed to convince him. 'You may think it deplorable, but that is the fact and I have colleagues – a minority,' he added with honesty, 'who are like minded.' The women murmured a protest at this confession that their case was being turned down by a minority in the Cabinet. 'Get rid of me by all means if you can,' Asquith continued, 'but at the moment I am head of the Government and I am not convinced.'

The fact that they could not convince the Prime Minister was all that was needed to frustrate the endeavours of all the processions, pamphlets, speeches and bravery of suffragists and suffragettes alike. In the judgement of Asquith's biographer, Roy Jenkins, 'there were only two effective obstacles to female enfranchisement before 1914. The first was the excess of militancy; and the second was the person of the Prime Minister, stubbornly unconvinced and occupying a commanding position in the House of Commons'.* In his opposition to woman's

* Collins, 1964, p. 248.

suffrage Asquith was against the majority of his party, let alone the majority of his own Cabinet. In various degrees of conviction Grey, Lloyd George, Haldane, Churchill, Birrell, Runciman and McKenna were all in favour of the women's demand for the vote. With him in his refusal to concede at all to the women's argument were Burns, Harcourt and Samuel.

The effect of militancy on Asquith was totally counter-productive. As Roger Fulford wrote in *Votes for Women*, 'the idea of converting a human being's reason by parades, marches and fighting the police was incomprehensible to him. The more the women marched, the less his reason marched with them. Therefore the work of the militants strengthened his opposition to the vote'.*

Nonetheless, and despite the infallibility of his political position, he could not entirely ignore the opinions of the majority of his Cabinet on the matter. Thus it was that Government time was occasionally afforded for Private Members' bills on woman's suffrage. That they never got further than a Second Reading was easily arranged by the Government's pleading pressure of other more vital business. Furthermore, those in the Cabinet in favour of giving votes to women were no more united in how to achieve their aim than were those in the suffragist and suffragette groups in the country at large. Churchill and Lloyd George, although both were in favour of woman's suffrage, voted against the Conciliation Bill in July 1910. Their reason was this: because the bill proposed a female suffrage strictly limited by age and property qualifications (as indeed it had to be to get any Conservative support at all – hence the 'conciliation' in the bill's title – and as indeed all Private Members' bills on the subject had always been in the past) they realised that the effect of the bill would be to enfranchise more Tory supporters than Liberals. Paradoxically, Arthur Balfour, who was Leader of the Opposition until 8 November 1911, found himself in the opposite state to Asquith. While the majority of his party were solidly opposed to woman's suffrage he himself was strongly in its favour. Thus, in terms of political expediency, if Lloyd George and Churchill were correct, Balfour was right and the majority of his party (who rejected him) were wrong.

* Faber, 1957, p. 184.

When the amended Conciliation Bill passed its Second Reading in May 1911, the Cabinet clearly expressed its majority view by agreeing that time should be given for a bill of similar intent to continue its progress through Parliament beyond its Second Reading. It had been the lack of this parliamentary time which had killed the original Conciliation Bill in 1910. Now it was agreed that in 1912 a week of Government time would be set aside for the committee stage. But when it came to the point of a Second Reading on 28 March the absence of thirteen Labour members in connection with a miners' strike and the abstention or transfer of support of all but two of the eighty-four Irish Nationalists in order not to imperil a government which seemed to be about to grant Home Rule, saw the bill lost by fourteen votes.

With the demise of the Conciliation Bill the last parliamentary hope left to the women was an amendment to the Manhood Suffrage Bill which was introduced by the Government on 17 June. As it stood it did not include women, but the suffragists were encouraged to think that an amendment could be moved to bring them within the ambit of the bill. In July the Prime Minister announced that the House of Commons would have a free vote on an amendment which would put women on the same new voting basis as men.

By this time militancy had taken over again. Four days after the unsatisfactory meeting with the Prime Minister on 17 November the suffragettes broke the truce. Leaving Caxton Hall they tried the usual gambit of reaching the House of Commons. As usual they were rebuffed and immediately retaliated with an organised window-breaking operation as a result of which 223 arrests were made and the following morning every available glazier in London was called out to replace the windows of government offices in Whitehall and of shops and post offices in the Strand. On 1 March there was another mass window-breaking in the West End, and again three days later. The following day the police raided the WSPU headquarters at Clement's Inn and in May Mrs Pankhurst and the Pethick Lawrences were tried at the Old Bailey and sentenced to nine months' imprisonment. In June the suffragette prisoners in Holloway Gaol went on hunger-strike and many of them were forcibly fed. Militancy and martyrdom were now the order of the day. It was not surprising that the Government's offer of a free vote on a women's suffrage amendment was denounced by the suffragettes as a 'gratuitous insult to women'. The suffragists, on the other hand, felt that with this concession the vote was as good as won. But it was the suffragettes whose declamation proved correct.

The amendment was to come up in late January 1913, towards the end of a session which had started in February 1912 and had already far outrun its normal time. On 22 January the Cabinet solved its internal arguments on the issue by agreeing to differ and deciding that whatever happened in the vote there would be no question of ministerial resignations. On the 23rd a totally new situation arose. Speaker Lowther suddenly took the feet from everyone by announcing that if the women's suffrage amendment were to be carried the whole bill would be so changed in its intent as to mean that it would have to be withdrawn and re-introduced. In other words it would have to be postponed until the following session of Parliament.

Although in the opinion of the Prime Minister and other parliamentary authorities the Speaker was entirely wrong in his judgement there was no way of overruling him. As Asquith reported to King George V, 'This is a totally new view of the matter which appears to have occurred for the first time to the Speaker himself only two or three days ago, and is in flat contradiction of the assumptions upon which all parties in the House hitherto treated the bill.' While he may as a lawyer and parliamentarian have been highly critical of the Speaker's bad judgement, there was no doubt that as a person and a politician Asquith was delighted at the result of it: 'The Speaker's *coup d'état* has bowled over the Women for this session – a great relief,' he wrote to his close friend Miss Venetia Stanley (later Mrs Edwin Montagu) on 27 January.

Faced with this broken pledge the only course that Asquith and the Cabinet felt able to take was to agree unanimously that the Manhood Suffrage Bill should be dropped and that an opportunity would be given for a Private Member's bill on women's suffrage early in the following session. Not unnaturally the women's movements, suffragists and suffragettes alike, were as one in regarding the whole thing as yet another Asquithian tergiversation.

When the bill did appear on the floor of the House for its Second Reading on 6 May there was enacted the curious parliamentary divertissement of the principal speaker for it being the Foreign Secretary, Sir Edward Grey, and the principal speaker against it being the Prime Minister, Herbert Asquith – one speaking immediately after the other. The bill was lost by 268 votes to 221. By now militancy was in full flood: there had been widespread letterbox damage, golf greens ruined, telegraph wires cut, arson and bombings, including the bombing of Lloyd George's newly built house at Walton Heath for which offence Mrs Pankhurst had accepted full responsibility and had been sentenced to three year's penal servitude on 3 April.

Although it was the militant suffragettes of the WSPU who captured the headlines, the suffragists of the NUWSS were just as active in their own way. Membership continued to increase. Public meetings became 'almost incessant', and in 1913, when the suffragette campaign was at its height, the suffragists organised another great march. In the middle of June, women set out on foot from all corners of the country and with bands playing and banners flying slowly converged on London along eight main routes. As they marched, others joined them and speeches were made in towns and villages along the route. Their reception was in the main friendly, not to say enthusiastic. The pilgrimage reached London on 26 July and ended with a mass rally in Hyde Park. 'The huge crowd,' wrote Ray Strachey, 'was not merely gathered to see the fun; it was gathered to support the demonstration; and the suffragists were at least able to feel that their task of converting public opinion was virtually accomplished.'*

Evidence of sympathy for the Cause could be seen in many ways: support from newspapers that had previously been hostile; support from Trade Unions; even support from sixty peers, with 104 against, when a Women's Suffrage Bill was introduced in the anti-suffrage fortress of the House of Lords.

But converted public opinion was not sufficient to initiate action. The Liberal Government, angered and embarrassed by the actions of Mrs Pankhurst and her followers, 'was obstinately blind to the feeling of the country. They seemed to think that severity towards the militants, and indifference towards the

* *Op. cit.*, p. 335.

Cause would make the whole thing lie down, and took refuge in masterly inactivity'.* Only a change of government, it seemed could bring any hope of progress. This was exactly the point the WSPU had been making. All that the processes of democracy achieved was 'masterly inactivity'. What was the point of persuading public opinion to support you if the political impasse remained. The Liberal Government must be harried from power. There must be direct action. 'I will incite this meeting to rebellion,' Mrs Pankhurst had shouted in the autumn of 1912. 'Be militant each in your own way, I accept the responsibility for everything you do!' And so, while the suffragists planned yet more campaigns and marches, the suffragettes went on with their 'outrages' and defied a Home Office order banning open air meetings of suffragettes. In August 1913 they began protest chanting in church; the following month they began to shout interruptions at theatres, starting at a performance of Shaw's *Androcles and the Lion.* In March 1914 they slashed the Rokeby Venus; in May a mass suffragette deputation to Buckingham Palace had a fierce battle with the police; organised window-smashing began again; and a suffragette arsenal of disputable contents was discovered at a Maida Vale flat in London.

Meanwhile there had been a rift in the Pankhurst clan. Antagonism between them had been growing for some time. Unlike her mother and elder sister, Sylvia was a pacifist and like her younger sister Adela never wavered in her loyalty to the Left – not at least as far as Adela was concerned until twenty-five years later. In 1912, Sylvia set up a suffrage headquarters in the poorest part of London and there organised the East London Suffrage Federation. Sylvia – and Adela – rejected the militancy and autocracy of the WSPU and like those of the NUWSS and the WFL the affairs of the ELSF were conducted in a democratic way. The rejection of militancy, however, did not go as far as the peaceful policy of the NUWSS under the leadership of Millicent Fawcett. While the destruction of property was banned, confrontations and demonstrations were the stuff of Sylvia's protest. And for this protest she paid with repeated imprisonment and the horrors of forced feeding. As Florence Nightingale had been to the wounded in the Scutari hospitals so

* *Ibid.*

was Sylvia Pankhurst to the down-trodden of the East End. They all loved her. She was 'Our Sylvia', and although her Federation was ostensibly non-violent she was protected where-ever she went – and especially when she was out of prison under the Cat and Mouse Act – by a bodyguard armed with clubs and knotted ropes.

There were others who had a different opinion of her. On Elsa Schiaperelli's wedding day at a London registry office she was disgusted to find Piccadilly being invaded by 'suffragettes, mad masculine furies, collectively and individually hideous, screaming for the vote and led by Sylvia Pankhurst'.*

This erstwhile art student, who had designed the emblem of the WSPU, rejected the contention of her mother's and sister's supporters that only women of property should have the vote. The vote was for everyone, especially the poor. If the laws under which women worked were bad, those laws could only be changed if women had the vote. Sylvia's disagreement with her mother and sister was based as much on political grounds as on a rejection of their violent militancy. The final break came in February 1914 when Christabel announced that Sylvia's East London Suffrage Federation was no longer connected with the WSPU. But it was Sylvia in the end who gained the day. Weakened as she was by hunger-striking, sleeplessness and forced feeding during her repeated terms of imprisonment, she decided on one last throw to register the seriousness of her cause. In June 1914 she announced that she would go on hunger-strike – 'to death, if necessary' – until the Prime Minister agreed to meet a deputation from the East London Federation. She was carried to the House of Commons on a stretcher and placed on the pavement with her supporters around her. Keir Hardie, her old friend and fellow Socialist, came out and told her that the Prime Minister would receive the deputation on the 20th. Asquith received the deputation as promised and, it is said, listened to the description of their hardships 'with real

---

* *Shocking Life,* Elsa Schiaparelli (Dent, 1954), p. 29. Schiaparelli's conclusion was that 'They got their vote and all their worries. Many men admire strong women, but they do not love them. Some women have achieved a combination of strength and tenderness, but most of those who have wanted to walk alone have, in the course of the game, lost their happiness.'

regret'. Spirits rose. Perhaps at last, the Cause had been won. In the event, the chain reaction in Central Europe blew the long years of struggle out of the window. But, by a strange paradox, it also achieved the object for which that struggle had been fought.

Chapter 14

. . . AND CHASTITY
FOR MEN

The argument of those in favour of votes for women, whether
they were suffragists or suffragettes, was that without the vote
women were condemned not only to political ineffectiveness but
also to economic, social and sexual degradation. Although the
political aspect of the Women's Social and Political Union was
greatly to the fore during most of its existence the social and
sexual aspects were never entirely forgotten. In particular the
sexual aspect was a strong element in Christabel Pankhurst's
suffragettism. In 1913 her pamphlet, *The Great Scourge and How
To End It*, was published under her mother's imprint. The great
scourge was the sexual diseases which were 'the great cause of
physical, mental and moral degeneracy, and of race suicide'. It
was a problem of 'appalling magnitude', from 75 to 80 per cent
of men being infected by gonorrhoea, and a considerable percentage, difficult to ascertain precisely, being infected with
syphilis.

Problem it certainly was, though whether it was quite on the
scale Miss Pankhurst suggested is open to question. Three out of
every four men in Britain with gonorrhoea! It takes a bit of
believing.

What was to be done about it? Suffragettes, she wrote, did
not discuss an evil and 'run away from it without suggesting how
it may be cured'. The proposed cure for the great scourge,
simply stated, was 'Votes for Women and Chastity for Men.'
One of the chief objects of the pamphlet was 'to enlighten
women as to the true reason why there is opposition to giving
them the vote. That reason is sexual vice. The opponents of

votes for women know that women when they are politically free and economically strong, will not be purchasable for the base uses of vice'.

It is more than doubtful whether 'sexual vice' was at all the reason why there was opposition to votes for women, even among the Paulines and Sentimentalists. Indeed it would be very surprising if such a path of logic presented itself to any man whether he indulged in 'sexual vice' or not. Political freedom and economic strength might certainly have the highly desirable effect of cutting down the numbers of poverty-stricken girls and women who were forced into prostitution in order to keep themselves or their families from the inferno of starvation and the lower depths. But there would still remain – such are the foibles of human nature – a significant number who would choose that occupation for other reasons. Furthermore, to suppose that 'sexual vice' was a prerogative of professionals was to display a charming ignorance of what went on even in Edwardian times. As mentioned earlier, the opposition to votes for women had other motives – and one in particular which was predominant in a Liberal government was political. Asquith believed – and J. B. Priestley for one was sure he was right – that 'female suffrage at that time would give the Tories a huge bonus'.*

Women, wrote Miss Pankhurst, were chary of marriage – and for 'several practical, common-sensible, sanitary reasons'. The best-informed and most experienced medical men said that 'the vast majority of men expose themselves before marriage to sexual disease and that only . . . 25 per cent at most escape infection'. Add to that the fact that 'sexual disease is difficult if not impossible to cure' and it was clear why 'healthy women naturally hesitate to marry. Mr Punch's "advice to those about to marry – Don't" has a true and terrible application to the facts of the case'.

That women whether healthy or not, were naturally hesitating to marry is not borne out by the marriage rate. From 1890 to 1913 the marriage rate in England and Wales increased from 223,000 to 287,000 annually without any significant variation in the arithmetical progression. In Scotland it increased from 27,000 to 34,000 annually and in Ireland it was almost steady

* Introduction to *Militant Suffragettes*, Antonia Raeburn (NEL, 1974).

throughout the period at an average of 22,000 a year. Even taking into account the increase in the population in Great Britain (there was a fall in the Irish population) these rates do not disclose any marked hesitation.

Miss Pankhurst's chief target in this thesis about sexual vice was, curiously enough, the Bishops.

'Perhaps our childless and celibate Bishops may say that it is a woman's duty, faced by the prospect if she marries, of being infected by her husband, to sacrifice herself and to marry all the same. They must not be surprised if such advice falls on deaf ears. . . . Why should women sacrifice themselves to no purpose save that of losing their health and happiness? Now that women have learnt to think for themselves, they discover that woman, in sacrificing herself, sacrifices the race. If the Bishops, and the whole pack of men who delight in advising, lecturing, and preaching to women, would exhort the members of their own sex to some sacrifice of their baser impulses, it would be better for the race, better for women, and even better for men.'

This lecture of Miss Pankhurst's was written in Paris. Since March 1912 she had been a leader in exile. On March 1 there had been a mass window smashing in the West End. At a given hour women had produced hammers from their muffs and pockets and smashed the plate glass windows of stores like Swan and Edgar's. Mrs Pankhurst, who had defiantly announced that 'the argument of the broken pane is the most valuable argument in modern politics', was arrested. Three days later there had been another concerted attack on the glass of the West End. The following day the police raided the headquarters of the WSPU at Clement's Inn and arrested the Pethwick Lawrences. Annie Kenney secretly became the chief organiser in London and Christabel, realising that if all its top brass were put inside the WSPU would be liable to collapse, escaped to France. Not for another six months was her hide-out revealed when the *Daily Sketch* found her in the Hotel de la Cité Bergère in Montmartre and took a picture of her walking past a gendarme in the Rue Montmartre; the picture filled the whole of their front page the following day, Friday 13 September.

Christabel Pankhurst ignored the Bishops' call for sacrifice.

She never married. She stayed in France until the outbreak of war in August 1914 brought amnesty for all suffragettes. Then she returned to England and in October 1914, with governmental approval, she went on a six-month tour of the United States, during which time her notoriety attracted large audiences whom she regaled with strong speeches on the need for the United States to enter the war on the side of the Allies. In November 1917 she re-formed the WSPU as the Women's Party with a very jingoist ultra-Tory programme. In December 1918 she was one of the seventeen women to stand for election to the House of Commons under an Act that passed through Parliament with hardly any opposition and became law only three weeks before the 'Khaki Election' took place. Of these seventeen only Miss Pankhurst had the 'coupon'. But although almost all those candidates who had this mark of coalition approval were returned to Parliament she was one of the few who were not. Nonetheless she polled 8,614 votes at Smethwick, and was defeated by only 775 votes by her Labour opponent.

The only one of the women candidates to be successful was the Countess Markiewicz, sister of Eva Gore-Booth who had been secretary of the Manchester Suffrage Society, and founder of the Irish National Boy Scouts. Countess Markiewicz stood as an Irish Republican and like others of her party, as she refused to take the oath, she never took her seat nor ever appeared at Westminster. Thus the breakthrough of women into the closer political context of Parliament was bedevilled by the animosities of Ireland which had already split the Liberal party over Home Rule and was to kill, maim and murder into the indefinite future.

Christabel Pankhurst never stood for Parliament again. She took her 'frightening combination of physical beauty with single-minded ruthlessness'* into another field where dedication was equally necessary. She became a religious preacher whose new message was the Second Coming of Christ.

While Christabel Pankhurst was using the factitious argument about sexual vice to explain why men were opposing the vote for women, there was an equally bizarre argument being put forward by some protagonists of the opposition of whom the

---

* Dr Brian Harrison's phrase from his article on 'The Unsung Heroines of Woman Suffrage' in *The Times*, 18 May 1974.

most notable – notable at least in the sense that he was a prominent immunologist and an accepted authority in his day and that he recorded his views in letters to *The Times* and reprinted them in his book entitled *The Unexpurgated Case Against Woman Suffrage* – the most notable seems to have been Sir Almroth E. Wright, who was caricatured by G. Bernard Shaw as Sir Colenso Ridgeon in *The Doctor's Dilemma*. The gravamen of his argument, written at length in euphemistic phrases and amusingly answered by a letter in *The Times* from Winston Churchill's wife under the initials C.S.C., was that because of menstruation, pregnancy and the menopause, women's physiological psychology was 'full of difficulties' for men. From that generalisation that 'the mind of woman is always threatened with danger from the reverberations of her physiological emergencies', Sir Almroth, in a letter that he wrote to *The Times* on 28 March 1912, went on to particularise about the suffragettes:

'It is with such thoughts that the doctor lets his eyes rest upon the militant suffragist. He cannot shut them to the fact that there is mixed up with the woman's movement much mental disorder: and he cannot conceal from himself the physiological emergencies which lie behind. The recruiting field for the militant suffragists is the million of our excess female population* – that million which had better long ago have gone out to mate with its complement of men beyond the sea.'

Sir Almroth then classified the militant suffragists into three types. The first were women who believed 'with minds otherwise unwarped, that they may, whenever it is to their advantage, lawfully resort to physical violence. The programme, as distinguished from the methods, of these women is not very different from that of the ordinary suffragist woman'. Thus did Sir Almroth excuse and dismiss at the outset from his conclusions those ladies of roughly his own class – the Pankhursts, Lady

* The population of England and Wales in 1911 was 36,070,000 of whom 17,446,000 were male and 18,625,000 female (an 'excess' of 1,179,000 females). The figures for Scotland were 2,309,000 male and 2,452,000 female (143,000): for Ireland 2,192,000 male and 2,198,000 female (+6,000) – a total 'excess' of females over males in the British Isles of 1,328,000. Several societies existed to further emigration of women.

Constance Lytton, and Mrs Pethick Lawrence – whose outright condemnation by him would have embarrassed his own sense of loyalty to the established hierarchy of the nation.

But having flicked the paws of those naughty ladies whom etiquette forbade him to calumnise, he let himself go on the next two classifications. Primarily there

'filed past a class of women who have all their life-long been strangers to joy, women in whom instincts long suppressed have in the end broken into flame. These are the sexually embittered women in whom everything has turned into gall, and bitterness of heart, and hatred of men. Their legislative programmes is licence from themselves, or else restrictions for men.'

For them militant suffragism was, in fact, a Lesbian secret society.

The third category were 'the incomplete. One side of their nature,' he stated confidently, had 'undergone atrophy, with the result that they had lost touch with their living fellow men and women. Their programme is to convert the whole world into an epicene institution – an epicene institution in which man and woman shall everywhere work side by side at the self-same tasks and for the self-same pay'. And if it was not a Lesbian plot then undoubtedly it was an overt expression of the penis jealousy and castration complex which, it was well-known all but a few women nursed in their physiological psychology.

But, Sir Almroth assured his readers, these dastardly female plots allied to their insatiable sexual desires, were all in vain. The wishes they embodied could never by any possibility be realised. 'Even in animals – I say *even*, because in these at least one of the sexes has periods of complete quiescence – male and female cannot be safely worked side by side, except when they are incomplete.'

Whatever happened, one wonders, when Sir Almroth was working beside a female nurse? In the next sentence he explains. 'While in the human species safety can be obtained, it can be obtained only at the price of continued constraint. And even then woman, though she protests that she does not require it, practically always does receive differential treatment at the hands of man.'

Sir Almroth's peroration gave warning to the monstrous regiment. 'It would be well, I often think, that every woman should be clearly told – and the woman of the world will immediately understand,' he added, making his social obeisance to those who dined with him or even dared to trust themselves working side by side with him – 'that when man sets his face against the proposal to bring in an epicene world, he does so because he can do his best work only in surroundings where he is perfectly free from suggestion and from restraint, and from the onus which all differential treatment imposes.'

While it is easy enough to mock at Christabel Pankhurst and Sir Almroth the sex war element in suffragettism should not be under-rated. Mrs Pankhurst, speaking at Massey Hall, Toronto in April 1921, under the auspices of the Canadian National Council for Combating Venereal Diseases, said the question of social hygiene was one which had occupied her for a long time. Though it might surprise her audience to know it, she said, in fact,

'. . . the main motive behind the suffragette campaign had been her horror at the prevalence of filthy sexual disease and moral squalor, and her determination to empower responsible women, through the weapon of the vote, to end such a state of affairs. . . . She and her daughter Christabel were just as convinced now as they had been in 1905 that prevention was more important than medical care, necessary as that was. Men must learn to control themselves. Despite all the "modern" ridicule, chastity was still a cardinal virtue'.*

That she was quite genuine in this avowal of the main motive behind militant suffragism is shown by what she said at the Old Bailey eight years earlier in April 1913 when she was tried after accepting responsibility for the bombing of Lloyd George's new house at Walton Heath. She was liable to be sentenced for up to fourteen years imprisonment, yet, she said, for the most revolting offences against little girls the maximum sentence was only two years. Her husband had been a barrister and she had learnt from him of the corruption that went on among those entrusted to administer the laws made by men. She quoted the

* David Mitchell, *The Fighting Pankhursts* (Jonathan Cape, 1967), p. 141.

case of an assize judge who, after passing trivial sentences on
men who had perpetrated hideous crimes against women, was
himself found dead in a brothel. Only that morning she had
been informed that there was 'in this very city of London a
regulated traffic, not only in women of full age, but in little
children: that they are being purchased and trained to minister
to the vicious pleasures of persons who ought to know better in
their positions in life'. To say that she had only been informed
that morning was no doubt legitimate oratorical licence, for
although many who read the report of her trial in the papers
may have been unaware of it Mrs Pankhurst herself with all her
experience must surely have been aware of the existence of the
White Slave Traffic and child prostitution long before 1913 –
Mrs Butler's campaign and W. T. Stead's trial had brought the
whole revolting business to light years before.*

'Suffragettes believe,' she went on, 'that the horrible evils
which are ravaging our civilisation will never be removed until
women get the vote. They know that the very fount of life is
being poisoned . . . that because of bad education, of unequal
standards of morals, even mothers and children are being
destroyed by the vilest diseases.'

It was not only the suffragettes who believed that without
votes for women 'the horrible evils' would never be removed.
The constitutional suffragists felt just as strongly. Dr Elsie
Inglis, who became honorary secretary of the Scottish Federation of Women's Suffrage Societies when it was formed in 1906,
was as vehement as Mrs Pankhurst about unequal standards of
morals and as a doctor she saw the effects at closer quarters than
the suffragettes' leader. 'I wonder when married women will
learn they have other duties in the world than to obey their
husbands. You don't know what trouble we have here with the
husbands,' she wrote to her father from the hospital where she
was training. 'Any idea that anybody is to be thought of but
themselves never enters their lordly minds, and the worst of it is
these stupid idiots of women don't seem to think so either: "'E
wants it, Miss", settles the question.'

Dr Elsie Inglis was one of the outstanding suffragists of her
time and was to become one of the heroines of the Great
War. She was born in 1864 at Naini Tal, a hill station in the

* See *The Victorian Woman*, Chapter 15.

Himalayas. Her father, John Inglis, born in 1820, was an 'old India hand', and her mother, Harriet Louis Thompson, was the daughter of another. By 1856 John and Harriet Inglis had a family of six boys and one girl, and in that year the whole family started home on furlough. Almost as soon as they had landed in England news reached them of the outbreak of the Mutiny and John Inglis returned to the Punjab where he was magistrate at Sialkot. It was several years before the ban on Englishwomen in India was lifted so that Harriet, leaving her 'first family' to be educated in England, did not rejoin her husband until 1863.

After ten years in Rohilkund and two as Chief Commissioner of Oudh, John Inglis retired. By now the Inglis's had a 'second family' of two daughters, Elsie and Eva. Of the 'first family' the daughter was now married and living in Edinburgh, while two of the sons had settled in Tasmania. On his retirement John Inglis took his wife and 'second family' to Hobart for two years to see his sons established. Then the four of them went to Edinburgh, where they had decided to settle. Here Elsie Inglis was to make her name as a doctor and as a champion of women's rights.

As was so often the case with outstanding women during the long struggle for emancipation it was her father's influence and encouragement which allowed Elsie Inglis's talent to unfold. She was born at the very time when the seeds of the women's movement which had been planted so many years before by pioneers like Mary Wollstonecraft were beginning to show their green shoots. It was, wrote one of Elsie Inglis's biographers,

'. . . the dawn of the movement which believed it possible that women could have a mind and a brain of their own, and that the freedom of the one and the cultivation of the other was not a menace to the possessive rights of the family, or the ruin of society at large. Thousands of women born at the same date were instructed that the aim of their lives must be to see to the creature comforts of their male parent, and when he was taken from them, to believe it right that he had neither educated them, nor made provision for the certain old age and spinsterdom which lay before the majority'.*

* Lady Frances Balfour, *Dr Elsie Inglis*, (Hodder and Stoughton, London, 1918), p. 25.

John Inglis's attitude towards his daughters was far from the common run. For them he wanted equal opportunities and the best – and highest – education. 'He gave them the best of his mind, not its dregs, and a comradeship which made a rare and happy entrance for them into life's daily toil and struggle.'* He was one of Bunyan's Greathearts, a man who, with John Stuart Mill, 'recognised that no community was the stronger for keeping its people, be they black or white, male or female, in any form of ignorance or bonded serfdom'.†

Elsie went to school at 23 Charlotte Square in Edinburgh and then for a year in Paris. Returning home she entered the Edinburgh School of Medicine for Women which had been founded by the Dr Sophia Jex Blake. In due course she and Jex Blake fell out over the management of the school and in 1892, while she was studying in Glasgow for her Triple Qualification, Elsie was one of the promoters of the second school of medicine for women in Edinburgh, the Medical College for Women.

The fact that she involved herself in this schism is not difficult to understand. All her life Elsie Inglis hated injustice and arrogance. Nor would she be turned aside by precedent or high-handedness from the achievement of something worthwhile that involved application and relentless routine; she never recognised the meaning of the word 'impossible'. Two small stories from her schooldays illustrate the attitude. In Tasmania, when such things were practically unknown, she instituted 'school colours' – two inches of blue and white ribbon sewn on to a safety-pin and worn on the lapel of the girls' coats. In Charlotte Square, an even more select environment then than it was during the author's schooldays elsewhere in Edinburgh fifty years later, Elsie asked that the school might be allowed to play in the Square gardens. In those days walks and the beginnings of tennis were the only ways in which people thought girls should take exercise in the fresh air. Elsie approached the awe-inspiring male directors of the school and got their consent – provided that all the neighbouring proprietors gave theirs. So with one other girl she went round every house in the square, spoke to the owners, and as a result the girls of Charlotte Square Institution (a dreadful appellation for a school!) were allowed

* *Ibid.*
† *Ibid.*, p. 85.

to play in the gardens of the square until a regular playing field was established. Small wonder that when, in 1914, Dr Elsie Inglis went to the War Office and offered her services as a doctor and hospital organiser she refused to be dissuaded from her object by the little Red Tab who said to her, 'My good lady, go home and sit still.'

Elsie Inglis completed her medical training at the New Hospital for Women in Euston Road, London,* and at the Rotunda in Dublin, in 1894. That same year, before she could 'hang out her shingle', her father died. 'I wish he could have seen me begin,' she wrote to one of her brothers in India. Almost immediately she went into practice in Edinburgh with Dr Jessie MacGregor, and in 1899 after the University of Edinburgh had admitted women to the examinations for degrees in medicine Dr Inglis graduated MB, CM. In 1901 she opened a nursing-home and maternity centre for working women. At first established in George Square, the Maternity Hospice, staffed by medical women, move in 1904 to the slums of Edinburgh's High Street. It was the only maternity training centre run by women in Scotland. For Elsie Inglis it was the child of her heart and joy of her mind; and for the poor women of Edinburgh it was the bright hope of kindness and care in trouble and pain.

Elsie Inglis was a Liberal Home Ruler and a member of the Women's Liberal Federation and was always impatient of the way party was put before franchise. 'I was sorry to see how the suffrage question was pushed into the background by Lady Aberdeen. However,' she wrote in 1893, 'I shall stick to the Federation, and bring them to their senses on that point as far as my influence goes. It is sham Liberalism that will not recognise that it is a real Liberal question.' Had Asquith only accepted that, what a lot of trouble and distress would have been avoided.

Despite this long-term interest, however, it was not until after 1900 that the women's movement took possession of her. From then until the war broke out in 1914 it was as important to her as her profession, but she never countenanced militancy. She was an admirer and follower of Mrs Fawcett throughout. Perhaps the strong emotional feeling she had about woman's suffrage can

* Founded in 1862, later called the Elizabeth Garrett Anderson Hospital for Women.

best be seen in an unpublished novel she wrote called *The Story of a Modern Woman*. Her heroine is listening to a suffrage speaker: 'The salvation of the world was wrapped up in the gospel she preached. Many of the audience were caught in the swirl as she spoke. Love and amity, the common cause of healthier homes and happier people and a stronger Empire, the righting of all wrongs, and the strengthening of all right – all this was wrapped up in the vote.' This was the rhapsody, but it was through her professional life that Elsie Inglis learnt to know 'how often the law was against the woman's best interest, and it was always in connection with some reform that she longed to initiate, that she expressed a desire for the vote'.* Her habitual greeting at New Year time was 'A good New Year, and the Vote *this* year.' She died six weeks too soon to see it.

It is difficult to pass an objective judgement on the suffragette movement. Did it help or hinder equality for women, and especially the struggle for women's votes? Who achieved more? The Pankhursts or the Fawcetts and the Inglises? One thing is certain: the publicity that the suffragettes aimed for and got has given them a place – many would say a disproportionately large place – in the history of the Britain of their time, whereas the suffragists tend to be forgotten. Nonetheless, in the opinion of one eminent modern authority, by August 1914 Mrs Pankhurst's 'violent strategy was in fact leading nowhere, and it is perhaps fortunate for her reputation that at that point the First World War began'.† In the end the whole movement fizzled out in an unnoticed corner while the manhood of the Western world destroyed itself with lemming-like obedience. In January 1918 a clause in the Representation of the People Act quietly gave the vote to women over thirty. A few months later women were made eligible for Parliament. Thereafter the political issue lost its edge.

Looking back over the previous century an article in the *Illustrated London News* of 5 January 1901 came to the conclusion that it would not be easy for the coming century to out-do the past one in the advance of the position, the opportunities, the freedom and the mental and physical growth of women. By the end of the Edwardian years little extra had been actually

* Lady Frances Balfour, *op. cit.*, p. 86.
† Dr Brian Harrison, *op. cit.*

achieved to disprove that opinion. But the pressure of changing
attitudes was building up to the point where the dams of
inhibition would undoubtedly be breached, even though strong
restorers of Victorian social archaeology in Britain would come
to the fore in the 1920s.

The British have usually had periodic fits of moral indignation and ideas of racial superiority – which does not suit them at
all and is alien to their basic tolerant selves. The two longest of
these fits in modern history so far have been Cromwell's
Commonwealth and the second two-thirds of Victoria's reign
which saw the totally unnatural accretion of an Empire. Odd
bursts thereafter have shown that the seeds are not exterminated.
More fascinating, perhaps, are the years – much shorter overall –
when the British shake themselves out of hypocrisy and complacency. The Edwardian decade was one of those periods of
transition. But before the convalescence was complete a totally
new disaster was enacted.

'The period from 1900 to 1914,' wrote Cole and Postgate in
their famous history of *The Common People.** 'is like the two first
acts of a play whose third act was never written. The historian
can trace the breaking-up of the Victorian age ... and the
development ... of various movements of revolt. But when the
struggle develops and it seems that some sort of denouement
must come, the action is violently and suddenly stopped.' Almost
overnight in August 1914 the preoccupations of the previous
day became of no importance: suffragettes, industrial unionism,
even the Irish question disappeared in a puff of smoke that came
from the barrels of a million guns.

Europe was at war.

* *Op. cit.*, p. 450.

Select Index

Select Index

Keyser, Sister Agnes 163
Kinematograph 12, 13, 110, 119, 120
Kirchner, Raphaël 133

Labouchere, Henry 85
Labour Party 18, 48, 51, 86–8, 92, 208
Labour-saving devices 73, 168
Ladies' clubs 165
Lady, The 140, 188, 193
Lady-helps 166
Lady shopkeepers 50, 150, 151
Laemmle, Carl 121, 122
Langhorne, Irene 126, 127
Langtry, Lillie (later Lady de Bathe) 47, 48
Latour, Anny 130, 133
Lauder, Harry (later Sir) 118
Lawrence, the Misses D. M. and P. 188, 189
Lawrence, Florence (the 'Imp' Girl) 121
Lesbianism 190, 219
Leslie, Penelope (Mrs G. A. Cavendish-Bentinck) 54–7
Leslie, Sir Shane 55–9, 63
Lewis, Rosa 159–64
Liberal Party (and government) 18, 54, 82, 83, 86, 89–93, 196, 198, 200, 203–7, 210, 211, 215, 217
Lipton, Sir Thomas 75, 76
Lloyd George, David 18, 204, 206, 207, 210
Londonderry, Marchioness of 53, 70, 71
'London Society', 24–31, 47–9, 51, 78, 112, 128
Lumsden, Louisa (later Dame) 187–9
Lytton, Earl of 203, 205
Lytton, Lady Constance 201–3, 206, 219

Macarthur, Mary R. 95, 96, 152, 154–6
MacDonald, Mrs Margaret 154
Magnus, Sir Philip 51
Male impersonators 117
Malthusian League, The 173, 174
Manchester, Duchess of 42, 53
Manchester High School 186
Manchester Suffrage Society 86, 88, 217
Manhood Suffrage Bill 206, 208, 209
Markiewicz, Countess of 192, 217
Marlborough, Duchess of (*née* Consuelo Vanderbilt, later Mme Balsam) 37–41, 46, 47, 71, 157, 158, 164
Marlborough House set 45–50, 53

Married Women's Property Acts (1870, 1882, 1893) 14, 87, 170, 171
Mary, Queen 50, 69, 101, 127
Masterman, C. F. G. 24, 31
Matheson, Cécile 95, 106
Maugham, W. Somerset 26, 110
Merry Widow, The 111–13
Mill, John Stuart 80, 87, 223
Monckton, Lionel 111, 112, 114
Moore, Mme Kate 43
Motor-cars 12, 31, 32, 65–9
Musical comedy 13, 110–14, 116, 122, 123, 126
Music-hall, 13, 110, 116–20, 122, 124
Music-hall stars 111–13, 116–18

National American Woman Suffrage Association (NAWSA) 39, 40
National Federation of Women Workers 154, 156
National Union of Women's Suffrage Societies (NUWSS) 85, 196, 202–11, 214, 221, 225
Newnes, George 193
New Zealand 69, 80, 102, 138
Nightingale, Florence 61, 150, 211
Northcliffe, Lord, *see* Harmsworth, Alfred
North London Collegiate School 186–8
Nursing 75–7, 138

Pankhurst, Adela 88, 89, 197, 211
Pankhurst, Christabel 41, 81, 88–95, 197, 198, 206, 211, 212, 214–17, 219, 220, 225
Pankhurst, Mrs Emmeline (*née* Goulden) 41, 87–91, 94–6, 137, 197–200, 203, 204, 206, 208, 210–12, 216, 219–21, 225
Pankhurst, Sylvia 88, 89, 197, 206, 211, 212
Paquin, Mme 128, 129
Parisian Haute Couture 128–30, 132
Parkes, Bessie Rayner (later Mme Belloc) 147, 148
Patterson, Mrs Emma 153, 154, 156
Paul, Alice 40
Pavlova, Anna 118, 120, 122
Pearsall, Ronald 117, 122
Pearson, Sir C. A. 13, 193
Percival, Alicia 185, 189, 190
Pethick Lawrence, Mrs 197, 201, 206, 208, 216, 219

229